THE NOVEL NOW

by the same author

*

HERE COMES EVERYBODY
*An Introduction to James Joyce
for the ordinary reader*
A SHORTER 'FINNEGANS WAKE'

THE NOVEL NOW

A Student's Guide to Contemporary Fiction

ANTHONY BURGESS

FABER & FABER
3 Queen Square
London

First published in 1967
by Faber and Faber Limited
3 Queen Square, London WC1
Reprinted 1968
This new edition 1971
Printed in Great Britain
by Western Printing Services Limited, Bristol
All rights reserved

ISBN 0 571 04757 2 (Hard Bound Edition)

ISBN 0 571 09796 0 (F.P.C.E.)

A LILIANA,
COMPAGNA AMATA DI
VITA E DI VIAGGI

Contents

Preface

The germ of this book was a little British Council pamphlet I wrote on the state of the British novel in the early nineteen-sixties. The audience I addressed then was not very different from the one I seek now. This survey (which is about the novel and the novel only) is not for the well-read reader who needs gaps – as in an otherwise perfect set of teeth – to be filled elegantly, nor for those who hunger after criticism in depth; it is for those, especially the young, who are starting to take the art of the novel seriously and want to organize their reading economically, which means systematically (to hurl oneself arbitrarily at the fiction shelves – space reserved next to the corn flakes and fish fingers in the string-bag for a nice slice of shock or dream – is to waste a lot of time and to insult the novel). Primarily I address students. I go further than my little pamphlet not merely as regards detail; I take American as well as British fiction, and I look at what novelists in Europe, Asia and Africa are doing. Most of the important novelists of the post-war period are dealt with; where there are omissions, these must be blamed not on oversight but on ignorance. I am weak on Canadian, South American and Australian fiction, find most Scandinavian novels unsympathetic, and have not read all the good novels that have come out of America and England. No man can read everything, and I discuss no author I have not read. Still, you have enough here for a start – the French anti-novelists, but not Mlle Sagan; Graham Greene, C.H., but not Nicholas Monsarrat, F.R.S.L.; Iris Murdoch, but not Barbara Cartland. To Mr Harold Wilson I apologize for saying nothing about Thomas Armstrong. To various novelists I know personally and whose work I admire impersonally, I apologize

PREFACE

for saying little or nothing about what they have done or are doing; this book is meant to be pocketable and handy, and it is easier, with such an aim, to concentrate on groups rather than individuals. It is not, despite the limitations of its author's taste and knowledge, meant to be a daring or idiosyncratic book; it seeks to instruct, not inflame. I trust that the instruction will be found fairly painless.

Malta, Rome, Singapore,   A.B.
Perth, Adelaide, Sydney,
Nandi, Honolulu,
San Francisco,
London, Rome,
Malta.
Spring, 1970

BIBLIOGRAPHICAL NOTE

Unlike in the first edition, the book-lists at the end of each chapter are intended as a bibliographical guide to the text, rather than a supplement to it, although where appropriate the lists have been added to, or brought up to date. The year of first publication is given, and this includes publication in both London and New York unless otherwise stated. When in the text an author has been given but no titles, the usual practice has been to provide the first and the latest novels, as a guide.

I

What is a Novel?

If we want to establish the meaning of a word, we rarely gain much help from probing into its origin or history. To dig out the Greek *tragos*, meaning 'he-goat', from the word 'tragedy' will not enable us to use that term with any greater accuracy. But with 'novel' things are a little different. We use the word as an adjective meaning 'new; recently introduced', and, though novels have been in existence for a long time now, there is, in comparison with the traditional forms of literature, still a sort of upstart quality about them. There are people who, despite the high example set by Cervantes and Flaubert and Henry James, insist on regarding the novelist as the lowest kind of literary practitioner: the novelist is more concerned with entertainment than with poetic or epic uplift; he doesn't ennoble the world but presents it as it is, with all its meanness, dirt and sexuality. He must, says W. H. Auden:

> Become the whole of boredom, subject to
> Vulgar complaints like love, among the Just
> Be just, among the Filthy filthy too,
> And in his own weak person, if he can,
> Must suffer dully all the wrongs of Man.

In other words, he does not stand in robed dignity like Homer or Sophocles, speaking fire; he identifies himself with the men and women of ordinary homes, streets, pubs, schools, prisons, using all kinds of language, flinching at no situation. What Auden sees

13

WHAT IS A NOVEL?

as a kind of martyrdom, many people regard as a kind of self-indulgence. Moreover, the novelist admits that he wants to give pleasure, while the poets and epic dramatists talk more about spiritual exaltation. Where the novel is 'new', it is 'new' in the sense that it seems to strike at certain traditional values–reticence, modesty, decency, dignity. These values have always existed in the past, but it is doubtful whether that past itself ever existed. The good old days, the Golden Age–no history book has a record of such a time.

But we cannot trace a beginning for the traditional forms of literature–the three kinds of poetry called epic, dramatic and lyric–while the start of the novel is pretty firmly set in history. The *Satyricon* of Petronius Arbiter belongs to Nero's reign, which is a long time ago, but at least its appearance can be roughly dated. We can call it the first European novel, since it is mainly in prose, tells a story, attempts rounded characterization, amuses, shocks, entertains. But lyric verse, epic poetry, tragedy and comedy seem to go back in pre-history. Compared with the *Iliad* or the *Oedipus* plays, even the poems of Horace, that unfinished prose master-piece of Petronius seems modern, a new form, novel, a novel. And yet it had to have antecedents, it had to derive from somewhere.

It is not fanciful to suggest that all our modern literary forms had their origins in the big traditional trilogy–the epic, the drama, the lyric. All these used verse, and to write verse was to write literature: prose was mainly for use, not for art, except for the art of oratory, which, being a device for moving people to action, not to pleasure or spiritual uplift, could not have that 'pure' aesthetic quality which we expect from literature. One of the important things about Petronius's piece of literary art–as also about Lucius Apuleius's *The Golden Ass* or Longus's *Daphnis and Chloe*–is that it is in prose. The process which has shunted the literature of the remote past towards the modern age has been a process of according more homage to prose and less to verse. Verse is still the medium in which the lyrical impulse tends to express itself, but, for the last three hundred years, the stage-plays that Europe has most valued have been written in prose. The epic–

the long verse account of the adventures of some national hero—also had to be de-versified, just like the drama, and in the turning of the epic into a prose story we seem to find the beginnings of the novel.

But not quite. Every coin has two sides. There were poets who wrote exalted odes and poets who turned out scurrilous satires. The theatre had its tragedies, but also its comedies. To balance the epic there had to be the mock-epic. We cannot always be hearing of man's higher nature, as exemplified in noble verses about great heroes who are brave in war and sagacious in peace. We need to be reminded of human insufficiency, to be told stories of anti-heroes. The first important European novel was of epic length and of mock-epic content. Cervantes produced in Don Quixote a man not sane but mad, not young and muscular but old and stringy, whose fantastic adventures lead him home not to wine and triumph but to bed and death. The epic structure is there as well as the epic length; as in the Odyssey, a journey holds the book together. But those qualities of irony and humour which, ever since Cervantes, we have expected to find in the greatest novelists, are derived from no true epic source. It is the tension between heroic form and unheroic content, between deliberately inflated language ('Sing to me, O Muse') and man's pitiable deflatability that produces the unclassical tones of laughter and pathos.

It is perhaps because of its mocking relationship to the epic that we expect one of the properties of the novel to be length. The novels we all accept as important are very long—*Don Quixote, Tom Jones, Tristram Shandy, Scarlet and Black, Madame Bovary,* all Dickens, all Thackeray, *War and Peace, Anna Karenina, Crime and Punishment, Ulysses, Doctor Zhivago.* This does not, of course, mean that great length is a prerequisite of artistic importance, but when we want to disparage some of our modern novelists—those who, like Forster, Waugh and Greene, can say what they have to say in fewer than a hundred thousand words—we tend to use terms like 'slightness', 'a less than panoramic vista' and so on. The epic hangover remains, and we're unwilling to dignify books of, say, fifty thousand words and under with the title of novel,

WHAT IS A NOVEL?

preferring to use the Italian term *novella* ('novelette' disparages not only length but content). The epic is dead as a literary form, and we like to feel that the novel is our modern substitute for it, bulky enough to take up epic space.

But we ought not to be too narrow in our view of what a novel should be. Cervantes and his followers, with their long, loose, comic-pathetic chronicles of adventures on the road, in inns and inn-bedrooms, represent only part of the tale. There was romance as well as adventure to bring into the novel (the prototype of the romantic heroine is probably to be found in Dido, Queen of Carthage, who makes a brief but tragic appearance in the fourth book of Virgil's *Æneid*); there was allegory and fable. Already in the eighteenth century it is evident that the novel–which can be a collection of letters, as in Rousseau, Smollett and Richardson, or a philosophical fable, like Voltaire's *Candide* or Dr. Johnson's *Rasselas* or Beckford's *Vathek*, or a big mad joke, like Sterne's *Tristram Shandy*–is becoming difficult to define. The nineteenth century knew a kind of massive stability, with the complicated, long, but plain moral story-telling of George Eliot, Dickens, Thackeray, Trollope, but the twentieth century has reacted violently against the great tradition. The period we're concerned with in this book–the twenty-five years since the Second World War–has produced more novels than any corresponding period in history, but no age has found it more difficult to define exactly what a novel is.

The term 'novel' has, in fact, come to mean any imaginative prose composition long enough to be stitched rather than stapled (a book and not a pamphlet), but Philip Toynbee and Eric Linklater have recently reminded us that a novel need not be in prose. If we lay down other conditions–the need for a plot, dialogue, characters–we shall find our rules transgressed at once by practitioners of the 'anti-novel'. Vladimir Nabokov's *Pale Fire* is in the form of a long poem with notes; Michel Butor is prepared to write a novel that looks like a short encyclopaedia; Alain Robbe-Grillet seems more interested in objects than in people. We can easily convey our meaning without dialogue–through letters or interior monologue, for instance. As for plot, more and more

16

WHAT IS A NOVEL?

novelists are revolting against what they regard as 'contrivance', the manipulation of coincidences to produce a neat conclusion. But I think that, if we take away plot, character, dialogue, even characters, we shall be left with something that is common to the most traditional and the most *avant-garde* novelist–a concern with interpreting, through the imagination, the flux of ordinary life; an attempt to understand, though not with the cold delibration of the scientist, the nature of the external world and the mind that surveys it. But surely, some will object, this is the job of the poet? It is, but the poet's method is one of extreme compression, while the novelist must still be influenced–however minimally–by the more leisurely jog-trot rhythm of the creators of the traditional novel–Cervantes, Fielding and the rest. The poet fights against time; the novelist yields to it. The poem tends to contract, the novel to expand. We cannot forget the novel's epic origin all that easily.

One reason why the novel has become so Protean a form is to be found in the huge range of outlook and ability of the people who practise it. To be a poet or dramatist requires particular endowments and a willingness to learn difficult technical skills. But–this is sad but true—almost anyone can write a novel of sorts, and almost anyone does. It is nowadays considered a duty for nearly every literate person to attempt at least the one novel which he traditionally has in him. The urge of the taxi-driver, burglar, deep-sea diver or professional photographer to write a novel is usually a purgative one–to set down on paper a load of experience and so free the memory of it. On the other hand, there are the people who have always had an itch to write without possessing any real vocation for the older, tougher, forms of verse and drama; the novel is the medium most readily available and most easily publishable.

Nowadays we hear less about the 'professional' novelist than we used to. Men like Flaubert, Henry James, Joyce dedicated themselves to an art which, in their desire to achieve the deepest possible imaginative penetration of life, they seemed deliberately to make difficult. Of the hundreds of novels that appear every month, very few are the work of professionals of this kind. If we have a huge number of near-amateur novelists at work, we can be sure of an expansion of the scope of the novel, but, at the same time, we must fear its debasement. One professional novelist–Evelyn Waugh–takes it for granted that this age will produce no Dickens or Flaubert or Henry James. At the beginning of his novel *The Ordeal of Gilbert Pinfold* (1957) he says:

'It may happen in the next hundred years that the English novelist of the present day will come to be valued as we now value the artists and craftsmen of the late eighteenth century. The originators, the exuberant men, are extinct and in their place subsists and modestly flourishes a generation notable for elegance and variety of contrivance. It may well happen that there are lean years ahead in which our posterity will look back hungrily to this period, when there was so much will and so much ability to please.'

We may question the 'elegance' if not the 'variety of contrivance'. But we cannot doubt that the twenty-five years since the Second World War have produced nothing to compare with the masterpieces of, say, the half-century before it. Just after the war, Cyril Connolly seemed to think that the creation of a great work was a matter of volition:

'. . . the true function of a writer is to produce a masterpiece and . . . no other task is of any consequence. Obvious though this should be, how few writers will admit it, or, having drawn the conclusion, will be prepared to lay aside the piece of iridescent mediocrity on which they had embarked!'

We should all like to believe that the 'iridescent mediocrity' and the 'elegance and variety of contrivance' are there because the contemporary novelist is prevented from getting down to some great work by economic pressure (since, after all, advances are more quickly earned on mediocrities than on masterpieces). But, deeper down, we know that it is not just a matter of the novelist's finding security and leisure, since a masterpiece will get itself written against all odds. The trouble is that novelists nowadays do not care sufficiently or believe enough. Masterpieces spring out of conviction.

Evelyn Waugh's 'exuberant men' all had unshakable faith in something–whether in European civilization, Christianity, pro-

18

WHAT IS A NOVEL?

gress, or even just (as with D. H. Lawrence) the redemptive power of sex. Whether their beliefs can be proved by time to be valid is neither here nor there; it is the conviction that counts and, with the conviction, the energy of creation that springs from it. Most of the novelists of today do not feel sufficiently strongly about anything to be urged into attempting some large-scale work of individual vision which, fusing the comic and tragic in a fresh image of man, shall not merely impress us, the readers, but radically change our view of life–as *Don Quixote* and *War and Peace* and *Ulysses* have changed it. In England we have had angry shouts against the unjust past or against the Welfare State, but these articulate no real conviction. In America Norman Mailer is protesting against a whole concept of life–the 'American dream' –but he does not seem to imply belief in anything to take its place. The two 'big' European novels which have, in a sort of delayed action, appeared since the war–Thomas Mann's *Doctor Faustus* and Boris Pasternak's *Doctor Zhivago*–both record failure on the part of Germany and Russia respectively to counter the self-destructive urge which appeared at a moment of historical crisis: they are both massive works, and they approach traditional greatness, but they are as much cries of despair as exuberant shouts of acceptance. Perhaps the times are no longer propitious to the production of masterpieces which both embrace and enhance life.

We must not, then, look for giants in the period we are going to study. We can no longer expect the one big book, the single achievement, to be an author's claim to posterity's regard. We shall be more inclined to assess the stature of a novelist by his ability to create what the French call an *œuvre*, to present fragments of an individual vision in book after book, to build, if not a *War and Peace* or *Ulysses*, at least a shelf.

Before starting our survey, we shall have to face two problems, and the first of these is the problem of categorization. The range of the contemporary novel is so great that any system of compartment-making will both work and not work. We can have novels by women, novels by writers under thirty, novels about sex, novels

WHAT IS A NOVEL?

about the Bomb, novels by believing Catholics, novels by renegade Catholics, novels by Frenchmen, novels by Serbs, novels by Brazilians. However we split up the contemporary novel, we shall have to admit merely to freezing its living stream and then hacking it into arbitrary lumps of ice. Works of art will not yield to scientific categories; what looks systematic in this survey will really be only the loosest kind of free association. The second problem is about omissions. There are many novelists whom there will be no space to consider, and most of these will be writers for whom the general public has a high regard. Very occasionally the best book and the best-seller coincide, but generally the books that make the most money are those which lack both style and subtlety and present a grossly over-simplified picture of life. Such books are poor art, and life is too short to bother with any art that is not the best of its kind. It often happens also that whole nations are at variance as to who are the important writers. It is a shock to see, in the Soviet Union, the fully annotated collected edition of the Works of A. J. Cronin, complete with scholarly introduction. The French regard Charles Morgan, not now greatly admired in England, as a modern English classic. Neither author–nor the huge-selling British Denise and American Harold Robbins (*The Carpetbaggers*)–can find a place there.

In his novel *Cakes and Ale* (1930) Somerset Maugham has something to say about this apparent irreconcilability of best-seller and best book:

'The elect sneer at popularity; they are inclined to assert that it is a proof of mediocrity; but they forget that posterity makes its choice not from among the unknown writers of a period, but from among the known. . . . It may be that posterity will scrap all the best-sellers of our day, but it is among them that it must choose.'

One must take this with a large grain of salt. There is no need to equate the known and the best-seller. Henry James, Virginia Woolf, Ronald Firbank have never ceased to be known among those who take the novel seriously, but their sales have never been spectacular. It is enough that the informed part of the reading public should be sufficient to bring an author back into print or, if he is still in print, keep him there. This is real best-selling. The other kind is too tempestuous to last for more than a season. A writer is often immensely popular because he has something to say which has a strong but elusive relevance to life here and now. But when here and now have gone, his message must go with them. The huge sales of the late Ian Fleming will, in a few years' time, be no more than a wistful lip-licking publisher's memory. Meanwhile the more quietly meritorious, the moderate sellers with something permanent to give, will go steadily but unspectacularly on, finding a lasting place in the history of the novel. It is with such writers that the following pages will mainly deal.

II

Giants in Those Days

The term 'contemporary' ought not, in any discussion of literature, to be taken too literally. George Orwell's *Nineteen Eighty-Four*, though published in 1949, still has the feel and ring of a contemporary book, while L. P. Hartley's *The Brickfield*, which came out in 1964, seems to belong to a much earlier epoch. Of James Joyce, who died in 1941, two years after the publication of *Finnegans Wake*, it has been said by his biographer, Richard Ellmann, that we are still learning to be his contemporaries, 'to understand our interpreter'. Our best definition of 'contemporary' would have to bring in time, but it would not have to neglect the things that give time significance – the facts of history, the thoughts, feelings, hopes and apprehensions that make one era different from another and often render mere calendar mensuration irrelevant and frivolous.

For most of us, contemporary history begins with the Second World War. In 1939, the realities of the totalitarian state were made clear to us; in 1945 the potentialities of nuclear warfare. In a sense, the whole six-year period was a single moment in time, a revelation that has so changed our ways of thinking that the years before seem bundled up with all the past centuries as a remote parcel of ancient history. The writers who mean most to us are those who, like ourselves, have experienced the same profound revolution of thought and sensibility or, if they are too young to have known the moment of change, breathe the new era like natural air. That is why a writer like George Orwell, though dead

22

more than twenty years, goes on being our contemporary. As for James Joyce, we take him rather as a major prophet, one who foresaw the 'abnihilization of the etym' without living through it. He is a modern novelist who has equipped our minds with the words and symbols we need in order to understand the contemporary world, and he will still be waiting to help when the fearsome future rolls in.

But our age alone will not enable us to understand our contemporaries. However a novelist may take his subject-matter from the present, he still has to learn his technique from the past, and, after the sifting of history, we recognize what pre-atomic giants are still standing there, ready to teach the post-Hiroshima age how to tackle its artistic problems. Some of these giants—like Sterne, Dickens, Stendhal and Flaubert—belong to periods so remote-seeming that we feel they can rarely exercise a *direct* influence on contemporary novelists. When any author nowadays writes in the manner of Sterne (as B. S. Johnson did in his *Travelling People*) or in the spirit of Dickens (as Angus Wilson often seems to do), we think we see a self-conscious harking back to the past and we regard it as somewhat artificial. The absorption of qualities from the giants of the true modern age is altogether different.

First among these giants must stand Henry James, who seems, in his courteous, over-civilized way, to open the door on to the modern novel. The modernity lies in the refined subtlety of sensibility, the eagerness to probe character and motive, the over-scrupulous prose-style with its thickets of qualifying phrases and clauses. Too many nineteenth-century novelists—and we have to include Dickens here—are content with artificially contrived plots, melodramatic climaxes, and characterization which approaches caricature. James's dates proclaim him a Victorian (1843–1916), but his concern with recording the details of life with fine brush-strokes—rather than with the broad slaps of poster-paint of many of his contemporaries—brings him into an age which the professional psychologists have made strongly aware of the infinite gradations of behaviour, feeling, and motive. But James is modern in another way—a way he shares with the poets T. S. Eliot and

GIANTS IN THOSE DAYS

Ezra Pound. With the breakdown of belief which the nineteenth-century rationalists instigated, intellectuals took either to the pessimism of Thomas Hardy and A. E. Housman or to the liberalism of men like H. G. Wells and Bernard Shaw. The continuity of Christianity seemed to have been lost; men sought the sense of continuity elsewhere. James, an American self-exiled to Europe, just like Eliot and Pound, found this continuity in European culture. Sensitive Americans saw the 'new age' already developing in their native country–an age in which material values would be paramount and in which religion would be either a parade of dead forms or an over-repressive puritanism. The old wisdom and artistic riches of Europe stretched all before these exiles from a land they thought of as spiritually barren; the soul was fed and was itself able to assert the value of a culture the new materialistic age was threatening. James, it has been said, has only one real theme, and this theme is there at the beginning (in *The American*) and towards the end (in *The Ambassadors*)–the impact of wise, subtle, seductive Europe on susceptible Americans. It is a sufficient theme for the development of the most complex psychological relationships. James's influence remains, fifty-five years after his death. It is to be sensed in the prose-styles of writers as different as Elizabeth Bowen and James Baldwin and, despite its spinsterish scrupulousness and its endless qualifications, the Jamesian sentence is a superb instrument for rendering the motions of the cautious, cultivated sensibility.

Marcel Proust (1871–1922) was also concerned with rendering European society–the somewhat narrow society of aristocratic Paris, to be specific, but from the point of view of an asthmatic recluse and in retrospect. If James's influence has been powerful on writers in English, Proust's has profoundly modified the whole course of the novel wherever the form is practised. *A la Recherche du Temps Perdu* is a *roman fleuve* or 'river-novel'–a colossal work of fiction built up over ten years in volume after volume. The philosophical implications of the work are important. Plot does not matter; what does matter is the close examination of time past, a total recall of events which makes them appear not as

24

mere memory but as part of a flux that still exists. Events do not just occur: they are real, and man comes to them. Sensation–not thought–is primal, but it is through concentrating on sensation that time and space and even the individual self fall away, revealing a kind of eternity–*le temps retrouvé*: time regained. The intensity of Proust's concentration on the data of the outside world (which includes people) burns white-hot and generates a unique prose-poetry.

Proust's rival for the claim of greatest influence on the twentieth-century novel is James Joyce (1882–1941), an Irishman who exiled himself to Europe to write exclusively about his native Dublin. His two great works are *Ulysses* and *Finnegans Wake*, the first of which pushes the novel-form to its limit, while the second pushes the English language beyond its limit. *Ulysses* deals with the events of a single day (16th June 1904) in Dublin, concentrating on three main characters–a Jewish advertising canvasser, his singer-wife, and a young poet who is a transcription of Joyce himself. We not only see and hear these characters; we are admitted into their innermost thoughts, and these are presented in the jerky telegraphese of the 'interior monologue'. Joyce shares with James and Proust a passion for the actual, but his preoccupation with form goes much further, reaching–so some of his critics say–the obsessive or maniacal. *Ulysses* is a comic re-telling of Homer's Odyssey; every chapter of the novel corresponds in some ways with an episode of the epic. When Bloom, the Ulysses of our day, goes to lunch, he is in the land of the Laestrygonians or man-eaters; in a newspaper office he is in the cave of Aeolus, god of the winds; in the brothel district of Dublin he resists the power of Circe, who turns men into swine. The parallelism is worked out in correspondences of action, but also in symbols: the cognate themes of the newspaper-office chapter are wind and rhetoric, which fact encourages Joyce to cram the episode with references to wind and, at the same time, to turn it into a sly textbook on the art of oratory. The nature of the prose of each chapter is dictated by the subject-matter. Thus, in the lying-in hospital in Holles Street, the mystery of embryology–the study of the growth of the foetus in the womb –is figured in a history of English prose-styles from Anglo-Saxon to futuristic slang, so that the chapter itself has the feel of a growing foetus. Stylistic experiment is as much the author's concern as is the telling of his story about ordinary Dubliners: *Ulysses* is a kind of encyclopaedia of prose-styles. It is also an encyclopaedia in a more general sense, since Joyce seeks to sum up the whole of European civilization on the margins of his fiction. Send the hero Bloom to a pub, there to hear the Sirens (two barmaids), and the whole art of music flowers—not only in direct references, hidden symbols, the channelling of Bloom's thoughts to music, but in the prose-style itself, which imitates a fugue. Each chapter sums up an art or a science as well as being governed by a significant organ of the body (the ear for music, the lungs for Aeolus, the womb for the maternity hospital). European civilization is finally embodied in a symbolic human frame.

Joyce seemed with this work to have taken the resources of the English language as far as was decent in a mere novel. Also he had plunged into areas of the conscious mind which previous novelists had been shy of touching. But in his *Finnegans Wake* he went the whole hog and dove into man's dreaming world. The entire action takes place in the sleeping mind (a single night, to balance the single day of *Ulysses*) of a Dublin publican, and in his dream the whole of world history is recapitulated. It was necessary for Joyce to invent an appropriate language for dream, and the difficult, allusive, multilingual, punning dialect of *Finnegans Wake* is the 'Jabberwocky' of Lewis Carroll's dream pushed to the limit. *Ulysses* is one dead end—an exhaustion of the resources of the realistic novel—and this is another. Neither book represents a really new starting-point for the novel; Joyce not only initiates a fresh approach to the form but himself realizes its potentialities. He is the pioneer, but he is also the pastmaster. All that his successors have been able to do is to chew on fragments crumbled from the gigantic cake. But Joyce has sanctified experiment, as well as brought a bigger-than-Jamesian integrity and dignity to the novelist's vocation, and present-day writers must always be aware of working in his shadow.

Other experimentalists look very small beside Joyce. Virginia

GIANTS IN THOSE DAYS

Woolf was his exact coeval (1882–1941) and is lodged with him as an originator, though it is evident that her *Jacob's Room* (1922) owes something to *Ulysses*, published entire in the same year but serialized previously. Her scope could never be as great as Joyce's (she was hampered not only by her sex but by her upbringing and environment), but, like him, she exploited the 'stream of conscious-ness' method and, like Proust, was obsessed with dredging the lastingly significant out of the flux of time. The purpose of fiction, as she saw it, was not to fabricate artistic shocks through plot-manipulation (the way of the conventional novel, now as then) but rather to show what patterns are already implicit in real life and how—using the devices of the poet more than the fiction-maker—these can be made explicit through cunning selection of detail. Thus in *Mrs. Dalloway*—which has very little real 'story'—we find different characters brought into a relationship not through dramatic machinery but by their sharing of common experiences—usually external and fortuitous, such as the sight of a sky-writing aeroplane or the sound of a public clock chiming. In *The Waves*, whose poetic prose now reads very awkwardly, we seem to get as far away from the novel-form as possible, but at the same time we don't enter the liberating world of a true poem. The characters in this book go in for soliloquies which make no dramatic contact one with the other; the unity comes from a rather artificial device—descriptions of the sun passing over the sea from dawn to dusk, which may be taken as symbolic of the passing of time: experience of a common flux is what binds the characters together.

The obsession with time which we find in Proust, Joyce and Virginia Woolf alike is not a yielding to it; it is an attempt to con-quer it. The flow of time means nothing in itself, and yet, in ordin-ary life, we are forced to travel along it. Virginia Woolf uses time (a servant now, not a master) to make her patterns, but she also sometimes mocks it, making it as unreal as the treadmill of history which *Finnegans Wake* turns into a single night's dream. So *Orlando* tells the story of a person who, fully adult in the Eliza-bethan age, is hardly any older in the nineteen-twenties and who, starting as a man, turns into a woman exactly midway through the

27

book. *Between the Acts*, her last novel, seeks to summarize all English history—and even to hint at the whole process of evolution—while recounting the events of a summer day and the preoccupations of a handful of characters.

It was Wyndham Lewis (two years the junior of Virginia Woolf) who pointed out—in *Time and Western Man*—that writers like her and like Joyce were, far from overcoming time, merely portraying its flux. Lewis was a painter as well as a writer, and he believed that it was by concentrating on the solid objects which do spacetime the honour of filling them that the tyranny of the flux could best be broken. Lewis's novels—*Tarr, The Apes of God, The Revenge for Love*—are so crammed with fastidiously recorded visual detail that they move with intolerable slowness: he works at a page as though at a crowded canvas. His method is not the most suitable for his aim, which he proclaimed to be a satirical one (satire should go swiftly and not heavy-footed), although the painter's habit of looking at a human being as a mere *thing* must, translated into his other art of fiction, produce a kind of savage humour. It was Bergson, the time-philosopher whom all these writers had read, who said that humour proceeds from the conversion of the human into the mechanical—a living soul becomes an object bumping against other objects. The humour of Lewis's books is usually too clotted with detail to hit home, but, because of the highly individual manifesto they exemplify—'I am for the Great Without, for the method of *external* approach', said Lewis—the books have to be read. They are the best possible foil to Virginia Woolf and Joyce. Their influence has not yet been great, but Lewis is too massive a writer to be ignored by posterity.

There were once signs that Ronald Firbank (1886–1926) might slip away and be lost through sheer slightness of achievement. His little novels—*Valmouth, The Flower Beneath the Foot, Prancing Nigger, Concerning the Eccentricities of Cardinal Pirelli*—appear at first reading to be merely amusing, trivial, exquisite but empty. A closer examination shows that—beneath the stage exoticism, the sly sex and intrigue, the perverseness, the tones of a homosexual 'queen', the wit, the consciously laid-on colour and atmosphere—

there are elements of tragedy, suffering and despair. The quality is of the live puppetry in Stravinsky's *Petrouchka* (a work that belongs to Firbank's time)–a desperation of feeling under the clownish gestures. But, apart from his content, Firbank has had much to give to a generation of novelists anxious to achieve weight through lightness. Joyce and Wyndham Lewis are big and heavy: everything is explicit in them, nothing left as a mere hint, a question mark at the end of a chapter. Firbank showed men like Anthony Powell and Evelyn Waugh how to make the blank pieces between chapters work for them (everything in Firbank takes place off-stage or between the acts) and, more important, how to convey everything through dialogue that cannot be conveyed through sheer silence. The dialogue of Firbank is light, natural, short-breathed, but there are always overtones and nuances which are the real indicators of character (Dickensian description would be gross and tasteless), just as the lightest of brush-strokes in the scene-painting reveal a whole world. Firbank's naughtiness and daring no longer shock a public that has fed on strong American meat, but his technique remains as fresh as this morning.

Compared with the exquisite Firbank and the great experimentalists, D. H. Lawrence seems lumpish, traditional, even pedestrian, but his brief career–1885–1930–is a glory of various creation. To say that he celebrated carnal love would be to oversimplify. Lawrence was reacting against liberalism, science, materialism, against a civilization that was turning bad, mechanical and repressive, and he sought a new faith in the natural instincts of men and women. It is this passionate affirmation of the life of the body and the emotions that gives distinction to work which is stylistically often slipshod, formless, repetitive. Lawrence accepts life not with his brain but with his loins and bowels, and he rejects the squalid emasculations of 'civilized' existence with a hatred so thoroughgoing as to seem morbid. The book that has done his reputation most harm is the once-banned *Lady Chatterley's Lover*, but even this inferior work–the near-final effort of a dying man– is hot with a message that the smut-seekers miss. Lawrence sees the growing life-denial of the modern world and he needs

GIANTS IN THOSE DAYS

a symbol of life's renewal; he finds this in the physical love of man and woman. Sex is holy: it is a door to the abode of the 'dark gods' –whose home is the loins, not the heavens–now only openly worshipped by primitive peoples. Like William Blake, Lawrence rejects reason; the intellect misleads. Only the instincts and the imagination show the world of reality.

The wonder of novels like *Sons and Lovers*, *The Rainbow*, *Women in Love*, *The Plumed Serpent* lies in their passion, but also in their power to evoke the impact of the natural world–the feel and smell and colour of living things. His rhythms drive home the doctrine (Lawrence was essentially a teacher) of man's kinship with the earth. The following comes from *The Rainbow*:

'But heaven and earth was teeming around them, and how should this cease? They felt the rush of the sap in spring, they knew the wave which cannot halt, but every year throws forward the seed to begetting, and, falling back, leaves the young-born on the earth. They knew the intercourse between heaven and earth, sunshine drawn into the breast and bowels, the rain sucked up in the daytime, nakedness that comes under the wind in autumn, showing the birds' nests no longer worth hiding.'

And so on. There comes a time in the lives of all of us when, no longer captivated by Lawrence, we seek to disparage and parody and sneer about 'deep dark bitter belly-tension'. But inevitably we go back to him, one of the great fresheners and renewers. His influence remains immense.

Lawrence portrayed not civilized man but natural man. There are two ways of looking at natural man, however: he can affirm life or death. If Lawrence's characters are driven by the force in their loins, those of Ernest Hemingway (1898–1961) are impelled to hunt, shoot, kill, themselves face death. The centres of higher thought are as repugnant to Hemingway as to Lawrence; they seem hardly to be reflected in a prose-style which is stripped to the bone, content with short words, impatient of Latinate abstractions. Hemingway learned the new plain language from Gertrude Stein (1874–1946), an American like himself, but he popularized the pared syntax and spare vocabulary of her verbal experiments

30

GIANTS IN THOSE DAYS

in a context of 'action fiction'. His best work is perhaps his first and last, beginning with *The Sun Also Rises* and *A Farewell to Arms* and ending with *The Old Man and the Sea* (a novella which, behind the action, seems to carry an allegorical meaning); his short stories–like those in the volume *Men Without Women*– perhaps show the paring-down process at its best. His technique is a little too easy to imitate, and many of the cheap 'tough' thrillers which infest the bookstalls are indebted to him. But his real qualities–disillusionment, stoicism, physical courage–hold their magic in a sort of historical perspective: he is very much one of the American writers who came out of the First World War.

Scott Fitzgerald (1896–1904) belonged to the same generation, but the whole post-war American age–not the exile from it, the lone hunter–is mirrored in his work. This makes his quality harder to summarize than Hemingway's. *The Great Gatsby* is, like so many American novels, about an American dream; here it is one dreamed by the romantic wealthy bootlegger who gives the book its name. He has become wealthy because, as a poor boy, he fell in love with a girl cocooned in wealth–her youth and beauty as it were preserved in it. The great levelling of the war, which turned him into a young officer, seemed to make her nearly accessible to one of his class and background; his tragedy is that his post-war elevation to riches does not make her wholly accessible. There are things he does not understand–that the past cannot be repeated, that the dream one has of oneself cannot be realized by the mere act of willing it. Gatsby is that jazz-age bloated America which was ended by the financial crash that ended the mad twenties. Fitzgerald is obsessed, like America herself, with a tycoon image which is also chivalric: it is there in *Tender is the Night* and in the unfinished *The Last Tycoon*, which is based on the career of the filmproducer Irving Thalberg. But, recording the tragedy of the fall of great men, he was aware of the adolescent nature of the image. His own personal tragedy was that he belonged to the dream and collapsed with it. Budd Schulberg's novel *The Disenchanted* portrays, in the character of Manley Halliday, the last sad days of this great American writer.

GIANTS IN THOSE DAYS

Fitzgerald's achievement was to fix an age in words and find fictional symbols for a national dream. Ford Madox Ford (1873–1939)–a British novelist of enormous talent and output, still shamefully neglected–recorded in his *Parade's End* a dream less optimistic and more quixotic. This work consists of four novels–*Some Do Not, No More Parades, A Man Could Stand Up* and *Last Post*–which trace the wartime career of Christopher Tietjens, the 'last Tory', devoted to ideals of impossible chivalry, unable to stem the rising tide of a new race of opportunists, systematically hounded by his wife and his godfather (also his general), absurdly generous, too much the gentleman to survive. And yet without him, we feel, nothing we fundamentally value can survive. Tietjens is, for all his static monolithic qualities, one of the great characters of modern English fiction and might be–if he were better known –one of the great myths of a society that seems to be losing its bearings. Ford's other important novel is *The Good Soldier*–described as 'the best *French* novel in English'. This probably means that it essays a subtlety in the portrayal of a most complex human relationship–four people knotted into an agony the world never sees–that, up to the time of its appearance in 1915, had never been seen outside France. Here, in the character of Edward Ashburnham, is another incarnation of Ford's English gentleman, to whom 'death rather than dishonour' is no mere empty slogan. Ford wrote too much (whatever that means; no man who writes to live can ever write too much), and he might be more favourably regarded if he had written nothing but *Parade's End* and *The Good Soldier*: they are suspect to many because they seem embedded in a mass of inferior pot-boilers. But they are among the finest fiction of the century.

E. M. Forster (1879–1970) could never be accused of writing too much. His first novel–*Where Angels Fear to Tread*–appeared in 1905, and his fifth, last and best–*A Passage to India*–in 1924. On this mere handful a very formidable reputation rests. The Forsterian technique is traditional, and some of his plot-elements seem to belong to the world of melodrama rather than to the sophisticated modern novel, but his originality and subtlety lie in the dry, often sceptical, frequently witty, always civilized commentary. Perhaps his themes are best summed up in the motto to *Howard's End*–'Only connect'–and the remark of Helen Schlegel in the same book: 'Personal relations are the important thing for ever and ever, and not this outer world of telegrams and anger.' Two worlds are always trying but always failing to connect–that of a society with formal conventions, some intelligence but no real grasp of life's purpose; that of the individuals who lie outside this society, generally inefficacious in action, aware of personal inadequacy, but, at moments of crisis, better able to act than the group that, superficially, is better endowed. The melodramatic situations are contrived so that human capacity can be tested to the uttermost. In *A Passage to India* the big dichotomy finds ready-made expression in the English society of Chandrapore and the Indian community. The two tentatively approach each other, both societies are tested after the alleged event in the Marabar Caves (Dr. Aziz is accused of rape by Adela Quested), contact is both gently sought and rudely forced, but contact fails. Even at the end, when Aziz and Fielding (who has attempted to love and understand the Indians) meet many years after Aziz's trial we hear the words 'No, not yet' and 'No, not there', echoing the irony of 'Only connect'. 'Only', indeed. As a whole corpus of Australian fiction seems to have sprung out of Lawrence's *Kangaroo*, so *A Passage to India* may be said to have fathered the Indian novel in English.

The novelists we have considered so far present the real world, however fantastically, and however they allow poetical symbols to intrude. We must come now to a movement in the novel which owes far more to ancient allegory than to modern naturalism. Despite one outstanding native example–T. F. Powys's *Mr. Weston's Good Wine*, in which God comes as a wine-merchant (his good wine is death) to the village of Folly Down–the most potent allegorist (though perhaps that is too simple a term) has been Franz Kafka (1883–1924)–an Austrian Jew born in Prague. Powys's morality can be explained easily enough in terms of Christian doctrine, as can Bunyan's *Pilgrim's Progress*, but

GIANTS IN THOSE DAYS

Kafka's three best novels—*The Trial*, *The Castle*, and *America*—and short stories like *The Metamorphosis* and *The Great Wall of China* are too complex for straightforward exegesis. The atmosphere is always nightmarish, though the style is usually flat and verbose, and the theme is always unresolved suffering. In *The Trial* the hero is arraigned on a charge which is never directly specified, is forced to contrive a defence (but what is he defending himself against?) yet at the end is politely executed. In *The Castle* a young engineer comes to work in a village, receiving his orders from unseen authorities who are hidden behind castle-walls. A Christian interpretation is possible—we are all subject to divine laws which we may not question, however little we understand; the human soul is isolated in a wood of terrible mysteries. But the Kafka world is hopeless, and Christianity is based on hope, as well as faith and charity. Any interpretation of Kafka in terms of orthodox religion, whether Jewish or gentile, tends to leave the essence of his work unelucidated; we have to look elsewhere for a key. Even his diaries, which record an acute psycho-neurosis, give only a partial answer. But the excessive domination he suffered from his father, his need to fight and yet placate authority, bring us close to a reason for the guilt and the hopelessness. In Kafka we are really digging at the roots of religion, finding a savage primal law set in the twisted dark streets of a modern Central Europe.

Kafka has influenced us all, not merely writers. When he first read *The Trial* aloud to his friends, their response was laughter. Nobody laughs now. We have all come to feel a powerful and desperate guilt since the revelations of Belsen and the blasting of Hiroshima: there are few of us now, Christian or not, who would reject the doctrine of Original Sin. And, with the breakdown of society as our fathers knew it, the creation instead of huge conurbations where everybody is lonely, the Kafka theme of man's essential isolation strikes at us poignantly. He was a pilot of the pain of contemporary man.

Thomas Mann (1875–1955) is revered more than his brother Heinrich (though the latter's *Professor Unrat* became universally known in its film-form—*The Blue Angel*), but it is difficult to assess

GIANTS IN THOSE DAYS

the extent of his influence on contemporary novelists. One of his great themes has been the conflict between the artist and the ordinary *bourgeois* man (*Tonio Kröger*), another the cultural sickness of Europe between the wars, given symbolic form in the sanatorium of *The Magic Mountain*. The massive tetralogy *Joseph and his Brethren* has seemed too Teutonically metaphysical for many readers, but the concentration of his thought, his profound philosophical concern with the future of Europe and the Germany that exiled him, found its supreme expression in *Doctor Faustus* (1949). This life of the 'German Composer Adrian Leverkühn as told by a Friend' boldly translates to our century the story of Faust's pact with the devil, the exchange of his soul for twenty-four years of power–with Leverkühn, the power of the supreme artist. The devil appears in the form of a disease; is genius then essentially a morbid thing? More particularly, has the greatness of Germany's achievement–in art, science, scholarship, above all music–been earned through deliberate self-damnation? This is the finest novel ever written about a creative artist, but it is far more than that: it is the deepest excavation of the German mind yet attempted by any writer of fiction.

I end our brief blow along the Giants' Causeway here–arbitrarily. The whole list of great names will seem arbitrary to any reader versed in the fiction of the last sixty or seventy years. Where is Joseph Conrad? He is up there, hard and bright, a fixed star, but he seems to belong to an age anterior to Henry James's, even though he died eight years after James. Any contemporary writer on the sea will be drawn to *Lord Jim* or *Youth*; no writer on the Congo can ignore *Heart of Darkness*. Some of Conrad's technical innovations–a shifting time sequence, the presentation of the action from the viewpoints of different characters (most notable in *Chance*)–have been influential. Still, Conrad seems to belong to an age which resists the new psychology and philosophy–Freud and Jung and Bergson–and his ornate prose is a final fruit rather than a new seed. It is this same unwillingness to recognize a new view of the universe–microcosm and macrocosm–and to mould style into modern rhythms that pushes back authors like

GIANTS IN THOSE DAYS

Galsworthy and Arnold Bennett into a past remoter than that of Proust or James or Joyce. (The same might, with some justice, be said of E. M. Forster, but we must beware of total consistency.) Apart from these bulky writers, there are solitary 'sports' like Fr. Rolfe–whose great novel *Hadrian the Seventh* has gained a new audience through its recent adaptation for the stage–who are too much bound up in idiosyncratic fantasies to be fruitful as influences. And there are novelists who, though important, seem to derive their importance from greater men. Let this chapter stand as a sort of penumbra to the light of our own times.

See Bibliographical Note on p. 12

F. Scott FITZGERALD (1896–1940)
This Side of Paradise. 1920
The Beautiful and Damned. 1922
The Great Gatsby. 1925
Tender is the Night. 1934
The Last Tycoon. 1941

Ernest HEMINGWAY (1898–1961)
In Our Time. 1924 (Paris) 1925
The Sun Also Rises. 1926
The Torrents of Spring. 1926
A Farewell to Arms. 1929
To Have and Have Not. 1937
For Whom the Bell Tolls. 1940
Across the River and Into the Trees. 1950
The Old Man and the Sea. 1952
A Moveable Feast. 1964

B. S. JOHNSON (1933–   )
Travelling People. 1963
Albert Angelo. 1964
Trawl. 1966

James JOYCE (1882–1941)
Portrait of the Artist as a Young Man. 1916
Ulysses. 1922 (Paris) 1936 (London)

James JOYCE (*continued*)
Finnegans Wake. 1939
Stephen Hero (Part of first draft of 'Portrait of the Artist'). 1944

Wyndham LEWIS (1884–1957)
Tarr. 1918
The Childermass. 1928
The Apes of God. 1930
Doom of Youth. 1932
Snooty Baron. 1932
The Roaring Queen. 1936
Count Your Dead: They are Alive! 1937
The Revenge for Love. 1937
The Mysterious Mr. Bull. 1938
The Vulgar Streak. 1941
America and Cosmic Man. 1948
Monstre Gai. 1945

Thomas MANN (1875–1955)
Royal Highness. 1915, tr. 1952
Confessions of Felix Krull. 1924, tr. 1955
Buddenbrooks. 1903, tr. 1924
Tonio Kröger. 1925, tr. 1928
The Magic Mountain. 1925, tr. 1927

Thomas MANN (*continued*)
  Joseph and his Brethren:
    The Tales of Jacob. 1933,
      tr. 1934
    The Young Joseph. 1934,
      tr. 1935
    Joseph in Egypt. 1936,
      tr. 1938
    Joseph the Provider. 1948,
      tr. 1949
  Lotte in Weimar. 1940, tr. 1940
  Doctor Faustus. 1948, tr. 1949
  The Holy Sinner. 1951, tr. 1952
  The Black Swan. 1953, tr. 1954

T. F. POWYS (1875–1953)
  Black Bryony. 1923
  Mark Only. 1924
  Mockery Gap. 1925
  Mr. Tasker's Gods. 1925
  Innocent Birds. 1926
  Mr. Weston's Good Wine. 1927
  Kindness in a Corner. 1930

T. F. POWYS (*continued*)
  The Only Penitent. 1931
  Unclay. 1931
  Make Thyself Many. 1953
  Goat Green. 1937

Budd SCHULBERG (1914–   )
  What Makes Sammy Run?
    1941
  The Harder They Fall. 1947
  The Disenchanted. 1950
  Waterfront. 1955

Virginia WOOLF (1882–1941)
  The Voyage Out. 1915
  Night and Day. 1919
  Jacob's Room. 1922
  Mrs. Dalloway. 1925
  To the Lighthouse. 1927
  Orlando. 1928
  The Waves. 1931
  Flush. 1933
  The Years. 1937
  Between the Acts. 1941

III

Utopias and Dystopias

One of the giants I deliberately ignored in the last chapter is H. G. Wells. This does not mean that the contemporary novel ignores him – rather the opposite. Wells is perhaps the only 'progressive' writer of the early modern age to have been both absorbed and reacted against. He has been absorbed as the pioneer of science fiction – a productive, vigorous and popular form. He has also been absorbed as the best of the post-Dickensian chroniclers of striving lower-middle-class youth, fighting to the top in a world peopled by repressive genuinely Dickensian grotesques. It is difficult to imagine a novel like Edward Hyams's *All We Possess* (1961) being written without the example of, say, *Tono-Bungay*. Hyams has a hero, Edward Tillotson, who climbs up various commercial and scientific ladders, knows setbacks and ultimate failure, messes up his sex-life and is convicted of financial malpractice. But there is one important difference between Hyams's approach to life and Wells's. When man fails to be true, beautiful and good, Wells blames history, society, human ignorance. Hyams, on the other hand, blames the human ego. In Wells, the enlightened self could, if all other selves were enlightened, build the New Jerusalem. In Hyams, man's duty is to recognize the hell of self and attempt to destroy it. His epitaph is taken from Simone Weil, one of the saints of our day: 'We possess nothing in the world – a mere chance can strip us of everything – excepting the power to say "I". That is what we have to give to God – in other words, to destroy. There is absolutely no free act which it is given to us to accomplish

UTOPIAS AND DYSTOPIAS

—only the destruction of the "I".' Such a doctrine would have been repugnant to Wells. Wells, a scientific liberal, rejected ideas like good and evil as ultimate propositions. There was no such thing as Original Sin; man was born free to build good—not to earn it or inherit it by divine grace. Wells believed that a Utopia was possible; he called himself a Utopiographer.

Many novelists set themselves the task—before and after the war—of exposing Wells's optimistic scientific liberalism as a sham. Science and education, said Wells, would outlaw war, poverty, squalor. All of us carry an image of the Wellsian future—rational buildings of steel and glass, rational tunics, clean air, a diet of scientifically balanced vitamin-capsules, clean trips to the moon, perpetual world peace. It was a fine dream, and what nation could better realize it than the Germans? After all, their scientific and educational achievements seemed to put them in the vanguard of Utopia-builders. What, though, did they give to the world? A new dark age, a decade of misery. Wells lived to see the break-up of his own rational dream and believed that homo sapiens had come to the end of his tether. It was time for evolution to throw up a new race. He died a disappointed liberal.

Liberalism breeds disappointment. The traditional doctrines of Europe do not. Accept that man is imperfect, that good and evil exist, and you will not, like Wells, expect too much from him. One characteristic of the contemporary novel is this acceptance of imperfect man, though not necessarily in a shoulder-shrugging what-can-we-do-about-it way. The human will, say some writers, is evil, it always chooses the bad; but we can, through a kind of spiritual discipline, unite ourselves with that Ground of Being (God, if you wish) that is good. It is time to mention the greatest anti-Wellsian of them all, Aldous Huxley.

Huxley's death in November 1963 was ignored by the great world because it had another death to think about—the assassination of President Kennedy in Dallas, Texas, U.S.A. This event, like the assassination of Gandhi which starts off one of Huxley's last novels, the bitter and terrible *Ape and Essence*, could be taken as a self-evident proof of the existence of evil—a Huxleyan starting-point

UTOPIAS AND DYSTOPIAS

which it was too late for Huxley to use. Huxley's awareness of good and evil found its first starting-point in the awareness of human division which found expression in an early novel *Point Counter Point*. His work before that had been gay, witty, erudite, vaguely pessimistic (*Crome Yellow*), concerned with the lack of belief and lack of direction in the cultured classes of the nineteen-twenties (*Antic Hay*), half-convinced that there was a way out of the human mess (*Those Barren Leaves*) which was closer to Indian yoga than to European Christianity. The statement of *Point Counter Point*, however, was that in man too many irreconcilables are yoked together for happiness in this world—flesh and spirit, passion and reason, instinct and intellect. The musical implications of the title applied to the fictional technique he used—many plots proceeding at the same time, very nearly independent of each other, on the analogy of the melodic strands of a complex piece of counterpoint—a Bach fugue, say. But the reader was also meant to perceive the counterpoint of different ways of looking at life—'with religious eyes, scientific eyes, economic eyes, *homme moyen sensuel* eyes', as Philip Quarles, the novelist within the novel, puts it. Huxley sees something of man's tragic condition in the fact that the different lines of approach never come together: they always remain parallel. The religious interpretation of man is at variance with the scientific; describe the sexual act in terms of pure mechanics and love and beauty dissolve. Man is bigger and more complex than H. G. Wells thought he was: there are also imponderables in him that neither science nor politics can explain.

Huxley's counterblast to Wells took the form of a Utopian novel called *Brave New World*. Huxley begins with a very Wellsian proposition: let science take over the world, let every natural impulse be controlled by science, let science condition us before birth and keep us conditioned in life. There is no doubt that science can produce world stability and individual happiness. And so, in Huxley's imaginary future world-state, children are bred artificially and made, in the very test-tube, content with whatever lot the State bestows on them. Human beings are graded like examination results: the Alphas do the intelligent work and the Deltas are the sweepers and cleaners. There is not much work to do and there are manifold pleasures, chief of which is sex, though a sex totally dissociated from the act of reproduction. There is no crime, there is no immorality: science had bred out the destructive element in man. This is a real Utopia, dedicated to the pursuit of happiness.

Into this world comes a young man bred in the old outlawed natural way, brought up among savages and on–ironical touch– a collected volume of Shakespeare's plays and poems, a book taboo in the new dispensation. The Savage (as he is called) rejects the new sinless and happiness-seeking order; he thinks that man ceases to be man when he is incapable of squalor, shame, guilt and suffering. A world in which there is no family hierarchy, no dignity in birth and death, and–perhaps worst of all–none of the human conditions which can produce a Shakespeare is the terminus of scientific progress. What is a Utopia to the people he is thrown amongst is its opposite–a Dystopia–to him. He crucifies himself for the sinlessness of the world.

The chilling point that Huxley makes in *Brave New World* is that science is already capable of creating a new type of human being thoroughly content with whatever his rulers give him. But is happiness enough? It was a question to be asked again in *After Many a Summer*, in which an American millionaire scared of death finances scientific research into longevity. The answer comes, however, not from modern science but from an eighteenth-century diary bought up in a job-lot library by the millionaire's British agent. The writer of the diary noted the longevity of carp and sought to prolong his own life by eating their raw minced guts. And it is discovered that, in the England of the late nineteen-thirties, he is still alive, hidden in a cellar, surreptitiously fed. The great secret has been discovered, though there is a snag: to live a couple of centuries you must reconcile yourself to reverting to the ape. But the millionaire is prepared to accept this: the important thing is to put off dying.

This nagging away–always erudite, lucid and witty–at man's purpose on earth, the nature of progress, the ends as well as the

UTOPIAS AND DYSTOPIAS

means of life, characterized Huxley's work to the end. He painted in *Ape and Essence* a picture of life in California after an atomic war – the end of civilization except for its squalor, taboos and stupid or deliberate worship of evil. The world, Huxley implied in his title and in some of the fantastic sequences of the book, is being run by apes. But, unlike Wells, he did not call for the extinction of man and the supervention of a new and more intelligent species: man could still follow the good if he united himself with the eternal Ground of Being. And his last novel – *Island* – presented a real Utopia.

As with so much of Huxley's later fiction, one is not sure whether or not to call this book a novel. It is less concerned with telling a story than with presenting an attitude to life, it is weak on character but strong on talk, crammed with ideas and uncompromisingly intellectual. Huxley gives us an imaginary tropical island where the good and happy life can be cultivated for the simple reason that the limitations and potentialities of man are understood. He presents a conspectus of this life, ranging from modes of sexual behaviour to the technique of dying. Nobody is scientifically conditioned to be happy: this new world is really brave. It has learned a great deal from Eastern religion and philosophy, but it is prepared to take the best of the art and science of the West. The people themselves are a sort of ideal Eurasian race, equipped with fine bodies and Huxleyan brains, and they have read all the books that Huxley has read.

All this sounds like an intellectual game, a hopeless dream in a foundering world, but Huxley was always enough of a realist to know that there is a place for optimism. Indeed, no teacher is a pessimist, and Huxley was essentially a teacher. In *Island* the good life is eventually destroyed by a brutal, stupid, materialistic young raja who wants to exploit the island's mineral resources. The armoured cars crawl through, the new dictator makes a speech about Progress, Values, Oil, True Spirituality, but, 'disregarded in the darkness, the fact of enlightenment remained'. The mynah birds fly around, crying the word they have been taught: 'Karuna. Karuna.' The word means 'enlightenment'.

UTOPIAS AND DYSTOPIAS

For forty years his readers forgave Aldous Huxley for turning the novel-form into an intellectual hybrid–the teaching more and more overlaying the proper art of the fiction-writer. Having lost him, we now find nothing to forgive. No novels more stimulating, exciting or genuinely enlightening came out of the post-Wellsian time. Huxley more than anybody helped to equip the contemporary novel with a brain.

From Huxley on, the creators of dystopias were impelled not by a pure science-fiction desire to tickle the imagination but by a moral concern which needed the form of a fable rather than of the psychological novel. George Orwell wrote a number of social novels and autobiographical tracts–*Down and Out in Paris and London, The Road to Wigan Pier, Keep the Aspidistra Flying, Coming Up for Air*–before coming to the notice of the whole world with *Animal Farm*, a brilliant political parable. The beasts on a farm revolt against the tyranny of the farmer, expel him, and take over the running of the farm themselves. Profits shall be ploughed back, there shall be no exploitation, all animals shall be equal. The pigs, who are considered more intelligent than the rest, form the executive of the new Utopia; things go well for a time. Soon, though, the high ideals of the revolution are forgotten, the tenets of democracy are discarded, and the pigs form an oligarchy. It is the story of the Russian Revolution; it is the story of any revolution. The slogan 'All animals are equal' has added to it: 'but some are more equal than others'. The pigs forget the other slogan–'Four legs good, two legs bad'–and enter into trading and social relations with human beings. At the end it is impossible to distinguish the human beings from the pigs.

Nineteen Eighty-Four, Orwell's last novel, is one of the few dystopian visions to have changed men's habits of thought. It is possible to say that the ghastly future Orwell foretells will not come about, simply because he has foretold it: we have been warned. The world of less than twenty years ahead is presented as divided into three super-states–Oceania, Eurasia and Eastasia. Britain is part of Oceania and is called Airstrip One. Winston Smith, a citizen of its capital, has been brought up, like everyone else, to accept the monolithic rule of Big Brother–a mythical and hence immortal being, the titular head of an oligarchy which sub-scribes to a philosophy called, ironically, English Socialism or Ingsoc. Only the 'proles', the masses, are free, free because their minds are too contemptible to be controlled; members of the Party are under perpetual surveillance from the Thought Police. Winston, the last man to possess any concept of freedom, revolts, but he is arrested and–through torture and brainwashing–rehabilitated. He learns the extent of the power of the Party, its limitless ability to control thought, even speech. Newspeak is a variety of English which renders it impossible to express an heretical thought; 'doublethink' is a technique which enables the Party to impress its own image on external reality, so that '$2+2=5$' can be a valid equation. The State is absolute, the only repository of truth. The last free man yields, of his own brainwashed free will, his whole being to it.

Huxley himself admitted, in re-introducing *Brave New World* to the post-war age, that *Nineteen Eighty-Four* gave a more plausible picture of the future than his own novel. Whether Orwell himself, were he alive today, would withdraw any part of his prophecy we do not know: he was mortally sick when he made it. The memorable residue of both novels is the fact of the tenuous-ness of human freedom, the vulnerability of the will, and the genu-ine–verifiable in real life–power of the scientist. One of the dangers of the scientific approach is its love of generalizations. Consider a man scientifically (as Huxley, with an ironical purpose, often does) and all that makes him a unique individual is system-atically eliminated. Thus, the scientifically run community can find no place for the eccentric or the exceptional. This is the moral of both *Brave New World* and *Nineteen Eighty-Four*.

It is also the moral of L. P. Hartley's *Facial Justice*, a novel which lives in an area where the dystopian vision and the pure moral fable overlap. Hartley's earlier works are in the Henry James tradi-tion–realistic, analytic, dealing with a known and traditional so-ciety–but his approach to morality was always highly individual. The *Eustace and Hilda* trilogy, which appeared between 1944 and

1947, presents its main theme symbolically in the first book of the three – *The Shrimp and the Anemone*. Eustace, as a young boy, looks into a pond and sees an anemone sucking away at a shrimp. He doesn't know where his sympathies lie: the shrimp is dying, but the anemone needs its dinner. While he is debating the morality of the situation, 'the unswallowed part of the shrimp grew perceptibly smaller'. As we read of the relationship between Eustace and Hilda, we learn that he is the shrimp and she the anemone; the boy and the girl, eventually the young man and young woman, are locked in a morbid dance of death which they are powerless to stop: they are destined to destroy each other. What sounds grim is, in fact, treated with great lightness and humour, and it is these qualities which enhance *Facial Justice*, which some, including myself, consider his most imaginative work.

Hartley presents us with an England recovering from World War III: there have been atomic attacks, and society has only recently emerged from skulking in caves. The new state is poisoned with a sense of guilt, and every one of its citizens is named after a murderer. Thus the heroine has been christened Jael 97. An attempt to build a moral world has resulted in an outlawing of envy and the competitive urge. There must be no great beauty, neither in body (which sackcloth covers, anyway) nor in face. A girl who feels herself 'facially underprivileged' can be fitted with a standard Beta face, neither ugly nor beautiful. Jael 97 is facially overprivileged: her beauty must be reduced to a drab norm. But, like the heroes and heroines of all dystopian novels, she is an eccentric. Seeing for the first time the west tower of Ely Cathedral, one of the few lofty structures left unflattened by war, she experiences a transport of ecstasy and revolts against the régime. But it is a régime with more liberal seeds in it than Orwell's.

One sees a great deal of our own age in Hartley's fantastic future, where the weather, with no room for either ice or fire, is always cool and grey and the state slogan is 'Every valley shall be exalted'. Perhaps every dystopian vision is a figure of the present, with certain features sharpened and exaggerated to point a moral and a warning. Constantine Fitzgibbon's *When the Kissing Had*

UTOPIAS AND DYSTOPIAS

to Stop (a corrupt future England falls into the hands of the vigorous and incorrupt Communists) and Diana and Meir Gillon's *The Unsleep* (the urge to 'live' finds a means of dispensing with sleep, with terrible consequences) are as much satires as are Orwell's and Huxley's fantasies, and only the present is worth satirizing. To give H. G. Wells his due, there was always a touch of the moralist in the best 'scientific romances'–there is trouble in the future world of *The Time Machine* and of *When the Sleeper Awakes*–but he held, in books like *The Dream* and even *The Shape of Things to Come*, that man ought to be optimistic about his ultimate future, for the perfect liberal society could be planned, could be built. Nowadays we are more cautious in our prophecies.

All these visionary novels are by English authors. But America has had its own bad dreams, like Sinclair Lewis's *It Can't Happen Here* (shamefully neglected) with its closely drawn picture of a democratic United States turning fascist. In a sense, this nightmare of the nineteen-thirties had been prefigured in the same author's *Babbitt*, just after the First World War, with its study of the socially repressive forces of American capitalism–expressed in small-town 'boosterism'. George F. Babbitt, a typical real-estate broker of his age and country, makes odd feeble gestures of revolt against the reactionary sanctimoniousness of Mid-West Zenith ('the Zip City') but gives in because his whole personal ethos derives from boosting, go-getting and tame social orthodoxy. He is already conditioned to the materialist heresy we may term Anericanism. This is a comic novel, but it shows the sharp teeth of the social critic.

Nevil Shute, the late popular novelist with the no-nonsense style, or lack of style, which bespeaks the trained technologist rather than the literary man, has written two flat but interesting novels set in the Australian future. *In the Wet* looks first at an England gone grey and spiritless with socialism and the over-levelling of a one-man one-vote universal franchise, and then transfers the British monarchy–beset by the snarling republicans of the Left–to Australia. It is a touching near-future projection, a marginal effort of the prophetic imagination.

UTOPIAS AND DYSTOPIAS

His *On the Beach*, on the other hand, gives us nothing less than the end of the world. Southern Australia awaits the drift, from the already extinguished Northern Hemisphere, of the radiation sickness that is the legacy of World War III. The people of Melbourne and environs live their few months of life with commendable Anglo-Saxon phlegm, having deliberately closed their minds to the coming disaster. But the disaster comes, and human life is snuffed out for ever. This is perhaps the only true 'close-ended' novel ever written. No character exists after the final page, but it would be cruel to suggest that no character exists before it either. Shute's talent was small and lucrative, but his books have ideas, and ideas are no despicable commodity in the post-Huxleyan novel.

See Bibliographical Note on p. 12

Constantine FITZGIBBON
    (1919–   )
  When the Kissing Had To Stop.
    1960
Diana and Meir GILLON
    (1915–   ) and (1907–   )
  The Unsleep. London, 1961
L. P. HARTLEY (1895–   )
  Eustace and Hilda:
    The Shrimp and the
        Anemone. London, 1944
    Sixth Heaven. London, 1946
    Eustace and Hilda. London,
        1947
  Facial Justice. London, 1960
  The Brickfield. London, 1964
Aldous HUXLEY (1895–1963)
  Crome Yellow. London, 1921
  Antic Hay. 1923
  Those Barren Leaves. 1925
  Point Counter Point. 1928
  Brave New World. 1932
  After Many a Summer. 1939

Aldous HUXLEY (*continued*)
  Ape and Essence. 1948
  Island. 1962
Edward HYAMS (1910–   )
  All We Possess. London, 1931
    (published as Tillotson, New
    York, 1931)
  The Mischief Makers. Harlow,
    1968
George ORWELL (1903–50)
  Keep the Aspidistra Flying.
    London, 1936
  The Road to Wigan Pier. London, 1937
  Coming up for Air. London,
    1939
  Animal Farm. London, 1945
  Nineteen Eighty-Four. 1949
Sinclair LEWIS (1885–1951)
  Babbitt. 1922
  It Can't Happen Here. 1935
Nevil SHUTE (1899–   )
  No Highway. 1948

47

UTOPIAS AND DYSTOPIAS

Nevil SHUTE (*continued*)
  A Town like Alice. 1950
  In the Wet. 1953
  On the Beach. 1957
H. G. WELLS (1866–1946)
  The Time Machine. 1895
  The War of the Worlds. 1898

H. G. WELLS (*continued*)
  When the Sleeper Wakes. 1899
  The Food of the Gods. 1904
  Tono-Bungay. 1908
  The Dream. 1924
  The Shape of Things to Come. 1933

IV

War's Sour Fruits

One of the gloomiest aspects of the fictional future time–as presented in works like *Nineteen Eighty-Four*, *Ape and Essence*, and *Facial Justice*, as well as Shute's popular vision of the end of man– is the aftermath of nuclear war. A good deal of ordinary non-visionary fiction has the shadow of the Bomb in it. And yet comparatively few good novels came out of that real, historical, war which ended with the blasting of Hiroshima and Nagasaki. The First World War produced many works of great merit–think of Hemingway's *A Farewell to Arms*, Richard Aldington's *Death of a Hero*, Erich Maria von Remarque's *All Quiet on the Western Front*, to give but a few examples–but the Hitler war failed to stimulate novelists as it failed to produce poets of the calibre of Siegfried Sassoon and Wilfrid Owen. Perhaps it was because the stamping out of a wretched tyranny was a necessary grim chore, and a guiltily belated one: it could not stimulate the imagination with that at least initial crusading fervour which had fired Rupert Brooke in 1914. Moreover, the First World War was to become so useless and wasteful that all that writers came to see in it was purely mythical–the old men cold-bloodedly destroying the young–and poets and novelists welcome myth, however ghastly. But the later war only stimulated the desire to keep records–usually of the universal experience of boredom followed by danger–and record-keeping rarely becomes art. Another thing: war (in Europe anyway) was not just something for soldiers: it was often more terrible for civilians, and it is difficult to think of a civilian novel set in wartime (like, say,

49

WAR'S SOUR FRUITS

Elizabeth Bowen's *The Heat of the Day*) as belonging to a special category called the War Novel. All British novels with a 1939–45 setting were, in one sense or another, novels about the war. Our concern here must be with fiction written by and about servicemen.

England's record was, until the coming of Evelyn Waugh's war trilogy, very meagre. Alexander Baron's *From the City, From the Plough* dealt adequately with the fighting on the Normandy beaches, and Walter Baxter's rather ill-written *Look Down in Mercy* told of the horrors of the war in Burma, though its homosexual theme is more compelling than its account of the general miseries of the soldier. America did better than Britain, perhaps because war seemed a fresher experience to citizens of an essentially unmilitary nation, also because the gap between fighter and civilian was more marked than in Europe and encouraged the recording of war as a special hell–in the old 1914–18 way–for the man in uniform.

The finest of the American war novels remains Norman Mailer's *The Naked and the Dead*, and yet what one chiefly remembers of this work is a theme which rises above war and which, in a totally different setting, George Orwell was working on independently at the same time as Mailer–namely, the emergence of a new doctrine of power. O'Brien, Winston Smith's torturer-instructor in *Nineteen Eighty-Four*, presents his victim-pupil with an image of the future–a boot stamping on a face for ever and ever. General Cummings in *The Naked and the Dead* tells Lieutenant Hearn to see the Army as 'a preview of the future', and it is a future very like Orwell's, its only morality 'a power morality'. He, representing the generals, and Sergeant Croft, representing a lower order of rule, are fighting fascism but are themselves fascists and well aware of it. Hearn, the weak liberal who will not, despite his weakness, submit to Cummings, is destroyed by his general through his sergeant. Cummings the strategist plans while Croft the fighting leader executes; Hearn, who represents a doomed order of decency and humanity, is crushed between the two extremes of the new power morality.

But the narrative presents, with great accuracy and power, the agony of American troops in the Pacific campaign. A representative group of lower-class Americans forms the reconnaissance patrol sent before a proposed attack on the Japanese-held island of Anopopei. We smell the hot damp dish-rag smell of the jungle and the sweat of the men. Of this body of typical Americans, however, despite the vivid realization of skin, muscle and nerves, only Hearn and Croft emerge as living individuals. With the men they lead we have a sense of deliberate contrivance, a desire to create human beings who are also types–the Jew, the Pole, the Texan and so on. Mailer works hard to block in the background of each man. He borrows a device from another American novelist, John Dos Passos, that of the episodic flashback, and he calls it 'The Time Machine'. The Time Machine is something of a mill or grinder: it seems to reduce the pasts of all the subsidiary characters to a common flour. Their lives are built on only one preoccupation and that is sex.

It is, however, a mark of Mailer's originality that he should be able to take over the technique invented by another writer and make it seem his own. In the nineteen-thirties, John Dos Passos was much read for his subject-matter. In works like *Manhattan Transfer* and the trilogy *U.S.A.* he painted the modern world in harsh left-wing tones, presenting not only ficititious characters to point his progressive thesis but also the facts of contemporary history. These were, so to speak, thrown at the reader in highly individual forms–rapid reportage under the heading 'The Camera Eye', a congealed mass of newspaper headlines, potted biographies of world figures. It was a suggestive technique, and it asked to be used in other contexts. Mailer's development of it provides a means of thickening the narrative line with another dimension, presenting each individual history as still real and relevant, not a wearisome recall beginning with some such formula as 'He thought back to the days when . . .' But the impression too often tends to be one of contrivance, of the deliberate fabrication of a past to convince himself, as well as the reader, that the characters have life.

For all its faults, *The Naked and the Dead* is the most massive·

picture America has given us of the futility of war, as also of that residue of intransigence which is to be found in all servicemen, however clamped down by inhuman discipline. The futility is figured in the capture of an island which proves to be of no strategic importance; the spirit of revolt is stirred by an accident–the patrol stumbles into a hornets' nest and runs away, dropping weapons and equipment, impelled into a realization that an impulse can contain the seeds of a choice. None of Mailer's later work can compare with this, his first novel, though perhaps the adverse critical response to his second–*Barbary Shore*–sent him sullenly to a wrong track in *The Deer Park* and *An American Dream*. Whatever its first critics said, *Barbary Shore* represents the only possible sequel to *The Naked and the Dead*, since it develops the theme of the 'power morality' adumbrated by General Cummings in that book. The theme is worked out in somewhat Kafka-like terms, in darkness, through mysterious symbols and intrigues. It is in many ways a more modern novel than *The Naked and the Dead*, but it is less direct and deliberately chooses the smallest possible *mise en scene*–a rooming-house–and a tiny cast of characters. After the expansiveness of *The Naked and the Dead* Mailer evidently felt the need for contraction. The themes of sex and death are in the book, as they are in every book of Mailer's, but they do not receive the full apocalyptical treatment. This was reserved for *An American Dream* where, says Mailer, his concern is with evil undisguised as war or power morality. The hero murders his wife and, before throwing her out of the skyscraper window, commits buggery with her German maid. There is further, though not always lethal, violence and more, though not really abnormal, sex before the hero drives off into the desert. A plot-summary can give no notion of the real content of the novel. The evil of the world expresses itself less in acts than in odours; Mailer uses smells to symbolize the absolute wrong that is an aspect of final reality. But where is good? There is no sign of it here. The book is far more pessimistic than *The Naked and the Dead*, where men grant themselves the power to opt out of the collective murder-suicide which is war.

WAR'S SOUR FRUITS

In his more recent work, Mailer shows himself once more concerned with collective violence—chiefly that associated with civilian protest against the Vietnam war. *The Armies of the Night* is a detailed account of his own part in the historic Washington peace demonstration, though its approach is fictional, with the character 'Mailer' presented in the third person. The curious, slangy, obscene *Why are We in Vietnam?* is a true novel, in which a bear hunt carries a light load of allegory. His book on the American lunar projects, straight reportage in that sometimes over-rich though always nutritious style which is recognisably Mailer's own, reveals that he is perhaps primarily a reporter on real life, not a creator of fictional worlds at all. But he is most likely to achieve his niche in the ultimate hall of literary distinction as a war novelist.

He is, among American writers, not unique in this. James Jones wrote a very bulky novel about American army life before Pearl Harbor—*From Here to Eternity*—which sits like a dead weight at the threshold of his career, forbidding literary progress or the search for a new subject. The size of the book is impressive, as is that (even more so) of his second novel *Some Came Running*, but sheer size is a commodity the Americans purvey easily. The content of *From Here to Eternity* is not epic enough to justify the length, though it is of horrifying interest—brutality, the gulf between officers and enlisted men, the spirit of growling revolt, sex at its grossest. The trouble with Jones's writing is that it totally lacks distinction, whereas Mailer is a skilled stylist. Massiveness in the novel is far from inconsistent with compression of style in writers who belong to the great Flaubert-Joyce-Proust tradition—and Mailer, for all his shortcomings, is such a writer—but with lesser men like Jones length is a property which derives from sloppiness, diffuseness, repetition.

Another long war-novel, *The Caine Mutiny* by Herman Wouk, stands somewhere between *From Here to Eternity* and *The Naked and the Dead*. It has some literary distinction—far more than Jones's book, far less than Mailer's—and its length is appropriate to its subject. To the officers of the U.S.S. *Caine* their captain

53

seems slowly revealed as not merely incompetent but mad: this needs the *longueurs* of many voyages and the accumulation of many incidents to show itself beyond question. An intellectual officer plugs away at the need to depose the captain, but to him it is a mere game–disaffection without action. The first officer, however, takes him seriously and assumes control of the ship. The mutineers are acquitted at the court martial which follows–thanks to a tricky lawyer–but there is no real triumph. The gulf between the American intellectual, fundamentally irresponsible, and the professional serviceman who protects his way of life is presented with bitter honesty. Wouk's later work cannot stand comparison with *The Caine Mutiny*, though it is always competent and very revealing of different aspects of modern America–the upper-class Jewish community in *Marjorie Morningstar*, the doomed best-selling author in *Youngblood Hawke*. But Wouk, though he has energy, lacks style and depth: his technique is uninteresting, just as his psychological penetration is shallow.

Satire on war in general is one thing, satire on World War Two is another. The horror of that war was the necessity of fighting it, and a special kind of doublethink is necessary to appreciate Joseph Heller's *Catch-22*, America's most recent major contribution to war fiction. Heller writes about American airmen on a small Mediterranean island during the Italian campaign, but his technique totally, and deliberately, lacks Mailer's naturalism. His approach is not merely satirical: it is surrealistic, absurd, even lunatic, though the aim is serious enough–to show the mess of war, the victimization of the conscripts, the monstrous egotism of the top brass. The Nazis, then, are not the target, only the colonels and generals of a system dedicated to an utter cynicism, keeping bomber-crews in the air (this is Catch-22) when they are near-mad with exhaustion, their tame psychiatrists accusing the men of 'a morbid aversion to dying' and 'deep-seated survival anxieties', the mess-officer stealing the carbon-dioxide capsules from the Mae Wests to make ice-cream sodas for the officers' mess, the sending-out of a stock letter to the next of kin: 'Dear Mrs., Mr., Miss, or Mr. and Mrs. ——: Words cannot express the deep per-

WAR'S SOUR FRUITS

sonal grief I experienced when your husband, son, father or brother was killed, wounded, or reported missing in action' (cross out whatever is inapplicable). As in the British fiction of the first war, the enemy is here in camp, not across no-man's-land or a stretch of water. Inevitably, in Heller's book, an American airman bombs his own base on behalf of the Nazis, and then the mad satire turns sour.

There are other American war-novels, perhaps no less distinguished than the works already mentioned. Gore Vidal wrote his *Williwaw* at the age of nineteen–a mature study of a vessel of the Army Transportation Corps negotiating a hurricane (or williwaw) in the Aleutians, though–as is only natural–weaknesses of style and characterization vitiate the work. Vidal was learning to write in *Williwaw,* and it was with post-war themes that he achieved complete articulacy–or rather themes like homosexuality (formerly taboo) which the post-war age regarded as legitimate material for serious novels. *The City and the Pillar* is a quiet portent. A homosexual hero eventually murders a friend who has turned heterosexual. Perhaps the vision of a male community, with women on the outside as dreams or enemies, was the gift of war to a new generation of novelists. Vidal came to full flower in his long historical novel *Julian,* with its Byzantine community of bishops and eunuchs and its painstaking portrait of the Emperor who was called the Apostate. He has not tailed off from a war-novel début, like so many of his American fellows; war gave him the primary writing stimulus and has made him something bigger than a war-novelist. The variety of talent he shows is quite remarkable. The notorious *Myra Breckenridge* is a piece of American myth-making that, drawing on film, sexual revenge, sex-change through surgery, and the inevitable pounding obscenity, presents in small space and great depth an image of the contemporary American psyche that posterity may well wonder at.

John Horne Burns, whose first novel–*The Gallery*–is a brutal but compassionate study of the Americans in Naples in 1944– might well have advanced as Vidal did, had he only lived. The interesting thing about American novelists who survived the war

55

WAR'S SOUR FRUITS

is the tendency for war-themes (or at least army-themes) to recur. William Styron wrote two massive and violent books—*Lie Down in Darkness* and *Set This House on Fire*—with, respectively, Deep South and exile-in-Italy settings, penetrating and tragic studies of human love, before writing his very brief *The Long March*. This deals brilliantly with a familiar American military theme—the enmity between temperamentally opposed officers, the self-destructive stoicism that follows on defiant obedience to a tyrannous discipline. We have seen it often presented, but rarely with such compressed eloquence.

There is a certain piquancy about considering the late Evelyn Waugh in this context of American toughs—he is quintessentially English—but his finest work is a trilogy of novels about the Second World War which, just before his death, he republished as a single novel in a single volume, and his earlier novels may be regarded as reaching towards such a consummation. To read a page of Waugh's prose is to revel in a cool, patrician, Augustan craftsmanship which is a world away from the Hemingway tradition. There is restraint, a lofty eschewing of the details of sex or violence, a love of the generalizing well-wrought period as opposed to the quick nervous presentation of sensuous experience as its happens. But there is in all Waugh's novels a hidden concern with violence that expresses itself in a ruthlessness which only the spirit of satire can excuse. In his first novel, *Decline and Fall*, a schoolboy has his foot shot by tipsy Mr. Prendergast with his starting-pistol, later the foot is amputated, finally the boy dies. These events are presented briskly, on the margin, without comment. Mr. Prendergast himself has his head cut off by a madman. These deaths may be taken as nursery-rhyme deaths—too ritualistic or comic to be true—and they are wrapped in fantasy of great wit and accuracy of observation. But, if we look below the surface, we shall find that Waugh is recording an age so lacking in roots or ethical convictions that enormities like even cannibalism (in *Black Mischief*) can find no category of judgement, hence no condemnation.

The world of the thirties that is sketched—with appropriate satire—in *Vile Bodies* is so lacking in purpose that it has to be

56

blown up by a war. It is a sort of dream-Armageddon and need not be taken too seriously, just as we must not be too shocked by the casual stubbing-out of Apthorpe's life in *Men at Arms*, the ghastly but comic fate of the hero of *A Handful of Dust*, or the disposal of the body of Aimee Thanatogenos (in the oven of a pets' crematorium) in *The Loved One*. Full-scale wars are enjoyed by this humorist even more than swift and grotesque individual calamities: they are harnessed to the comic machine. The African revolution in *Black Mischief* and the thinly disguised Abyssinian war of *Scoop* are mere pretexts for humorous extravagance, but Waugh always seemed to need a vision of violent action as a corrective for his report from an England without faith or purpose. In a way, he likes to present purgatory in his novels, and this is appropriate for a writer who is a Catholic convert. The early heroes are young innocents who engage the teeth of the world but come through, thanks to a divine dispensation, triumphant on the other side. The hero of *A Handful of Dust*, his finest pre-war novel, is the first of Waugh's mature and suffering gentlemen. Tony Last, with his estate and responsibilities, a beautiful wife and fine son, sees few clouds ahead in his near-feudal summer. Then the world collapses. His wife loves another, his son is killed at a hunt. The country gentleman leaves his estate and goes up the Amazon to seek a lost city. This appears in delirium as the world he has lost, the world our civilization had abandoned. He ends in hell, not purgatory, reading Dickens aloud over and over again to a half-caste illiterate. His heirs turn his estate into a fur-farm.

The gravity of vision which lay under the comic brilliance was waiting for larger expression. With the coming of war, in which Waugh served with distinction (he liked the pun on his name; one of his travel books was called *Waugh in Abyssinia*), his comic genius exploded in a book about the 'phoney war' which caught something of the mess, boredom and waste, as well as the shadow of the horror—*Put Out More Flags*. In *Brideshead Revisited*, which came at the end of the war, there was a firm and romantic Catholic statement expressed in a most luxurious prose and full of the yearning for a more gracious and self-indulgent age that was excusable in a time of privation and austerity (Waugh, inexcusably, thinned out the richness in a later re-working of the book). *Brideshead Revisited* is an optimistic novel. The world decays, war kicks out the old values, but the Christian faith endures. The time was coming when Waugh had to make this statement at even greater length and in greater depth, but first he had to comment on two new worlds–that which had come out of the war (*Scott-King's Modern Europe*), that which seemed to be moving farther and farther away from its cisatlantic origins (*The Loved One*–a satire on American burial customs, a denial of the possibility of an Anglo-American *rapprochement*). Then came the first volume of the war novel which was to be called *Sword of Honour*.

Men at Arms introduces Guy Crouchback, a Catholic gentleman with a *castello* in Italy and a private income. His wife has left him and his religion forbids divorce and re-marriage. He is lonely and is growing dim and dull, having opted out of the current of life. The coming of war fires him with a crusader's zeal, gives him a purpose he has long lacked. But he is in his late thirties, nobody wants him, the war seems able to get along well enough without him. Eventually he joins the Halberdiers as a subaltern, trains and sees action. Waugh does not push Crouchback too much into the foreground at first. There is a fine galaxy of comic characters–the incredible Apthorpe, the Brigadier, the uniformed clubmen, the politicians–as well as some more lovable than any Waugh has previously given us–the honest professional soldiers, old Mr Crouchback with his firm and simple faith. But the pathos of Guy Crouchback's position is woven strongly into the fine war report-age and the superb comic action. His wife, divorced again, rejects his advances; his new bride, the army, is proving a slut; disillusionment about the true purpose of the war is already beginning.

The other volumes–*Officers and Gentlemen* and *Unconditional Surrender*–show the deepening of the disillusionment. The age of the gentlemen is fast going; men whom Crouchback has admired prove cowardly or treacherous; the new type of hero, the man of the people, is being painfully forged. It is the failed officer and impostor Trimmer, a former ship's hairdresser, who takes on this role, and he even begets a child on Crouchback's wife (still that in the Church's eyes), who emerges before her air-raid death as a character of raffish nobility. The child is born in true wedlock, however; Crouchback and his wife re-consummate it, ensuring that a great Catholic family has an heir, though–by an irony appropriate to the new age–this child is really a proletarian by-blow. Crouchback lives through the débâcle at Crete, is sickened by aspects of the 'people's war' in the Balkans, feels the death-urge, regrets the passing of an old order of chivalry and gentleness, but, with the stoicism of his kind, makes unconditional surrender to history. He reminds us in many ways of Christopher Tietjens in Ford Madox Ford's four novels of the First World War–the in-corrupt and disregarded gentleman of Christian ideals. What Ford's tetralogy did for the First World War, Waugh's trilogy (it is hard to think of it as otherwise despite its final unification without sectional titles) does for the second. It is not merely the story of one man's war; it is the whole history of the European struggle itself, told with verve, humour, pathos and sharp accu-racy. Smaller post-war works of his–like the admirable and fan-tastic *Ordeal of Gilbert Pinfold*–we took with the gratitude with which we had taken the earlier books. But *Sword of Honour* we take with wonder as well.

See Bibliographical Note on p. 12

Alexander BARON (1918–   )
  From the City, from the Plough.
  London, 1948
Walter BAXTER (1915–   )
  Look Down in Mercy. London,
  1951
John Horne BURNS
  The Gallery. New York, 1947
John Dos PASSOS (1896–   )
  Manhattan Transfer. 1925

John Dos PASSOS (*continued*)
  U.S.A. New York, 1937
  (42nd Parallel, 1930; Nine-
  teen-nineteen, 1932; The Big
  Money, 1936)
Joseph HELLER (1923–   )
  Catch-22. New York, 1961
James JONES (1921–   )
  From Here to Eternity. New
  York, 1951

WAR'S SOUR FRUITS

James JONES (*continued*)
Some Came Running. New York, 1958

Norman MAILER (1923–   )
The Naked and the Dead. New York, 1948
Barbary Shore. New York, 1951
The American Dream. New York, 1965
Why are We in Vietnam? New York, 1967
The Armies of the Night. New York, 1968

William STYRON (1925–   )
Lie Down in Darkness. Indianapolis, 1951
Set this House on Fire. New York, 1960
The Long March. Indianapolis, 1951

Gore VIDAL (1925–   )
Williwaw. New York, 1946
The City and the Pillar. New York, 1946
Julian. London and Boston, 1964
Myra Breckenridge. London and Boston, 1968

Evelyn WAUGH (1903–66)
Decline and Fall. London, 1928
Vile Bodies. 1930
Black Mischief. 1932
A Handful of Dust. 1934

Evelyn WAUGH (*continued*)
Scoop. London and Boston, 1938
Put Out More Flags. London and Boston, 1942
Brideshead Revisited. London and Boston, 1945
Scott-King's Modern Europe. London, 1947
The Loved One. London and Boston, 1948
Helena. London and Boston, 1950
Men at Arms. London and Boston, 1952
Love among the Ruins. London, 1953
Officers and Gentlemen. London and Boston, 1955
The Ordeal of Gilbert Pinfold. London and Boston, 1957
Unconditional Surrender. London, 1961 (as The End of the Battle, Boston, 1962)
Sword of Honour (Men at Arms, Officers and Gentlemen, and Unconditional Surrender, revised in one volume), Boston, 1966

Herman WOUK (1915–   )
The Caine Mutiny. 1951
Marjorie Morningstar. 1955
Youngblood Hawke. 1962

V

Good and Evil

Evelyn Waugh told the first readers of *Decline and Fall* that the book was meant to be funny. He told the readers of the first version of *Brideshead Revisited* that the book dealt with an 'eschatological' subject – in other words, with death, judgement, hell and heaven, and the Catholic faith that calls these 'the four last things ever to be remembered'. This kind of preoccupation in fiction makes Waugh a 'Catholic novelist', and it relates him to another great convert whom he admired (there is a fine incidental tribute in *Men at Arms*) but whom he is totally unlike – Graham Greene.

If Waugh is concerned with the Catholic Church as a great mystical body which enshrines not only ultimate truth but also the essence of a civilization which modern materialism threatens, Graham Greene is much more interested in the actual doctrines of the Church – particularly the fundamental doctrine that states that good and evil are not mere relative terms like right and wrong but unchanging absolutes. The early novels of Greene – like *The Man Within*, *England Made Me*, *It's a Battlefield* – are clever and technically interesting, but it was not until the appearance of *Brighton Rock* that the true voice of the novelist, the Catholic novelist, was heard. It is sometimes said that Greene's Catholicism is not strictly orthodox, that he adheres to the Jansenist heresy. If this means that he broods more on man's inborn depravity than on his ability to be regenerated, this is true: he is more interested in presenting evil than good. The hero of *Brighton Rock* is a young lapsed Catholic who runs a 'bookmaker's protection'

GOOD AND EVIL

racket in the seaside resort of the title. He is dedicated to evil–betrayal, violence, murder–but with a full awareness of the eternal–or eschatological–meaning of his acts. At one point he says, rather improbably, '*Credo in unum Satanum*'. He is pursued by a blowsy decent stout-drinking woman who is convinced that he murdered her one-day seaside friend and who is much concerned with the righting of wrongs. Greene makes the paradox clear: she is animated only by relative values–since right and wrong are man-made–while the young ruffian is bound to the absolutes of good and evil. If one accepts evil one is at least expressing a belief in an ultimate reality: the Devil presupposes God. If one is scornful of these concepts and satisfied with the standards of merely human law, then one belongs to a lower order of mankind. The boy gangster–despite his unremitting pursuit of evil–can be seen with the eyes of eternity; his pursuer–despite her decency and desire for justice–cannot. In a sense, it is better for one's soul to pursue evil rather than right. It is a dangerous paradox, but it produced a superb novel.

A complement to *Brighton Rock* is *The Power and the Glory*, in which a priest, outlawed by an atheistical revolutionary régime in Mexico, holds fast to his function, bringing the divine word and the sacraments to the very people whose name has been invoked by the revolutionary leaders. He is a ragged and wretched man, far from perfect. He sinned by begetting a child, he has fleshly appetites, he is cowardly. But he is the vessel of the divine, and that is enough. He has the power to change bread and wine into the body and blood of Christ (one of his difficulties is the obtaining of wine for the sacrament, since this 'people's state' is prohibitionist): his human frailties are of no account in the light of this miraculous gift. Once again Greene is fascinated by the contrast between the divine and human views of man. And, even more than in *Brighton Rock*, with its seedy pubs and cafés and lodging-houses, he is drawn to painting the depravity of man's world in images which are also symbols. In *The Heart of the Matter* he goes to West Africa in wartime, and his hero, Scobie, is a police officer with no illusions about the depravity of white and black men alike. It is perhaps because of this knowledge of the human condition that he is able to achieve a near-divine love of his parishioners (a policeman is a kind of priest). Needless to say, he is a Catholic. The heart of the matter that Greene presents in his story is a kind of theological riddle: cannot a man whom the Church must call a sinner perhaps really be a saint? Scobie has a Catholic wife, but–out of compassion–he learns to love a young girl who has known the suffering of shipwreck and the loss of a husband. Scobie commits adultery but cannot repent of the sin, for he would, by giving up his adultery, be condemning a defenceless soul to new agonies of privation. He makes a sacrilegious communion, accepts that he is damned, and is only too ready to throw away chances of God's mercy: he does not deserve God. He commits suicide, and must now, according to strict doctrine, be in hell. But it is left to a priest to wonder how much the Church knows of any human soul–men only confess the unimportant things–their sins–and how far the Church is able to legislate about divine reward and punishment. The reader at least is convinced that Scobie, who chose evil with his eyes open, is more aware of its opposite, good, than the merely lukewarm and conventionally pious.

In *The End of the Affair* Greene goes further. An adulteress who has not even Scobie's faith dies an unrepentant death (again, it is the adultery that cannot be repented of), but after her death curious and inexplicable events occur: a man who loved her is cleansed of a hideous birthmark; a sick boy with a school-book of hers (saintly relic) makes an impossible recovery. Strangest of all, the narrator, whose passion for her remains so intense that he curses the forces that have taken her away, starts to be aware–for the first time in an agnostic life–of God's existence. God is someone to be hated, but–as the inevitable priest remarks–he is a 'good hater': the hatred of God is, paradoxically, a blessed beginning.

Greene's most recent novels–*The Quiet American*, *A Burnt-Out Case* and *The Comedians*–return from the London of *The End of the Affair* to the exotic settings which he loves best–Saigon and Africa and Haiti. They probe, like all Greene's works, into the problems of good and evil and the wretchedness of the human condition. But *The Quiet American*, with its setting in a cockpit of modern war, with its careful plotting and sufficiency of violent action, stands close to another kind of novel which Greene delights in producing–the adventure story which will admit contrivance, coincidence, the bizarrely thrilling for its own sake, and merely touches the periphery of the great ultimate moral concerns. These novels–*Stamboul Train*, *A Gun for Sale*, *The Confidential Agent*, *The Ministry of Fear*, *Our Man in Havana*, *Travels With My Aunt*– he calls 'entertainments'. The term seems to diminish them; in fact, they are superbly written and their engineering is masterly. They make excellent films but remain essentially literature. It is these books, and the equally brilliant adventure-stories of Eric Ambler, that keep the British 'thriller' up to scratch. The precedent of the Greene 'entertainments' is before such writers of spy-novels as John le Carré (*The Spy Who Came in From the Cold*; *The Looking-Glass War*), and even Ian Fleming, with the popular James Bond books, could hardly fail to learn something from Greene's technical brilliance in this secondary *genre*. A fine writer will exert influence at many levels.

Another British novelist much concerned with Evil (though hardly at all with Good) is William Golding. He came late to the novel-form with a book about children which has some of the qualities of a dystopian fable, since it attempts to show how self-defeating are all efforts to build an idyllic and just community. In his boys' book *Coral Island*, R. M. Ballantyne shipwrecked a number of decent Church-bred lads and watched them create from scratch a fair replica of British civilization. Golding's book *Lord of the Flies* remembered Ballantyne and presented the same situation –the shipwreck (or rather planewreck) of educated Christian middle-class boys on a desert island; he even gave his three main characters the same names as Ballantyne's young heroes. But where Ballantyne was optimistic Golding is disillusioned: take off the brakes of enforced control and boys, like men, will choose chaos rather than order. The good intentions of the few are overborne by the innate evil of the many. Instead of a boy-scout camp we get young savages–painted, naked, gorging on pig-flesh, given

GOOD AND EVIL

to torture, murder, human sacrifice to false gods. The title refers
to Beelzebub, most stinking and depraved of all the devils: it is
he, and not the God of the Christians, who is worshipped. A
child is a stark caricature of a man; he does not, despite Words-
worth and Rousseau and the other romantics who believed in the
noble savage, trail clouds of innocent glory: he turns quickly to
evil. This is the main thesis of all Golding's novels–the primacy of
evil and the near-impossibility of good. *The Inheritors* (perhaps
his best novel) is a devastating subversion of H. G. Wells's view
of *homo sapiens* as maker, hero, liberal conqueror. The world of
Neanderthal man approaches a golden dream of innocence; *homo
sapiens* comes along to disrupt it–evil is built in him, part of his
nature; he is led instinctively to worship of Beelzebub.

Such a doctrine is not strictly Christian. Christianity accepts a
fall and the possibility of redemption. Golding cannot, however,
posit an Eden–not for man: man did not fall from grace; he was
never in a state of it. But choice is, in the later novels, available to
his wretched adult modern heroes–to the eponym of *Pincher
Martin* and to Sammy Mountjoy in *Free Fall*. Martin is a torpe-
doed sailor clinging to a rock in mid-Atlantic, or so it seems. But a
brilliant piece of naturalism turns out to be a modern *Book of the
Dead*. Martin has already died and is, with typical human perverseness, engaged in rejecting the divine vision and opting for
hell. The power of choice is always biased; man chooses the worse.
All Martins in the navy are called 'Pincher', but the nickname of
this Martin is very apt: he has nothing of his own, every shred of
his make-up has been pinched, stolen. He was baptized Christopher, but he has refused the office of bearer-of-the-Christ; he
wants to be himself, but he is nothing. This is his hell–not imposed but freely elected: an eternity of total emptiness.

The title of *Free Fall* sums it all up–one's fall is free, one wills
the descent into evil. Sammy Mountjoy lived as a child in paradise
(that is the meaning of his name). Like Dante, he saw elements of
divinity in a girl called Beatrice, but he perverted love into lust.
He looks back on his loveless evasive life, full of wrong choices
and failures to understand, from the point of view of a man who is

being interrogated by a Nazi officer. 'All day long,' he says, 'action is weighed in the balance and found not opportune nor fortunate or ill-advised, but good or evil.' But even with the knowledge of what ought to be chosen, regeneration has nothing to do with free will. Sammy is released from his prison cell, since he does not know enough to betray his comrades, and hears the stellar music of Dante. Beatrice has been reduced to idiocy in an asylum; Sammy enters paradise. He does not understand, nor do we. Our only freedom is to fall; the rest is out of our hands.

Golding's next and, to date, last serious novel, *The Spire* (for we cannot take *The Pyramid* all that seriously), is concerned with the Dean of a medieval cathedral, Jocelin, and his vision of a four-hundred-foot spire erected to the divine glory. But is this vision really God-derived, and is the motive one of pure worship? The addition of the spire to the cathedral (which seems to have affinities with Salisbury) involves the commission of more evil acts than can justify even the most holy-seeming project. The spire itself is an 'unruly member'–a phallus–and the church becomes the scene of sexual enormities and pagan rites; Jocelin himself falls into the sin of lust; the money he acquires for the building is from a corrupt source; the whole work seems founded on a pit of human filth. Yet the spire is completed, though the vision may not have been innocent. Indeed, the dying Jocelin says: 'There is no innocent work. God only knows where God may be.' Golding's revelation is not just of the primacy of evil; it is of ultimate forces that no man can ever hope to understand.

It is proper to mention here an Australian novelist who, through his concentration on man as a moral creature, has brought the Australian novel into world literature at last, making it rise above its picturesque regional associations. Before Patrick White, Australian fiction was mainly limited to romances of the outback or derivations from D. H. Lawrence's *Kangaroo* (the first major novel ever to have an Australian setting). The Australian continent is so huge, various, and bizarre that (a 'wilful, lavish land', as the school poem puts it) it always tended to become the centre and not just the setting: there were never any fictional characters big

GOOD AND EVIL

enough to oust it. (And, skilful as writers like Hal Porter, Frank Hardy and Dymphna Cusack may be, they are bedevilled by a certain colonial provincialism.) With Patrick White's *Voss* one felt that at last Australia, grumbling like a big dog, was being made to lie down; with *Riders in the Chariot* one has the impression of a complex universal drama–without one whiff of provincialism– in which the Sydney locale is a mere accident.

It is a bitter novel with very full characterizations: an elderly female recluse living in a decayed mansion, drawn to animals and trees and distrustful of human beings; a Jewish intellectual work- ing as an unskilled factory hand, having found refuge from Nazism but not from guilt for his wife's death; an aborigine–no comic abo going walkabout but an integrated human being with a pas- sion for art; a Rabelaisian laundress with a huge family and a drunken husband. All these are united in the possession of a common vision of good, symbolized secretly by the chariot of the title: they are all riders in it. Against the vision of good is set the fact of evil, most shockingly manifested in the scene where the Jew is 'crucified' on the eve of Good Friday by his drunken cobbers. The novel is big-boned and over-earnest and it does not always avoid melodrama, but White's sincerity shines through blind- ingly: he is genuinely concerned about people and the ultimate forces which take possession of them. This concern is as powerful as ever in *The Solid Mandala*, but there is a disturbing note of mawkishness as well–something we do not expect from White.

Admirers of the work of Pamela Hansford Johnson (Lady Snow) have not always seen a preoccupation with the problems of right-doing, sometimes resolving itself into questions of the final sanctions of morality, which lies hidden under the complexities of her novels, as well as their wit, accurate reportage and delight in the surface of life. Her first book, *This Bed Thy Centre*, appeared when she was only twenty-two, but its recent reissue reminds us that she has been pretty consistent in her preoccupation with moral dilemmas. *The Humbler Creation* presents an Anglican clergyman who is saintly, but, driven by the intolerable frustra- tions of his family life, falls into adultery. As with Graham Greene

GOOD AND EVIL

(whom she in no way really resembles) we are tempted towards moral judgements that orthodoxy would not condone. *The Last Resort* seems to touch a theological level with its rumination (in the person of the narrator) on the difference between ourselves and the company of the saints and martyrs: they commit themselves to the big terrible decisions; we hold back. And however amoral and free we like to think ourselves, there are always nagging doubts about the religious furniture that lies, gathering dust but still very solid, up there in the attic. *An Error of Judgement* deals with a consultant physician who has done fine work and is revered by his patients. But he is aware that he took up medicine only because pain fascinates him: his profession could be a means of inflicting it, or at least withholding its palliatives. He abandons his practice and takes to a job whose altruism seems obvious—trying to rehabilitate delinquent youth. But he meets one young man who has committed a sadistic crime of particular ghastliness; he has not been caught, he is quite ready to commit the same crime again. Like a vet, the doctor 'puts down' the young brute with brandy and sleeping tablets. What sort of judgement do we make? The orthodox answer is not satisfactory, but could any answer be? No novel of any complexity can ever have the directness of a moral tract, but the virtue of Pamela Hansford Johnson's work often lies in its power to present the great issues nakedly—forcing us not so much to a decision as to a realization of the hopelessness of decisions. If, that is, we are not saints and martyrs.

I ought to stress that all Miss Hansford Johnson's novels are notable for a kind of grave lightness of touch; they are never without humour. Her comic gifts are seen as well as anywhere in *The Unspeakable Skipton*, whose hero is a mad, egoistical novelist working on a book that will never end and never be published. All kinds of beastliness are, to him, in order if they provide material for his fiction: like Dante, he puts his enemies in hell. There is nothing good about him, and yet there is this monstrous dedication to art which lifts him to a kind of empyrean: he is as far above ordinary decent plodders through life as the saints and martyrs are. He is, perhaps, a devil, and is not a devil a perverted angel—

having more traffic with the divine order than people who are not Skipton and are all too speakable?

There are several English novelists who, without adopting a specifically Christian point of view, are concerned with the human dilemma in its various manifestations and are brave enough to suggest their own answers or to imply that no answer seems possible. P. H. Newby–and this is a pity–has become best known for his two comedies *The Picnic at Sakkara* and (its sequel) *A Guest and His Going*, which illustrate the very contemporary dichotomy of an Egyptian, Muawiya Khaslat, who is drawn personally to a human being (the teacher Edgar Perry) but detests everything he stands for; in a wider sense, these books are also about the agonizing divisions between races and cultures. But Newby's best novels are about a more fundamental bewilderment–that of man himself, lost in a desert without a compass. *A Step to Silence* and *The Retreat* (like the two novels mentioned above) form a diptych with a single hero. Oliver Knight faces the mess of the prewar world, the growth of fascism, Munich not far off, but this public world is also a reflection of the smaller one with its more privy agonies–growing up, the initiation into adulthood, the difficulty of finding standards to judge things by. When he becomes adult and joins the R.A.F., his bewilderment is made worse by the artificial pressures of war. He becomes a fugitive from the double mess, is genuinely lost. Newby seems to imply that all a man has in a world without maps is his individuality, his instincts, his capacity to be himself. Knight, and lost heroes like him, is more unfortunate than Graham Greene's self-damned Scobie. Scobie at least is aware of the ultimate significance of human action; he knows what he is doing and where he is going.

In a more recent novel, *The Barbary Light*, Newby presents the complicated evil in a man not in terms of infantile traumata, a curable illness, but as the product of a pattern of distrust. The hero, as a boy in Cardiff, boards a ship with the full permission of the crew, who tell him that they are Africa-bound. But, a mile or so along the coast, he is put ashore: the whole thing was a joke. Yet the joke is not harmless. A boy's disappointment breeds a sick attitude to the world. And yet, so Newby seems to imply, it was just one door into an inevitable sickness which we all, in our different ways, have to suffer. Life itself is the sickness. Newby's prose-style, with its hallucinatory concentration on detail, is the perfect medium for presenting life's fitful fever.

All the writers I have considered here are capable of seeing man as a tragic figure, and yet there have been few novels in our century which can be justly called great tragedies. The archetype I have in mind is Marlowe's Faustus (not Goethe's Faust), equipped with total knowledge of the consequences of human action and yet able to make a self-destructive choice. Graham Greene's characters are perhaps too small; Thomas Mann's Adrian Lever-kühn seems driven more by disease than by free will. But Malcolm Lowry produced, in *Under the Volcano*, a Faustian masterpiece which, though first published in 1947, still awaits general recognition. Like *Ulysses*, it presents in detail the events of a single day in a single place–the Day of the Dead in a town in Mexico, Popo-catepetl and Ixtaccihuatl looking down. It is the last day on earth of the British Consul, Geoffrey Firmin, and he is dying of drink. Like any tragic hero, he is fully aware of the choice he has made: he clings to his sloth, he needs salvation through love but will not utter the words that will bring it, he allows his diseased lust for drink to push him from bar to bar. In other words, he seeks damnation. Indeed, he is already living it, for this Mexico is presented as a vision of hell. At the end of the book he is murdered, and his body is thrown into the ravine between the volcanoes, with a dead dog after it.

We do not despise or even dislike Firmin, despite his self-condemnatory weaknesses. As with all tragic heroes, he sums up in himself the flaws which are latent or actual in all human beings, though on a spectacular scale. Like Faustus, he excites pity and terror. He has tasted of the world as it is–the late nineteen-thirties, with the war in Spain rehearsing the bigger war to come– and sees the manifestations of contemporary history as symptomatic of the whole rottenness which is built into the human condition. He wants to opt out, as would we all if we could see

GOOD AND EVIL

with the clarity that the gods grant, a compensatory gift, to men destined to destroy themselves. The tragic hero always has free will, but it is never total: he did not make the world. In a sense, even Macbeth is a witness or martyr.

Lowry's own life ended in drink and disillusionment, but posthumous evidence of a huge talent continues to appear. His volume of stories—*Hear us O Lord from Heaven Thy Dwelling-Place*—appeared five years after his death, but it still waits to be accepted as one of the most courageous fictional experiments since James Joyce. Its musical *leitmotiv*, its endless inner monologues, its marginal glosses that explain nothing, above all its narrative skill, are in the service of a mind restlessly probing into the roots of life, well aware of the good there but even more aware of the evil.

See Bibliographical Note on p. 12

Eric AMBLER (1909–   )
   The Dark Frontier. London, 1936
   A Kind of Anger. 1964
William GOLDING (1911–   )
   Lord of the Flies. London, 1954
   The Inheritors. London, 1955
   Pincher Martin. London, 1956
   Free Fall. London, 1959
   The Spire. 1964
   The Pyramid. 1967
Graham GREENE (1904–   )
   The Man Within. 1929
   Stamboul Train. London, 1932
   It's a Battlefield. 1934
   England Made Me. 1935
   A Gun for Sale. London, 1936
     (as This Gun for Hire. New York, 1936)
   Brighton Rock. 1938
   The Confidential Agent. 1939
   The Power and the Glory. Lon-

Graham GREENE (*continued*)
     don and Toronto, 1940 (as Labyrinthine Ways, New York, 1940)
   The Ministry of Fear. 1943
   The Heart of the Matter. 1948
   The End of the Affair. 1951
   The Quiet American. London, 1955
   Our Man in Havana. 1958
   A Burnt-out Case. 1961
   The Comedians. 1966
   Travels with my Aunt. 1970
Pamela Hansford JOHNSON (1912–   )
   This Bed thy Centre. 1935
   The Last Resort. London, 1956
   The Unspeakable Skipton. 1959
   The Humbler Creation. London, 1959
   An Error of Judgement. 1962

GOOD AND EVIL

John LE CARRÉ (1931–   )
   The Spy Who Came In From The Cold. 1963
   The Looking-Glass War. 1965

Malcolm LOWRY (1909–57)
   Ultramarine. London, 1933
   Under the Volcano. 1947
   Hear us O Lord from Heaven Thy Dwelling-Place. Philadelphia, 1916 (short stories)
   Lunar Caustic (edited Earle Birney and Margerie Lowry). New York, 1963
   Dark as the Grave Wherein My Friend is Laid (ed. Douglas

Malcolm LOWRY (*continued*)
   Day and Margerie Lowry). New York, 1968

P. H. NEWBY (1918–   )
   A Step to Silence. London, 1952
   The Retreat. 1953
   The Picnic at Sakkara. 1955
   A Guest and his Going. 1959
   The Barbary Light. London, 1962
   Something to Answer for. London, 1968

Patrick WHITE (1912–   )
   Voss, 1957
   Riders in the Chariot. 1961
   The Solid Mandala. 1966

VI

Great Individuality

If Malcolm Lowry derives from any other author at all, that author is James Joyce, though the Joycean elements have been absorbed and converted into something quite un-Joycean. The same may be said of three other novelists of equal originality, all of whom—if we take the most superficial view imaginable—can be called a sort of Irishmen. These novelists are Joyce Cary and the late Flann O'Brien (that was not his real name), and Samuel Beckett (who writes in French). Their writings possess in common, besides the willingness to experiment in the big Joyce laboratory, very little except the fact of the strong individual voice that shouts or sings alone: Beckett is obsessed with *la merde universelle*, which we may translate as 'the universal muckheap'; Cary proclaims, with William Blake, that everything that lives is holy; O'Brien is a powerful phantasist who makes his own patterns out of the material of everyday life.

Joyce Cary's name is Irish, but his subject-matter is either African or English. Until 1932, when he was forty-four, he was an officer in the Nigerian Political Service; only after his retirement did his career of novelist begin. Inevitably, he drew on his colonial experiences when he began to write, and we may call his first four books his 'African novels'—*Aissa Saved, An American Visitor, The African Witch* and *Mister Johnson*. Of these, the last is probably the best. Johnson is a Negro clerk who has received a mission-school education: in him the two tides, the black and the white, come together. But, as Cary shows, such a meeting cannot be a

73

real confluence: the elements will not mix. Johnson entertains fine dreams of being a European, a whole new world before him (as, theoretically, before all the African colonies), but he is naïve, childlike, exuberant, unable to distinguish between the real and the fantastic. He is a comic-pathetic figure, but not one on whom we feel inclined to look down: he is gay and stoical–with much of the ideal man of the imagination, very much a Caryan obsession, bursting out of his escapades. Eventually his 'white' aspirations have an ironical fulfilment: he comes to know British justice in the most intimate way possible–by being sentenced to death.

In all the four African novels, Cary presents, in its simplest form, his big theme of the conflict between alien modes of thought and living. In the later novels–such as *The Horse's Mouth*–we are to see the creative imagination (the most precious part of a human being) grappling with repressive, life-denying, forces; here we see the primitive mind engaging the white man's way of life, unable wholly to understand, rejecting much, borrowing only to pervert, always failing to be absorbed into a system colder, less fanciful and mythical, than its own. Having made his statements about primitive people, Cary passed on, logically enough, to books about childhood. *Charley is my Darling* depicts the life of working-class children during the evacuation period of World War Two; *A House of Children* revisits the upper middle class of the Victorian era, remembering (rather than re-enacting) the life of a large family. Both books brilliantly convey childhood's capacity (shared with the primitive) for living in the imagination. And now Cary was to move into his most interesting period, mounting the third stair. The time had come for the adult world of modern England.

Cary always wrote his novels in groups. The trio consisting of *Herself Surprised, To Be a Pilgrim*, and *The Horse's Mouth* concerns itself with three main characters, each of whom takes the foreground in turn. Sara Munday tells the story of *Herself Surprised*, and this story is mostly about her love-life with Wilcher–a fierce failure of a man–and with Gulley Jimson, the improvident painter of genius. Sara's style is in the prose tradition of noncon-

GREAT INDIVIDUALITY

formist writers like Daniel Defoe–the long bubbling narrative which describes amorous adventures with the gusto of repentance, the conviction of sin. Sara is, from the angle of orthodoxy (and religiously she is very orthodox), a sinner, but she is one of those sinners who proclaim the wonder of the life of the flesh, like Juliet's Nurse or the Wife of Bath. 'Everything that lives is holy', says Cary, after Blake, and Sara is holy in her wholehearted capacity to give of herself, reserving her moral doubts till later. Wilcher, who moves downstage for *To Be a Pilgrim*, finds a kind of salvation in Sara. He comes of a family of proud and fearless progressives–men and women who sought freedom in politics as well as religion, liberal nonconformists in fact–but he finds that the vein of self-confidence and strength has dried up in himself. He is a sort of comic-pathetic ageing Hamlet, condemned to imagination without action, and his failure to assert himself hides from the world his very real mental powers and his profound, inherited, faith. In order to understand the processes which have produced him and render him different from the more forceful members of his family, Wilcher has to recapitulate the history of that modern England that rose on Queen Victoria's grave and foundered with the Second World War. The result is an astonishing summation of an important aspect of English life.

We are concerned with nonconformism in religion and politics and nonconformity in social life. The greatest nonconformist of them all is Gulley Jimson, who takes over the narration of the trilogy for *The Horse's Mouth*. This seems to me Cary's finest achievement. Jimson is a painter of genius, and Cary, a writer of genius who once studied painting, understands him thoroughly. Jimson's god is William Blake, whom he quotes endlessly in his long interior monologues; like Blake, he believes that imagination represents a higher order of reality than what people call the real world. Only his art means anything to him, though it means little to the age in which, an old impoverished man, he lives on as a cheerful anachronism. He gets money, paint, canvas where he can: art is his only morality. To point his indifference to the world, he brings the story to its final climax by painting a huge mural on the

GREAT INDIVIDUALITY

wall of a building that is already being pulled down. The book is crammed with characters and picaresque escapades; its fire and gusto never once flag. It is a comic hymn to life, but it is noble as well. Depicting low life, it shines out with an image of the highest life of all–that of the creative brain. Having reached this peak of his art, Cary's imagination began to decline. The trio of novels about Chester Nimmo–*Prisoner of Grace*, *Except the Lord*, *Not Honour More*–has a kind of desperate, bustling vitality which dare not slow down or become quieter: if it did, we should be tempted to find the characters hollow.

Samuel Beckett is one of the great controversial playwrights of our age, whose *Waiting for Godot* goes on infuriating audiences or moving them profoundly but never leaves them indifferent. As a novelist he is just as important, though his novels often repel with a total lack of action, colour, solidity: they are the very antithesis of the novels of Joyce Cary. Though an Irishman like Cary, Beckett must be regarded as primarily a French novelist, since French is his elected first language (his three earliest books– *Belacqua*, *Murphy*, and *Watt*–are the only ones to have been written in English). The choice of French perhaps came the more easily to an Irishman, who, seeing English as an imposed and alien tongue, would not find any other European language much more foreign as a creative medium: the fact that Beckett, like Joyce, settled in Paris has not all that much to do with it–Gertrude Stein, Hemingway, as well as Joyce became Parisians but remained writers in English. One descries a mixture of motives in Beckett's choice. In English he tended to the poetical:

'The leaves began to lift and scatter, the higher branches to complain, the sky broke and curdled over flecks of skim blue, the pine of smoke toppled into the east and vanished, the pond was suddenly a little panic of grey and white, of water and gulls and sails.'

That (from *Murphy*) is beautifully done, but it represents the end of the line. It is too easy, especially for an Irishman, to be poetical in English, and Beckett wanted a dry austerity, the ultimate bone–the sharp exactness which French, of all languages, can give. Also there was the fact that Joyce, whom Beckett knew well and whose works he understood as well as any man, had pushed English to the limit: a writer of Beckett's temper needed a fresh start, a fresh medium.

If Joyce is concerned with recording the richness of life, Beckett is obsessed with rendering its misery. This is not perverseness, the deliberate grinding of the bad tooth; it is rather an attempt to discover what man is really like when he is stripped to show his essential condition, which is one of struggle against unheroic odds. 'My characters have nothing,' says Beckett, and this is true. Again, he says: 'I'm working with impotence, ignorance. I don't think impotence has been exploited in the past. . . . My little exploration is that whole zone of being that has always been set aside by artists as something unusable—as something by definition incompatible with art.' All of the wretches who give their names to Beckett's novels—Watt, Molloy, Malone (of *Malone Dies*)—as well as those who never reach the glory of a title, are reductions of mankind—tramps, outcasts, poverty-stricken old men. They wear rags, they are diseased, they smell, they are rejected by us, thrown out of doss-houses, told to get off the bus. They are not only disgusting, they are absurd. And yet they are human beings like ourselves, humiliated by charity, demanding something better than condescension or contempt. The point about them is that they manage to survive, finding the odd hole in the ground to sleep in, the odd crust to gnaw. Ultimately they are stoical, expecting nothing from God, aware that the stars they sleep under are indifferent, insentient matter. Indeed, neither religion nor philosophy can offer any comfort. Beckett does not believe in God, though he seems to imply that God has committed an unforgivable sin by not existing. All that stripped, poverty-eaten, diseased, stinking humanity possesses is the ability to do better than God—namely, to exist; also, it has a voice, though the outer world cannot hear it: '. . . within, motionless, I can live, and utter me, for no ears but my own . . .'

To write about characters who have so little requires very great literary skill. Beckett is a master of form: his books have a shape that suggests music. Out of the nothingness of life he can call up fantasies of great power, and his unheroic heroes grow, by the very starkness of their lives, into genuine pieces of mythology. His language, whether English or French, is highly idiosyncratic, and he is not afraid of making his sentences exactly mirror mental states, as in this from *The Unnamable*: 'I seek, like a caged beast born of caged beasts born of caged beasts born of caged beasts born in a cage and dead in a cage . . .'—or this (Pim is describing his life of wandering) in *Comment C'est* (*How It Is*): 'my life above what I did in my life above a little of everything tried everything then gave up no worse always a hole a ruin always a crust never any good at anything not made for that farrago too complicated crawl about in corners and sleep all I wanted I got it nothing left but go to heaven'. Such art, such integrity, such deliberate limitation of subject-matter must keep Beckett in the proud company of novelists who are not 'popular', but there is no denying his originality. His novels, like all important works of art, have the stamp of the inevitable on them: they had to be written and, though we suffer reading them, we are glad that they have been written.

My third Irishman, Flann O'Brien, was an Irish journalist and Gaelic scholar whose real name was Brian O'Nolan. Of his very few books, *The Hard Life* and *The Dalkey Archive* are slight but funny (they have also been largely ignored by English critics), but *At Swim-Two-Birds* is probably a masterpiece. Of it, Philip Toynbee has said: 'If I were cultural dictator in England I would make *At Swim-Two-Birds* compulsory reading in all our universities.' The book was first published in 1939, which enabled James Joyce, with two years of life to go, to say: 'There's a real writer with the true comic spirit', but there is still no move to make *At Swim-Two-Birds* required reading anywhere. Still, its audience is growing, and university students in Dublin, its town of origin, quote from it as from a new Holy Writ.

It owes a great deal to Joyce, but it is not massive and its touch is light; it even approaches the whimsical. The narrator is an Irish student who, in the intervals of lying in bed and pub-crawling, is writing a novel about a man named Trellis who is writing a book about his enemies who, in revenge, are writing a book about a man named Trellis. In a way, then, the book is a book about writing a book about writing a book. The student-narrator is interested not merely in literature but in Irish mythology, which fact enables him to bring in Finn MacCool, legendary Irish giant, and indulge in comic-heroic language which sounds as though it is translated from the Erse:

'The knees and calves to him, swealed and swathed with soo-gawns and Thomond weed-ropes, were smutted with dungs and dirt-daubs of every hue and pigment, hardened by stainings of mead and trickles of metheglin and all the dribblings and drippings of his medher, for it was the custom of Finn to drink nightly with his people.'

Flann O'Brien did, in fact, discover a means of counterpointing myth, fiction and actuality through the device of a sort of writer's commonplace-book. The technique is one of straight juxtaposition. The narrator has his first experience of drink and allows an extract from a Christian Brothers' literary reader to comment on its evils at clinical length. His typescript novel about Dermot Trellis, occupier of the Red Swan Hotel, is given in instalments and *in extenso*. There is no feeling of recession, of one order of reality (myth or novel or narration) lying behind another: all are presented on the same level. This is what gives the contrapuntal effect.

What O'Brien seems to be after in this very funny novel is an extension of the scope of the form but, as the same time, a limitation. All good novelists grow tired of plot with its wearisome manipulations, coincidences, simplifications. To keep narrative interest without having to impose overmuch action on the characters was Joyce's aim, and it was also O'Brien's. It is best to push action either on to the margins (where it is merely heard about) or into passages of parody, extracts from heroic annals, newspaper reports and the like–all of which have a valid connection with the life of the hero, but only the life of his mind. Much of the action of *Ulysses* is relegated to dream, imagination or–most important–to parody of the literature of action. Action in *At Swim-Two-Birds* (other than pub-crawling) is reserved to the counterpoints of the main narration. This may be called a limitation, but it provides scope for the only kind of extension that means much to an Irish

GREAT INDIVIDUALITY

writer – extension in the use of language. Here again this novel comes close to *Ulysses* in calling on a huge vocabulary, a large variety of literary styles, including poetry, textbooks and newspaper reportage, and that world of myth which underlies actuality. And there are plenty of opportunities for exhibiting the low glory of Dublin street- and pub-talk:

'Here's to your health, said Kelly.

'Good luck, I said.

'The porter was sour to the palate but viscid, potent. Kelly made a long noise as if releasing air from his interior.

'I looked at him from the corner of my eye and said:

'You can't beat a good pint.

'He leaned over and put his face close to me in an earnest manner.

'Do you know what I am going to tell you, he said, with his wry mouth, a pint of plain is your only man.'

O'Brien's last published novel, *The Third Policeman*, is a kind of fairy story with a real hell in it. It is frightening and ungenial but has undeniable power. Potential readers should not, however, rush to this without getting hold of his masterpiece first. *At Swim-Two-Birds* cannot safely be ignored.

See Bibliographical Note on p. 12

Samuel BECKETT (1906–   )
  More Pricks than Kicks. London, 1934 (republished, London, 1970)
  Murphy. London and Toronto, 1938
  Molloy. Paris, 1951, tr. 1955 (London, New York, Paris)
  Malone Dies. Paris, 1951, tr. New York, 1956

Samuel BECKET (*continued*)
  The Unnameable. Paris, 1953, tr. New York, 1958
  Watt. Paris, 1953
  How It Is. Paris, 1961, tr. 1964
Joyce CARY (1888–1957)
  Aissa Saved. London, 1932
  An American Visitor. London, 1933

GREAT INDIVIDUALITY

Joyce CARY (*continued*)
  The African Witch. London,
    1936
  Mister Johnson. London, 1939
  Charley is my Darling. London,
    1940
  A House of Children. London,
    1941
  Herself Surprised. London,
    1941
  To be a Pilgrim. London, 1942
  The Horse's Mouth. London,
    1944

Joyce CARY (*continued*)
  Prisoner of Grace. 1952
  Except the Lord. 1953
  Not Honour More. 1955
Flann O'BRIEN (1911–66)
  At Swim-Two-Birds. London,
    1939
  The Hard Life. London, 1961
  The Dalkey Archive. London,
    1964
  The Third Policeman. London,
    1967

VII

The Novel as a River

Some novelists are happiest when they can organize what they
have to say about man and his problems not into single separate
books, each with a new hero, background and plot, but into a
whole sequence which contains many volumes but goes on telling
the one story. The French use the term *roman fleuve* for a novel
which flows on and on in this manner, perhaps the author's life-
work, perhaps a work that only death finishes – the reader's or the
writer's. The river-novel often, it must be said, appeals more to the
writer than to the reader. Knowing the beginning of a novel, we do
not like to wait too long for the end; indeed, there are people who
like to read the end first. A *roman fleuve* looks like an *œuvre* (or
body of various work), but it is not: it is only a single big novel
whose various sections must never, as they come out, be judged as
separate books; thus the author, delaying the end, has it in his
power also to delay the critic's verdict. Capture an audience for
your first volume, and you are sure of keeping much of it for your
last. You are spared the burden of perpetual fresh invention and
some of the problems of form; what would be long patches of
boredom in the short novel are called 'expansiveness' in the novel-
sequence. Plan a really long one of these, and you have planned
your writing life.

When, however, we consider the pleasure and enlightenment
that Anthony Powell and C. P. Snow (Lord Snow) are giving us,
we are not inclined to take these strictures too seriously. Both
Snow and Powell seem to have set themselves a very lofty aim –
that of rivalling Marcel Proust in producing imaginative chronicles

THE NOVEL AS A RIVER

of an era and, to some extent, a class. The very title of Powell's novel-sequence – *The Music of Time* – recalls the *A la Recherche du Temps Perdu* of the French master, and the technique of invoking past time through a seemingly trivial object or incident (with Proust it was a cake dipped in tea) appears at the very beginning of *A Question of Upbringing* – the first novel in the Powell sequence. Nicholas Jenkins, the narrator, sees workmen warming themselves at a brazier at the corner of the street. 'As the dark fumes,' he says, 'floated above the houses, snow began to fall gently from a dull sky, each flake giving a small hiss as it reached the bucket. . . . The grey, undecided flakes continued to come down, though not heavily, while a harsh odour, bitter and gaseous, penetrated the air.'

Snow falling on fire makes Jenkins think – 'for some reason' – of the world of antiquity – 'legionaries in sheepskin warming themselves at a brazier . . . centaurs with torches cantering beside a frozen sea'. And then the classical associations take him back to the days when he learned the classical languages; it is still winter, but we are back at school, and the story is able to commence with the appearance of Widmerpool, one of the main characters, as a schoolboy. In his earlier novels (single, not part of any sequence) – like *Afternoon Men* and *Venusberg* – Powell had used an impersonal approach, making no judgement on characters or events. It is essential to the scheme of *The Music of Time* that there should be a narrator-commentator, for the whole complex story must resist the crass ticking of the clock, the chronological method, and submit to one man's extra-temporal pattern. Jenkins watches the characters move, but they do not march through time, as we seem to in real life; their movements must be frozen, as in a picture, or ordered into the steps of a dance. Time can only provide the music if the narrator's hands can move freely up and down on its keyboard. J. W. Dunne, the time-philosopher, was, I think, the first man to present this image: if we view time mechanically (as most of us do), then we are merely playing a dull chromatic scale starting at bottom A and ending at top A; if we view time creatively (as Powell does), then time is capable of a great number of melodies. But Powell's general title conceals the pictorial element in his technique: the dancers often hold a pose, or a *tableau*, as though a film of a ballet had been chopped up into stills.

So far Powell has produced the following instalments of his sequence: *A Question of Upbringing, A Buyer's Market, The Acceptance World, At Lady Molly's, Casanova's Chinese Restaurant, The Kindly Ones, The Valley of Bones, The Soldier's Art, The Military Philosophers*. Who and where are the dancers? Their stage is where the world of the artist overlaps with that of polite, or fashionable, society; they are bohemians, aristocrats and people of affairs. We are not allowed to see everything they do; Jenkins selects for us such gestures as fit best into his choreography, and he himself is reticent about matters which readers of popular novels expect a narrator to be only too eager to disclose–his love-life, his marriage. The fastidiousness of selection is matched by the polished formality of the style. It is a style apt for high comedy, and the slow unfolding of the comic situation is something that Powell does superbly. But high comedy is only one aspect of the comic genius, and one sometimes frets less at the limitation of art than at what seems to be limitation of temperament. Can the author really justify the vastness of the plan in the face of such smallness of scope? In that opening to *A Question of Upbringing*, Jenkins thinks of 'Poussin's scene in which the Seasons, hand in hand and facing outward, tread in rhythm to the notes of the lyre that the winged and naked grey-beard plays'. And then he imagines 'human beings, facing outward like the Seasons, moving hand in hand in intricate measure'. It does not seem, on the face of it, to be a large enough concept for an epic scale.

The 'damped', euphemistic quality of much of the sequence is summarized in the title of *The Kindly Ones*: the 'kindly ones' are the Eumenides of Greek legend, the Furies. Powell is introducing us, and his characters, to war–both the great wars of the twentieth century (here we see how the musical technique, contemptuous of chronology, is able to bring the two into a single measure). The first war is heralded by a big comic build-up suitable for a second-act curtain in a nightmare farce–the maid Billson deranged by talk of a ghost and Albert the cook's impending marriage and entering the dining-room stark naked ('I really thought familiarity was breeding contempt,' says Jenkins's mother. 'I certainly hoped so, with parlourmaids so terribly hard to come by.') The second war is fanfared with a charade of the Seven Deadly Sins, enacted in the mansion of Sir Magnus Donners. There is, as always, this 'purification' of relationships and events by the freezing into formal *tableaux*.

The character-interest of *The Music of Time* is very considerable, though all the personages are drawn from, as it were, the tenor register; there are large areas of the keyboard which are never struck, and it is especially notable that Powell cannot take the lower classes seriously. But Widmerpool and Moreland and Sir Magnus and the many others (some of whom are farcical eccentrics in the Waugh manner) are earning places in the fictional pantheon, ensuring immortality for a work that has not yet been wholly revealed as a work. Yet it is conceivable that posterity will be uneasy about this long chronicle so lacking in variety of tone or pace, with its strangely formalized dialogue, its leisurely descriptions, the small area of its interest. We, its contemporaries, must wait for the last bar of *The Music of Time* before delivering more than a tentative judgement.

C. P. Snow's novel-sequence, *Strangers and Brothers*, has just been completed at this moment of writing. There are eleven constituent books, and the order of their appearance is not quite the same as their reading order; unlike Powell's novels, Snow's have to be approached in terms of a straightforward chronology. The period of modern history dealt with by each volume is indicated, in the following list, after the title: *Strangers and Brothers* (1925–33); *The Conscience of the Rich* (1927–36); *Time of Hope* (1914–33); *The Light and the Dark* (1935–43); *The Masters* (1937); *Homecomings* (1938–48); *The New Men* (1939–46); *The Affair* (1953–54); *Corridors of Power* (1955); *The Sleep of Reason* (the nineteen-sixties–particularly the time of the Moors Murders); *Last Things* (the end of the decade). The first volume, it will be noted, gives a title to the whole.

THE NOVEL AS A RIVER

The eleven novels we have take the form of the autobiography of Lewis Eliot (eventually Sir Lewis; he never achieved a barony). He is the son of decent working-class people in the Midlands; his birthplace is possibly Leicester, Snow's own town, and his birth-time is round about the First World War. He enters a split world, the nature of which is indicated in the title *Strangers and Brothers*. Eliot has a deep, intuitive understanding of his brother and of two friends–one older, one younger–who stand in a kind of fraternal relationship to him; other people are strangers –literally strange to him, to be observed as external phenomena, their speech and actions recorded and, as he sees them in greater depth, analysed. The recording, commenting side of Eliot is not (as it is with Powell's Nicholas Jenkins) all we are allowed to see of him; he is an emotional man, though the emotion must be kept under control. His first wife, part of whose attraction lies in her her being a member of a higher social class (hypergamy, or marrying above oneself, is a great contemporary British theme), is incurably neurotic and represents a handicap to his career. He sees this dispassionately, without resentment, being involved deeply in the tragic situation of loving someone who desperately needs, but cannot take, help. A similar situation is present in his relationship with his younger friend, Roy Calvert, a brilliant scholar of manic-depressive tendencies (the theme implied in the title of *The Light and the Dark*). Death ends both relationships. His wife commits suicide; Calvert, who could easily have been placed in essential government work, becomes a pilot and is killed in the bombing offensive on Germany. About this latter, Snow writes with a bitterness probably echoed by all the fighting forces of the United Kingdom: the terribly erroneous strategic doctrine of the aerial offensive against 'interior lines of communication' seemed to arise from some mysterious human darkness, against the light of reason; its ghost still frightens us today.

Eliot's career, professional and social, has a varied pattern. At the beginning, he is 'Lucky Lewis'. With the aid of a small legacy from an aunt and at the instigation of his older friend, a solicitor's clerk, he becomes a barrister. After a slow start–helped by a

THE NOVEL AS A RIVER

friend who is a member of a circle of wealthy English Jews, hindered by his wife's neurosis and his own ill-health, fortunately curable–he starts building up a practice; at the same time, his law lectures at Cambridge bring him in touch with the world of academic politics examined so closely in books like *The Masters*. War breaks out, and he becomes a temporary civil servant, a secretary of committees; his immediate superior is a figure of power and decision, while his Minister is a member of an aristocratic family he already knows (the fields of observation are steadily widening). He now meets his second wife. In *Homecomings*, in many ways the most moving volume of the sequence, they become lovers. Determined to have children and fearing that Eliot is emotionally damaged to the extent that he cannot give, nor receive, love, she marries someone else and has her child. But she realizes her mistake, is divorced, and then marries Eliot. She represents yet another new background: her father is a painter, successful and substantially well off, contemptuous of or indifferent to attitudes of society. One of the imponderables, for which the world of the Light cannot legislate, now attacks the Eliots: the illness of her first child suggests a spiteful revenge on them for ignoring the conventions. But the Power relents, leaving their relationship more firmly cemented than before.

And now, in *The New Men*, another world of experience opens. Involved in the development of a nuclear deterrent, Eliot shares the horror of many of his scientific friends at its possibilities and he watches his brother give up a promising career on the administrative side of scientific research because of his principles. For a time his brother is a 'stranger' to him, but this too is part of his development. He has learnt to judge 'strangers' successfully by typing or categorizing them; now he has an insight that his intuitive understanding of people may be wrong; he realizes that there is a greater depth to them and, at the same time, perhaps a greater simplicity than he had previously imagined. In *The Masters* and its direct sequel *The Affair*, curiously linked to and yet isolated from the other aspects of his experience, Eliot is seen observing the mechanism of 'closed politics'–the process of decision-form-

THE NOVEL AS A RIVER

ing in committees or other small authoritarian groups: this is a source of great fascination to him. It appears to him that, in the long run, men do what they want to do; they decide what their background, feelings and experience make them decide, reasons convincing to themselves and others being easy enough to find. Strangely, this does not work out too badly: spiky points of integrity, honesty, justice thrust forward: one is left feeling that, since one has to be governed, this way may be one of the least harmful–and hateful–modes of doing it.

This is how a mature mind must look at the world of affairs. Eliot has, in effect, outgrown the liberal nonconformist background still represented by his older friend George. George still clings to the postures of revolt against provincialism, the leader and tutor of a small, everchanging group of young people who are eager to be initiated into what is for them a new, liberal, adventure of the spirit. He is never accepted in the bigger world that Eliot has joined. Eliot himself has acquired, without smugness or self-congratulation, a 'correct' background of friends and associates: they are 'sound', and so is he. He basks modestly in the respect of worthy men and in the fulfilment of what he sees as a fundamental necessity for all human beings–the sense of power. His capacity for insight has diminished somewhat, but this may be taken as the penalty of self-control, the development of techniques for dealing with his own emotional and professional problems. It is the ruled, who are really free, who exact this price from the rulers and runners, professionals and pundits.

In *Corridors of Power*, Snow moves Eliot into the world of high or open politics. We see here, restated, two recurrent themes of the whole series–the way in which unpredictable sexual attraction may defeat or bring close to defeat calculating, rational men– often the best of them; and the astonishing way in which attitudes and opinions can be reversed in the most unlikely characters. These themes are sound enough, and soundly developed, but the novel itself seems weaker as a whole than its predecessors. This may have something to do with a more reverent attitude to politics than most of us can assume: politicians, most of us feel, are to

THE NOVEL AS A RIVER

be satirized rather than taken seriously. The passage of Sir Lewis Eliot through the wonderland of high life–country houses parties, dinners in penthouses, fateful teas at the Athenæum–is treated with an awful gravity: the rulers have all the life and the ruled have ceased to exist. But it is hardly possible to pretend that the enormous tensions which hold society together and move it through history can be very seriously affected by the fortunes of individual politicians: even today the communicator has more real power than the executor. It is, in fact, one of the revelations of the whole sequence that few of the men of power shown are really aware of the sources of their beliefs and attitudes; mostly they seem to believe that they themselves have made them, in the sense that their experience of life has taught them accurately all they need to know–after all, are they not successful? All that can save them–and us–is the descent into humanity. But humanity cannot, so *The Sleep of Reason* seems to tell us, always be relied on to be human. The central event of this novel is obviously derived from those Moors Murders of which Lady Snow wrote in *On Iniquity*, and there is a stirring of theology, a sense of sin, which we had not expected in a novel by his rational lordship.

There are many exciting things about the *Strangers and Brothers* sequence–the confidence with which it taps the current of time, so that, in writing it, Snow has always looked forward to a future not yet in existence as well as back to a known past; the mature knowledge of men and affairs, given extra authority by our knowledge that Snow is no slippered writing recluse but a man actively involved in the practical mechanics of high policy-making; the reserved personal relationships of the 'strangers' and the whole-hearted ones of the 'brothers'; the 'resonance between what Lewis Eliot sees and what he feels'. There are certain dangers in so massive an achievement. Snow seems to have robbed the novel-form of its power to feed the senses: the world of colour and texture and scent has disappeared–most conspicuously in *Corridors of Power* –and life seems reduced to a number of paradigms, as though this were a grammar-book and not a novel. But perhaps that is a small price to pay for this feeding of a new side of the imagination, this

THE NOVEL AS A RIVER

opening up of a region of human life which has, heretofore, been practically closed to the fictional voyager.

I must mention one other long British novel-sequence (I reserve the trilogies and tetralogies to another chapter, for a reason which I will give there). This is Henry Williamson's *A Chronicle of Ancient Sunlight*, a work which, despite its power, is failing to engage the critical and public attention it merits. Perhaps Williamson's technique, which–compared to that of Snow or Powell–is somewhat old-fashioned, tends to diminish the power and poignancy of the content. This is concerned with the life of Phillip Maddison, first seen as a young boy living on the near-rural outskirts of London, his growing-up slowly and meticulously recorded and–at the same time–the England of the period before the First World War most accurately and fragrantly caught. Maddison becomes a soldier and later an officer, and the three volumes *A Fox Under my Cloak*, *The Golden Virgin* and *Love and the Loveless* perhaps give us one of the most encyclopaedic fictional accounts of what that first war was like. In a more recent instalment of the sequence, *It Was the Nightingale*, Maddison enters that otter-world with which Williamson (on the strength of the remarkable *Tarka the Otter*) will always be mainly associated: much of the book is taken up with the search for a pet otter which, to Maddison, is a remnant of the life he spent with his wife, dead in childbirth. This book is at times almost unbearably poignant. Williamson's style may be romantic, but it always avoids sentimentality; its sensuous response to nature is fresh and often surprising. The sequence–fifteen volumes long–is at last complete, but it still awaits that burst of critical response which will proclaim, if not a masterpiece, at least a work we would not willingly be without.

Finally, let us go over to America. Only the death of William Faulkner put an end to what amounts to the most massive novel-sequence of the century. Faulkner wrote about nothing but the American South, and he very nearly wrote about nothing but an invented region of that South–Yoknapatawpha County, Mississippi. And yet, because of the difficulty of his prose style, he is regarded less as a great regional novelist than as an irritating and wilful experimentalist. He is, in many ways, more difficult than Joyce, with his endless sentences, under-punctuated, and his turgid interior monologues, but the very complexity of his prose—mirroring, as it does, complex states of mind—makes us take his Deep South more seriously than that of, say, Erskine Caldwell.

Faulkner is interested in the degeneration of representative white families in the South: that degeneration is part of history and, sordid as it must be, it has to be recorded. In *The Sound and the Fury* (which literally opens with a 'tale told by an idiot', in idiot's prose) we watch the fall of the house of Compson—a family once great, even before the Civil War, in the town of Jefferson, Mississippi. The fall has, since Faulkner, come to be regarded as typical of all such families, with its pattern of drunkenness, rejection of work and life, praise of a mythical past, seedy senatorial oratory. Benjy Compson, the idiot, is a potent and terrible symbol of decline. The Compsons are, however, not the only white Southerners to fall: there are the Sutpens in *Absalom, Absalom!*, and there is irony in seeing their degeneration partly through the eyes of the Compsons. The sources of damnation in the Sutpens are easily summarized—a mean ambition to power (aristocratic, slave-owning), which sees human beings as a kind of property, and cognate with this, the animality which turns black women into things to be used—the mixing of blood, the breeding of shame and more slaves. The story goes far back; Faulkner is obsessed, as he must be, by history. But his history is an aspect of the present, not a romantic *Gone With the Wind* dream-world.

There is another important family in Faulkner's chronicle—the Snopeses, poor-white, sustained by no aristocratic values, victims of injustice as well as built-in shiftlessness, but tough as the Compsons and Sutpens are weak. Their story is mainly told in the trilogy consisting of *The Hamlet*, *The Town* and *The Mansion* (this last, Faulkner's final major book, appeared in 1961). Mink Snopes sums up the dimly-sensed philosophy of the whole clan in *The Mansion*: 'He meant, simply, that *them—they—it*, whichever and whatever you wanted to call it, who represented a simple fundamental justice and equity in human affairs, or else a man might just as well quit; the *they, them, it,* call them what you like, which simply would not, could not harass and harry a man for ever without some day, at some moment, letting him get his own and equal licks back in return.'

The tough, repetitive meditations go on and on, and sometimes the reader tires. But Faulkner has a massiveness and sometimes a majesty not easily found elsewhere in contemporary American writing. Mink Snopes, lowest of poor-whites–'that had had to spend so much of his life just having unnecessary bother and trouble'–at least sees something of human glory at the end of the chronicle:

'. . . the beautiful, the splendid, the proud and the brave, right on up to the very top itself among the shining phantoms and dreams which are the milestones of the long human recording– Helen and the bishops, the kings and the unhomed angels, the scornful and graceless seraphim.'

See Bibliographical Note on p. 12

William FAULKNER (1897–1962)
Soldiers' Pay. New York, 1926
Mosquitoes. New York, 1927
Sartoris. New York, 1929
The Sound and the Fury. New York, 1929
As I Lay Dying. New York, 1930
Sanctuary. 1931
Light in August. New York, 1932
Pylon. 1935
Absalom, Absalom! New York, 1936
The Wild Palms. 1939
The Hamlet. 1940 (Snopes, vol. 1)

William FAULKNER (*continued*)
Intruder in the Dust. New York, 1948
Requiem for a Nun. New York, 1951
A Fable. New York, 1954
The Town (Snopes, vol. 2). 1957
The Mansion (Snopes, vol. 3). 1959
Anthony POWELL (1905–)
Afternoon Men. London, 1931
Venusberg. London, 1932
A Dance to the Music of Time:
A Question of Upbringing. 1951
A Buyer's Market. London, 1952

THE NOVEL AS A RIVER

Anthony POWELL (*continued*)

The Acceptance World. London, 1955

At Lady Molly's. London, 1957

Casanova's Chinese Restaurant. 1960

The Kindly Ones. London and Boston, 1962

The Valley of Bones. London and Boston, 1964

The Soldier's Art. London, 1966

The Military Philosophers. London, 1968

C. P. SNOW (1905–   )

Strangers and Brothers:

Strangers and Brothers, 1940

The Light and the Dark. 1947

Time of Hope. London, 1949

The Masters. 1951

The New Men. London, 1954

Homecomings. 1956

The Conscience of the Rich. 1958

The Affair. 1960

Corridors of Power. 1964

The Sleep of Reason. London, 1968

Last Things. 1970

Henry WILLIAMSON (1897–   )

Tarka the Otter. London, 1927

Henry WILLIAMSON (*continued*)

A Chronicle of Ancient Sunlight:

The Dark Lantern. London, 1951

Donkey Boy. London, 1952

Young Phillip Maddison. London, 1953

How Dear is Life. London, 1954

A Fox under my Cloak. London, 1955

The Golden Virgin. London, 1957

Love and the Loveless. London, 1958

A Test to Destruction. London, 1960

The Innocent Moon. London, 1961

It Was the Nightingale. Longale. London, 1962

The Power of the Dead. London, 1963

The Phoenix Generation. London, 1965

A Solitary War. London, 1966

Lucifer before Sunrise. London, 1967

The Gale of the World. London, 1969 (final part)

VIII

Other Kinds of Massiveness

Every novelist practising today feels prodded by the ghost of Dickens to attempt the big canvas, crammed with characters. But few novelists seem inclined to shut themselves away for a long time, forgotten by the world of readers, cameras, and microphones while they toil at the large panoramic book in one volume. It is often not economical to do this, except perhaps in America, where subsidies, scholarships and academic sabbaticals are often available: apart from the desirability of keeping one's name freshly known with a succession of books of no great length, there is the question of how much a reader will pay for a novel. The retail price of a book of eighty thousand words is (at the moment of writing) £1.75; can one charge a proportionate amount more for a novel of, say, half a million words? It is better to bring out one's great work in instalments, like Snow and Powell. This way the best of both worlds lies: eventually the single volumes will appear bound into larger units (the first three novels of *The Music of Time* are already available as one big book). This is the contemporary equivalent of the Dickensian procedure of publishing in weekly or fortnightly parts and, for that matter, the Joycean way of letting the world see *Ulysses* in magazine serial form or *Finnegans Wake* in pamphlet fragments.

The *roman fleuve*, if it reaches Snovian or Powellian or Williamsonian proportions, must, however, always end as a fair segment of a shelf and not as a single volume. There is another kind of novel-in-instalments which does not go so far and appeases the

OTHER KINDS OF MASSIVENESS

ghost of Dickens-the work that is planned, rather like a symphony or concerto, in three or four movements-the trilogy or the tetralogy. Four movements seems to be the outer limit, as with a symphony; three movements, as with a concerto, is the minimum. The novelist who plans one of these works is doing something quite different from the *romancier fleuve*: he is more aware of symmetry than the man who looks down a long stretch of winding river; each novel has a fixed and foreseen relationship with every other novel in the little sequence; the sense is of a solid pyramid or tower rather than of an unpredictable work of nature.

With the *Sword of Honour* trilogy Evelyn Waugh shilly-shallied, first saying that he planned three novels about Crouchback at war, later saying that two would 'do the trick'. But a law of art drew him to the threesome we have (now a single volume): we cannot conceive of such a project as being other than predestined to take a triune form. When I myself began to write my *Malayan Trilogy* (called *The Long Day Wanes* in America), I saw very clearly how a symphonic scheme (the second movement is a scherzo) would enable me to record, each as a very nearly complete entity, the different stages of an expatriate Englishman's love affair with Malaya, as well as the stages of the process which brought Malaya from British protection to independence. A single long novel would not do: there had to be the feel of a very substantial pause between movements which could, at a pinch, be taken as separate and isolated compositions.

This, I think also applies to Olivia Manning's very interesting trilogy-a sequence about two English expatriates in the Balkans. The constituent books are called *The Great Fortune*, *The Spoilt City* and *Friends and Heroes*. There has been a fair space between the composition of the second and the last, but the unity of feeling is marvellously maintained. The trilogy seems to me perhaps the most important long work of fiction to have been written by an English woman novelist since the war; it seems also (in the wider sense that was not applicable to my chapter on the war-novels of servicemen) to be one of the finest records we have of the impact of that war on Europe. Miss Manning's two

OTHER KINDS OF MASSIVENESS

chief characters, Harriet and Guy Pringle, are living in Bucharest at the beginning of *The Great Fortune*: Guy is working for a British cultural mission in Rumania. In the first year of the war Harriet (who is the observer of the two; she observes her own husband as well as the big public events in which both are caught up) watches the slow corruption of a doomed civilization. The observation finds comic, as well as poetic, expression: the Rumanians are drawn with exasperated tenderness and are sometimes caricatured, but they remain real and rounded. In *The Spoilt City* we move towards the occupation of the city by the Germans after the fall of France; in the final novel Harriet and Guy are in Athens, in a fresh centre of disturbance, though accompanied there by a preposterous *émigré* aristocrat, their friend..

The minute and accurate record of the Balkans under the stress of war is only one aspect of the trilogy; the other aspect, perhaps more important, is Harriet Pringle's attempt to understand her husband–a process which is incomplete even at the end of *Friends and Heroes*. He is a complex character, big, cultured, quixotically helpful, vital, often foolish, demanding–indeed, one of the most fully created male leads of contemporary fiction. He needs three large volumes for his setting forth and, summing up the variable contradictoriness of man, he balances the Balkan civilizations which are breaking up, though only, as we know, to be remade. He is a kind of civilization in himself.

Miss Manning's talent is very considerable, and her Balkans trilogy is the important work towards which her earlier novels– *The Wind Changes*, *School for Love* and *A Different Face*–have been leading. It is rarely that one finds such a variety of gifts in one contemporary woman writer–humour, poetry, the power of the exact image, the ability to be both hard and compassionate, a sense of place, all the tricks of impersonation and, finally, a historical eye.

Another British writer (male) who has built a solid fictional structure–this time a tetralogy–about a foreign place, is Lawrence Durrell, whose *Alexandria Quartet* started with *Justine* in 1956, continued with *Balthazar* and *Mountolive* in the one year 1958,

96

OTHER KINDS OF MASSIVENESS

and concluded with *Clea* in 1960. Durrell calls the work a 'four-decker novel whose form is based on the relativity proposition', and such a description, to which references to 'space-time continuums' have been added, is both frightening and misleading. Durrell is evidently interested in creating a new kind of fiction, and, like Huxley in *Point Counter Point*, he finds it necessary to include a novelist among his characters, so that we shall be reminded occasionally what kind of novel is being written. Indeed, he adds to the novelist-narrator Darley–who relates the story of three-quarters of the sequence–a secondary novelist, Pursewarden, and a dead novelist, Arnauti. It is Pursewarden who says most about this theory of relativity: we view life, he tells us, from a necessarily limited point, but the limitation has nothing to do with our personal make-up, only with the ultimate facts of space and time. We observe from a given point-instant, but *what* we observe becomes different if we alter our position: 'Two paces west and the whole picture is changed.'

What this amounts to is that, one novel of the *Quartet* being concerned with time, and the other three with the 'three sides of space', we can never see the whole of any given character or event in one novel alone. Each novel is meaningless on its own, we seem to be told, as length or breadth or height or time (which needs space to measure) is meaningless outside of a mathematics book. *Justine* explains *Balthazar* on one level, while *Clea* explains it on another, deeper, level; *Mountolive* merely keeps time moving. It does not seem to me that there is anything really original in this technique; in an ordinary novel–dignified by none of Durrell's theorizing–we make similar discoveries about people and events, the final discovery coming at the end. This is especially true of one of the lowliest forms of popular literature–the detective story–and it is from the detective story that a novel as sophisticated and profound as Graham Greene's *The End of the Affair* partially derives. In a railway-bookstall crime novel a man may die in the first chapter; in a later chapter we find a plausible explanation for his death; in a later chapter still we learn the real reason for it. In *Balthazar* Pursewarden commits suicide; in *Mountolive* the reason

OTHER KINDS OF MASSIVENESS

seems to be given—his position in the Foreign Office and his liking for anti-British Nassim (Justine's husband) in conflict; in *Clea* we discover that he has had an incestuous passion for his blind sister. To learn more and more as we go on is what we expect from any good novel, and we need no benefit of 'relativity'.

It is conceivable that the tetralogy might have seemed more original if it had been set in a British middle-class environment; certainly the freshness of the technique of *Point Counter Point* comes out strongly by reason of its plain London setting. But Durrell has chosen a highly exotic *mise en scène* in which anything can happen—pederasty, incest, all the convolutions of lust, all the varieties of betrayal. His Alexandria is a dream-city caught in 'poetic' prose which seems to emphasize its unreality:

'Notes for landscape-tones. . . . Long sequences of tempera. Light filtered through the essence of lemons. An air full of brick-dust—sweet-smelling brick-dust and the odour of hot pavements slaked with water. Light damp clouds, earth-bound yet seldom bringing rain. Upon this squirt dust-red, dust-green, chalk-mauve and watered crimson-lake. In summer the sea-damp lightly varnished the air. Everything lay under a coat of gum.

'And then in autumn the dry, palpitant air, harsh with static electricity, inflaming the body through its light clothing. The flesh coming alive, trying the bars of its prison. A drunken whore walks in a dark street at night, shedding snatches of song like petals. Was it in this that Anthony heard the heart-numbing strains of the great music which persuaded him to surrender for ever to the city he loved?'

It is a prose-poetry whose rhythms tend to flaccidity and which sometimes melts into a romantic wash a little too close to the old lending-library sadistic-sentimental exotic escapism beloved of the dreaming shop-girl. For all that, there are passages which are powerful and masterly—sharply and exactly observant. But the final impression is of something shimmering in a rather old-fashioned *fin de siècle* way, suggesting languor and satiety after elaborate self-indulgence. The decadence smells of stale incense.

Durrell has followed his tetralogy with a dilogy or duo—the

OTHER KINDS OF MASSIVENESS

novels called *Tunc* and *Numquam*. They have Alexandrian properties—exotic scenes, deformities, lush sex—but they have little to do
with reality. The hero-narrator builds an all-powerful computer
which is taken over by a firm that proposes to run the world.
Durrell has some good bawdy sixth-form fun with the sexual
aspects of its plans, and he presents some acceptable grotesques as
well as a couple of gorgeous women (one of whom, when dead,
the computer remakes from scratch). But there is an unsatisfactory
disparity between the farce-fantasy and the high-toned play of the
language.

The projected trilogy of Edward Upward seems, from its first
volume, to be old-fashioned in rather a different way. Upward is
one of the near-fabulous names of the nineteen-thirties, the 'Chal-
mers' of Christopher Isherwood's autobiography *Lions and
Shadows*, to be associated with W. H. Auden and Stephen Spender
and Cecil Day Lewis in their 'heart's heyday' of revolutionary
optimism, now long since left behind. In the summer of 1962—
nearly thirty years after his last book, *Journey to the Border*—
Upward published *In the Thirties*, which was at once greeted by
Isherwood as a masterpiece: 'I believe that it may well be the first
part of one of the greatest and most original novels of our time.'
Less partisan critics may well have more reservations.

In the Thirties presents the beginning of the progress of a young
poet, Alan Sebrill, whose creative frustration leads him to join the
Communist Party, who leaves the Party in the late nineteen-forties
without, however, abandoning his revolutionary ideals, and in
whom finally allegiance to poetic rather than political truth pre-
vails. What is disappointing about this first volume is the apparent
conviction that the record of what it was like to be a young Communist in the thirties is enough in itself, it does need not to be
shaped into a work of art. It is full of matter, but this means it is
unselective. That Upward can write is attested by phrases like 'the
spume like fine lace curtains undulating in a black wind, or like
the shredded fat hanging down over a bullock's heart in a butcher's
shop', but he is too often deliberately pedestrian, as though puri-
tanically afraid to allow style to get in the way of subject. After

OTHER KINDS OF MASSIVENESS

the greyness of these evocations, it is a relief to dip into the jam-pot of *The Alexandria Quartet*. But perhaps *In the Thirties* fails chiefly because of Alan Sebrill himself–a less than compelling character with whom it is no pleasure to identify ourselves.

Upward came to the contemporary scene after a long silence, but the return of Richard Hughes broke a creative void of twenty-five years. Hughes's literary reputation had, we thought, been settled and sealed by *A High Wind in Jamaica* and *In Hazard*–masterly, very adult novels about children. But in 1961 he announced that he had embarked on a long historical novel-sequence to be called *The Human Predicament*, and he published the first instalment, *The Fox in the Attic*. This is set in 1923. Its hero, Augustine–a character not, as yet, much more compelling than Upward's Alan Sebrill–opens the action, walking into modern history with a dead child on his shoulder. This dead child seems to symbolize the past but is also a device to set the story moving: the small Welsh town where Augustine lives (this town is wonder-fully rendered) blames him for the child's death, so he goes off to stay in a German *Schloss*. Now the narrative enters the stream of post-1918 German history, and its central event is the failed Munich *Putsch*, its chief 'public' character the emergent Adolf Hitler.

We cannot yet judge *The Fox in the Attic*, for it looks forward eagerly, as we do ourselves, to a sequel, and we wonder whether we shall have to wait another twenty-five years before it is given to us. All we can say so far is that Hughes's mastery of narrative, man-agement of situation, rendering of time and place are as powerful as in the earlier books. The viewpoint often seems to be drenched in the yet-uncorrupted innocence of a child, and the description of the foyer of the big German hotel, for instance, with its subtle odours of dyspepsia, carries overtones of the whole messy world that adults are building.

The authors I have mentioned so far in this chapter have re-corded, or are in process of recording, modern Europe, either in its centre or on its fringe. Alexandrian Africa belongs to the Mediterranean and is not too far from the Bucharest and Athens

OTHER KINDS OF MASSIVENESS

of Olivia Manning. Doris Lessing has devoted much of a penta-teuch to a problem that never appears in Durrell's world – that of the relationship of black and white, ruled and ruler, in a British dependency. Her work is called *Children of Violence*, and its constituent novels are *Martha Quest*, *A Proper Marriage*, *A Ripple from the Storm*, *Landlocked* and *The Four-gated City*. One may say that Mrs. Lessing has two other themes, besides the one of colour, though all three are really cognate – she is concerned with the rights of a woman in a world of men, she looks to the politics of the left wing to bring justice to women and blacks alike. This sounds a crude programme for a novel-sequence of such length, and it can give no indication of the subtlety and complexity with which the heroine, Martha Quest, is presented, nor of the way in which simple issues grow more and more complicated with the coming of the Second World War, the influx of other elements from Europe. But the true strength of *Children of Violence* lies in the firm grip which is kept on the fundamental issues; it is a crusader's novel.

In 1962 Mrs. Lessing showed herself capable of achieving a single-volumed novel of great length, though this work – *The Golden Notebook* – resolves itself into four elements: it is, so to speak, a one-movement symphony like Sibelius's Seventh, in which contrasting sections take the place of separable movements. The novelty of shape is dictated by the didactic purpose (there is a parallel here with the expressionist drama of writers like Brecht, the urge to teach too strong to tolerate the old easy-going forms of literature). The heroine of *The Golden Notebook* is a novelist suffering from 'writer's block'. Instead of attempting a new novel, she fills four notebooks with four kinds of observation, though her preoccupations are twofold – with the Communist revolution of the nineteen-thirties (she became a Communist in South Africa because only the Communists seemed to have any 'moral energy') and the emergence of the 'free woman'. She is evidently close to Martha Quest in spirit and ideals, though she is perhaps duller – a fit mate for Alan Sebrill. Her conception of herself as a 'free woman' leads her to say some hard things about male arrogance, crassness, sexual impotence and incompetence, and her own sexual

OTHER KINDS OF MASSIVENESS

frustrations (which are, of course, to be blamed on men) fill up a good part of one notebook. She is intelligent, honest, burning with conviction, but she ends up as a bit of a bore. So, for that matter, does Mrs. Lessing's own experiment. The four notebooks merge into the single conception of the 'Golden Notebook', and we are told that we have really, after all, been reading a novel. We are not convinced, however. There has been too much diversion of aim, too little digestion of deeply held beliefs into something acceptable as a work of art. The crusader's best medium is the manifesto, which is not quite the same thing as a novel.

Still, here is a bold enough attempt at something bigger than the eighty-thousand-word effort which is what nowadays passes for a full-length work of fiction. Only two male novelists now living in England have courage to create long works on the scale of *The Golden Notebook*, though their aims could not be more different from Mrs Lessing's, nor from each other's. These novelists are J. B. Priestley and Angus Wilson, and they demonstrate how it is possible for two distinct contemporary traditions to derive from a common source. That common source is the Victorian novel–distilled, for Priestley, through Hugh Walpole, though there can be no doubt of the superiority of the pupil to the master. Where Walpole is capable only of diluted romance, seasoned with a few grotesques, Priestley is full-blooded, genuinely comic, full of social awareness. So is Angus Wilson, who drinks his Dickens straight but is drawn also to the subtler George Eliot; he has, in addition (as we shall see) opened a world for the English novel that the Victorians pretended did not exist.

If posterity remembers Priestley for *The Good Companions* and for nothing else, it will have done him only a partial disservice. That lengthy picaresque chronicle of the adventures of a concert party (a form of entertainment troupe that seems now to have died out) has many faults–sentimentality, long-windedness, a too hearty taking of the open road–but its virtues seem solid enough, even after forty-two years. Priestley has captured certain aspects of English life in the late nineteen-twenties–the Yorkshire mill-town, the Midland English village, the black industrial depression,

102

the still strong nonconformism, the optimism of men with little money – and set down sturdily fashioned characters among the Dickensian grotesques. The huge structure holds well and the narrative is never too slow. The same virtues of credibility, humour in the English tradition, and a genuine concern with the changing patterns of social history also inform novels like *Angel Pavement*, *They Walk in the City* (though this has some deplorably implausible episodes in the middle) and the more recent *Lost Empires*, a novel about the old-time music-hall, even deader and more regretted than the wandering concert party. Between these hefty works, Priestley has attempted shorter novels, often of great excellence, like *Bright Day* and his recent admirable 'international-conspiracy' thrillers, as well as that shrewd glance at modern bureaucracy, *Sir Michael and Sir George*. Unlike so many novelists who grew up in an earlier age, Priestley has insisted on living in the present, and – with such concepts as 'The Grey Ones' (the title of a short story in the collection *Another Place*) and 'Admass' – he has actively influenced post-war England's attitudes to itself. That he is rarely taken seriously in contemporary surveys of the novel (there is no place for him in, for instance, Walter Allen's *Tradition and Dream*) is perhaps due to his failure to make any fictional experiments (he has reserved experiment for the stage) and his willingness to be content with a burly, no-nonsense, unintellectual approach to life in his novels (he is intellectual enough in his plays and essays). Yet it would be foolish to disregard his achievement and make little of his vast creative energy.

Angus Wilson, on the other hand, is a darling of the intellectuals, though he, like Priestley, has been happy with a traditional approach to form in the novel. Content, however, is a very different matter. Wilson digs deep into the roots of human morality and comes up with good and evil, while Priestley clings to a rather easy-going liberal concept of life. Also, Wilson has disclosed the peculiar horrors that await the male homosexual in modern British society, and he has bared that whole half-world with uncompromising honesty. His first novel, *Hemlock and After*, deals with an ageing novelist, Bernard Sands, famous, married, with grown-up

OTHER KINDS OF MASSIVENESS

children, who discovers–at the very moment when his life's work is to be fulfilled–that he cannot control the homosexual tendencies in his nature which, all his past life, he has been able to repress. He at once becomes a prey to evil forces which no amount of Priest-leyan liberalism can laugh away. Even the natural world shows itself as mainly toothed and venomous, while the human world displays grotesques of a malignity undreamt of by the Victorians. Contemporary English society, with its creamy tolerant surface covering tired values, can find no answer to the problem of evil; the death of Sands comes in bitterness and what looks like failure. But, as the title reminds us, there is something after the hemlock– the works achieved (Sands was a great novelist) as well as the evilly thwarted good intentions.

Anglo-Saxon Attitudes presents an even bigger panorama of con-temporary English life, some of its sillier aspects most cruelly caught. And one may say now that Wilson's capacity for accurate 'taking off' of stupidity is unrivalled anywhere: he is a great mimic, though he sometimes delights too much in mimicry–sometimes he seems merely to mimic Dickens instead of creating characters out of the current of the life he knows. But there are plenty of genuine Wilsonic creations in *Anglo-Saxon Attitudes*, as well as a plot of rich ramifications growing out of an event of stupid malignity which does not even take place in the course of the observed action. During an archaeological 'dig' before the First World War, a pagan phallic symbol is, as a cruel joke, placed in the grave of an Anglo-Saxon bishop. The chief character, an ageing professor of history, Gerald Middleton, suspects into late life that the views of medieval scholars on Early English religion have been modified by a hoax, and the long and intricate narrative is concerned with un-winding the complicated strands that lead back to its enactment. Many people, of all classes and sexes, are involved: the unravelling proves to be an enrichening. As in *Hemlock and After*, there is sharp observation of the deep moral dichotomy that underlies the surface of the life of our times; there is wit; there is learning; there is cruelty.

The Middle Age of Mrs. Eliot very boldly attempts the full-

OTHER KINDS OF MASSIVENESS

length delineation of a woman of our times, with considerable success–perhaps too much. In concentrating on what, for a male novelist, is a very dangerous undertaking, Wilson seems sometimes to forget that he is writing a novel, that one of his functions is to entertain. Meg Eliot is a barrister's wife–well-off, smart, given to good works, a little too self-assured. Nemesis strikes at her on a trip to the Far East: her husband is accidentally shot dead, and she finds herself alone and without money, forced to make a new life and learn to understand her true nature, which years of self-satisfied marriage have obscured. It is one of the most remarkable *tours de force* of modern fiction, but it is closer to a clinical examination than to a novel.

Like most highly imaginative artists, Wilson tends to be happier when indulging a vein of fantasy than when merely being an accurate recording-machine. *The Old Men at the Zoo* moves farther away from traditional naturalism than do his other novels: he has a future setting, and some of his events seem divorced from probability–in other words, reality and myth come together. The narrative starts with threats of war–a federated Europe growling at isolated Britain–and against this background political wrangling goes on at the London Zoo – how it shall be run, what its future shall be. It is a tiny enclosed world, but it is important, and the problems of loyalty experienced by Simon Carter, the Zoo's secretary, have universal application. With the coming of war, though, the Zoo collapses, and Wilson's naturalism collapses (or, if you please, is transfigured) into something like mythical fantasy. The 'Twilight of the Gods' setting in which Sir Robert Falcon, the new director of the Zoo, meets his end; the horrible cannibalistic eating of the animals in a time of famine; the gladiatorial proposals of conquering Europe when, taking over Britain, she also takes over the London Zoo–these are brilliantly rendered, but they go far beyond the scope of ordinary fictional plausibility. We are in a world of private nightmare, as Dickens so often was, but Wilson has the un-Dickensian courage to give the nightmare its head. To me, *The Old Men at the Zoo* seems the best thing that Wilson has ever done.

OTHER KINDS OF MASSIVENESS

Late Call brings us back to the present, a pertinent study of another aspect of contemporary Britain–the New Town. Sylvia Calvert, fat, suffering from high blood pressure, has to retire from hotel management, and, with her husband–a ranker-officer of the First World War who subsists on anecdotes of his past, grumbles about the present, and bets on horses–she goes to live with her widower-son Harold, a secondary-modern headmaster and pillar of New Town society. Wilson's aim is partly to show the rootlessness of a community which has opted out of the old values (including the concepts of good and evil). Of the vicar of the New Town church–which, inevitably, does not look like a church–Harold says: 'You never get any of this dry-as-dust theological stuff from him that's done so much to keep people out of the churches. Quite the contrary. Last Easter he gave a sermon on the eleven plus.' Wilson seems to imply that the New Town would be better for some of that dry-as-dust theological stuff.

What is there for Sylvia Calvert in this community of liberal ideals and bowling-alleys? There is escape into television and the odd nice historical novel from the public library, but the only true release is into country untamed by the New Town, where a farm cat slinks by with a half-dead rabbit in its mouth and a tree is struck by lightning. Bernard Sands looked with horror on this naked revelation of ultimate forces in *Hemlock and After*, but it is whether we like it or not, reality. It is this concern with the terrifying and exalting essences underlying the *TV Times*, the drama club committee meeting, the kitchen crammed with gadgets, that Angus Wilson continues, ever more deeply, to show. His eye catches the surface of life miraculously, but after that there is the descent into the dark mines of the human spirit.

Finally, I ought to mention the longest one-volume novel ever written. It appeared in England in 1966, after much transatlantic trumpeting–*Miss Mackintosh, My Darling*, by an American lady (and descendant of the great Mormon), Marguerite Young. It was a very very long novel, and few had time to read it all. Its size was, for many, both the sole source of its interest and its main disrecommendation. But Angus Wilson, who read it from first page

106

to last, propounded that it was a good book. The common reader may respect his judgement without necessarily wishing to confirm it.

See Bibliographical Note on p. 12

Anthony BURGESS (1917–   )
    See Chapter XVI—page 218
Lawrence DURRELL (1912–   )
    Alexandria Quartet:
        Justine, 1957
        Balthazar. 1958
        Mountolive. London, 1958
        Clea. 1960
    Tunc. 1968
    Nunquam. London, 1970
Richard HUGHES (1900–   )
    A High Wind in Jamaica. London, 1929
        (as Innocent Voyage. New York, 1929)
    In Hazard. 1938
    The Human Predicament:
        A Fox in the Attic. 1961
Doris LESSING (1919–   )
    Children of Violence:
        Martha Quest. London, 1952
        A Proper Marriage. London, 1954
        A Ripple from the Storm. London, 1958
        Landlocked. London, 1965
        The Four-gated City. 1969
    The Golden Notebook. 1962

Olivia MANNING
    The Wind Changes. London, 1937
    School for Love. London, 1951
    A Different Face. London, 1953
    The Great Fortune. London, 1960
    The Spoilt City. 1962
    Friends and Heroes. 1965
    The Play Room. London, 1969
J. B. PRIESTLEY (1894–   )
    The Good Companions. 1929
    Angel Pavement. 1930
    Bright Day. 1946
    They Walk in the City. 1936
    Sir Michael and Sir George. 1964
    Lost Empires. London and Boston, 1965
    The Image Man. London, 1968
        (Out of Town and London End)
Edward UPWARD (1903–   )
    Journey to the Border. London, 1938
    In the Thirties. London. 1962
    The Rotten Elements. London, 1969

OTHER KINDS OF MASSIVENESS

Angus WILSON (1913–   )
 Hemlock and After. 1952
 Anglo-Saxon Attitudes. 1956
 The Middle Age of Mrs. Eliot
  London, 1958

Angus WILSON (*continued*)
 The Old Men at the Zoo.
  1961
 Late Call. London, 1964
 No Laughing Matter. 1967

IX

Other Miners

To say that, whether he likes it or not, the novelist must always be concerned with human society is a truism. But our age has seen a good deal of a particular fictional way of looking at human society—an examination not just of the values inherent in it but of the values that tend to be imposed upon it. The novels I mentioned in my chapter on Utopias and Dystopias are satires on the kind of repressive government that the mind in nightmare can weave out of the examples set by Germany and Russia. But there have been other attempts to write political novels, and these have not always drawn on fantasy or prophecy; they have been in the stream of straightforward naturalism. The political novel can be merely a study of how our governors behave, and the admirable fiction of Maurice Edelman, a Member of Parliament as well as a man of letters, is firmly based on what he observes and knows. *Who Goes Home?* and *A Call on Kuprin* show us, among other things, what really goes on in the House of Commons; *The Minister* and its sequel *The Prime Minister's Daughter* are about the ways in which the public life of an ambitious politician can be threatened by disclosures of his private life. C. P. Snow's *Corridors of Power* (which acknowledges the professional help of Maurice Edelman) is also a political novel in this here-and-now way of straight reportage. But politics to most writers is not just a dirty word but a frightening word; it very easily draws to itself, as a fictional subject, the connotations of a totalitarian nightmare.

Arthur Koestler has written in Hungarian and German, as well as English, and his novels have always been about the problems of revolutions, the ways in which power can corrupt not only its wielders but its victims, and (drawn from personal experience) the living nightmare of the prison and the concentration camp. *Darkness at Noon*, which presents the Soviet purges not as an historical abstraction but as a reality suffered by a devout revolutionary who now believes the revolution to have been betrayed, is not, like *Nineteen Eighty-Four*, a demented vision of the future but a faithful rendering of fact. *Thieves in the Night* shows the Palestinian Jews trying to build a society in the face of injustice and their own awareness of how suffering may corrupt rather than ennoble. *The Gladiators* takes the story of Spartacus and that slaves' revolt which the Roman historians tell us so little about, trying to make it an allegory of modern revolution (in a new State founded on hatred of oppression, how far is its ruler permitted to use oppression himself to maintain law and order?). Two terms seem inseparable from any discussion on Koestler and other practitioners of his kind of political novel; they are 'nightmare' and 'allegory'. These two words send us straight to Franz Kafka, whose fantasies have nothing to do with politics but who, nevertheless, once seemed in danger of becoming the one true mentor of political novelists in England.

Rex Warner followed Edward Upward in seeing the usefulness of Kafka-like hallucination in fiction about a collapsing capitalist world. Upward's *Journey to the Border* uses a kind of influenza delirium to present its story about a young man desperately seeking the right things to believe in – the right things being, inevitably, revealed as the tenets of Communism. Warner wove hallucination into allegory, and his philosophy was not quite so explicit as Upward's. *The Wild Goose Chase* is about three brothers who go off looking for the wild goose of political freedom but find themselves caught in the net of a weird fascist state whose laws have logic only in the realm of madness. Two of the brothers succumb to the régime; the other brother goes on searching for reality. The adventures he meets are exciting and frightening and totally unreal, and the end of the story is pure symbolism – the collapse of the

OTHER MINERS

Anserium (repository of the tame geese) and the winging heaven-wards of the wild geese which stand for man's free spirit. Interesting as fantasy, the novel fails as allegory: we take no lesson away from our reading of it, political or otherwise.

This cannot be said, however, of Warner's *The Aerodrome*, whose symbols are compelling and still, twenty-five years after the book's first appearance, relevant to our moral and political condition. An ordinary English village is presented as a figure of human life: its inhabitants are imperfect, sometimes even depraved, but we accept our own share in their Original Sin. To this village comes a totalitarian body called the Air Force (it resembles the R.A.F. only in its ranks and uniform) whose mission is less to fly than to clean up the dirty world. It admits no sin or indiscipline; it aims at making human beings cold, mechanical, perfect. The choice of two evils is laid before us; which will we take? The Air Force is not a sectarian symbol–it can be Fascism or Communism or any organization devoted to sterilizing man into a clean obedient citizen; the imperfect world it confronts is man as he is. It is a pity that Warner finds it necessary to manipulate a plot of great and implausible complexity to keep the action bubbling: this detracts from the undoubted power of the simple allegory.

Warner has written other novels touched with the finger of Kafkaesque nightmare–*The Professor*, *Why Was I Killed?*, *Men of Stone*–but he seems to have worked out the allegorical vein. Since the war we have known him better as a classical scholar and translator of Xenophon and Thucydides, but he has emerged also as a fine historical novelist with his *The Young Caesar* and *Imperial Caesar*. It is notable that the posture of Kafka disciple does not last for long with any of our writers who first made their names with nightmares. William Sansom's volume of stories, *Fireman Flower*, which took a lot of its material from Sansom's own experience in the National Fire Service in wartime London, conjured Kafka visions out of burning buildings and imitated the master's flat wordy style with such skill that it was evident Sansom had a large talent for mimicry. This was confirmed in his first novel, *The Body*–a superb book, perhaps his best.

OTHER MINERS

It is a book on a very old theme–that of jealousy. A middle-aged hairdresser comes to believe that his wife, equally mature though still ripely attractive, is having an affair with a hearty, convivial, practical-joke-loving neighbour. His jealousy, like Othello's, has no foundation, but, unlike Othello, he is driven not to madness but to an obsession with seeing his cuckoldry confirmed. He watches closely and his eyes are sharpened; the details of the external world come through with a clarity which is abnormal but, I think, not hallucinatory. Sansom's ear, matching his eye, renders the idiom and rhythms of post-war lower-middle-class English with a terrible exactness. The final image that emerges in the self-tortured mind of the husband is of the human body growing old and unsavoury–the broken toenails, the rough skin, the bad breath; it is what the sharpened eye is led to observe at last and it leads, in its turn, to a kind of philosophy. By a paradox, Sansom mines into the human spirit by staying on the surface.

His love of the surface of physical life sometimes carries him away: a lust for word-manipulation serving not (as with Joyce) a musical end but a pictorial one is a characteristic of his short stories as well as his novels, and the occasional banality of some of his plots–hidden under the decoration–comes out more clearly in those slighter works. But the novels always hold the attention and often educate the reader into taking a fresh, rain-washed, look at the world of sensation, especially visual sensation. *The Face of Innocence* and *A Bed of Roses* are straightforward tales about the involutions of love and marriage, disclosing no new psychological subtleties; but we enter the world of the sun–the South of France in one, Spain in the other–as if for the first time, so remarkably vivid is the scene-painting. His outstanding virtues are displayed alongside his faults in, at their most typical, *The Last Hours of Sandra Lee*, in which poetry is conjured out of the very paper-clips in a London office and the cadences of speech continue to be wonderfully caught. Yet the heroine delights us with what she looks like, not with what she is; she is a triumph of the cosmetician's art, a lay-figure and not a human being.

If Sansom, after his Kafkaesque beginning, has brought a kind

OTHER MINERS

of lyricism to the novel, Henry Green has been after other poetical qualities–chiefly that unity, close-knit and taut, we find in the sonnet-form. His novels stay in our minds as entities, not as mere pretexts for the strutting of characters or self-indulgent scenic description. The economy and directness are conveyed in his very titles, which–after his first novel, *Blindness*, a schoolboy production–are all pure participles, telling us what the novels are about–*Living*, *Party Going*, *Caught*, *Loving*, *Concluding*, *Doting* (he breaks this rule of his maturity only in *Back* and *Nothing*–though the latter at least looks like a participle). *Living* comes out of Green's own experience as a worker in the Midlands factory which belongs to the Green family, and it is perhaps the most piquant, exact, and heartening novel of industrial life we possess. After all, it is unusual to find an Eton and Oxford man with a large literary talent entering a *milieu* most often serving, so far as literature is concerned, anti-capitalist growls; this novel has to be unique. The point about *Living* is that it is about living: the workers are not statistics in an industrial report but people with their own concerns and aspirations. They are like the pigeons which they keep in their lofts–homebound and yet free–and which flutter and whirr throughout the novel as a unifying symbol.

Party Going looks like a piece of expressionistic symbolism, but it has no message. Fog delays the departure of a boat-train, and the station hotel is filled with passengers indefinitely waiting–singing workers on the ground floor, rich young people in the rooms above. We have the impression that the workers will take over the hotel, as in some Brecht or Toller play about revolution, but Green avoids action. The one memorable thing that happens seems significant: an old lady finds a dead pigeon in the station and she wraps it up in a parcel. It would be dangerous to attach a simple meaning to this or to the effect it has on the delayed passengers: we may perhaps take it as symbolizing the incursion of an eccentric, individualistic act on societies which carry on with their inherited patterns of behaviour. But Green is writing a poem here, and once meaning is extracted from a poem, the poem itself collapses. We ought to remember, though, when the novel

113

appeared – 1939, when the peace-dove fell dead at our feet, and the fog of war stopped everybody's party-going. *Caught* ought to be contrasted with Sansom's *Fireman Flower*. The title-story of Sansom's collection deals with life in the Fire Service in London, but it is quick to open up a fantastic Kafka world; Green's study of the same life is more naturalistic, but there is a Kafka touch there too – men and women thrown together by circumstances they have not willed, all aware of the difficulty of making contact with each other. The real Kafka nightmare is about trying to understand and make oneself understood, the failure of communication. When Green's characters are released from the bondage of this failure (as Kafka's never are), it is through violence from without, the coming of the London blitz. *Caught* is about the war, but it is also about the eternal human condition; its title, like all Green's titles, is exact and informative.

Thus, *Loving* is about loving. The period is still the war, indeed it is exactly contemporaneous with *Caught*, but this time the characters have escaped from London to Ireland, there to be entangled in a net of loving and intrigue. Here, more than in the earlier novels, Green uses symbols (those doves again, but this time with peacocks) to show subtleties of motivation that direct statements would only make crude. But with the later, post-war, books Green has become more concerned – rather like Sansom – with the exact rendering of the surface of urban life, particularly the rhythms and idioms of London English. This has its own fascination and value, but something of the old magic has been lost. Still, Green's books remain solid and glittering as gems; they could not be cut without being impaired – they are not, like so many contemporary novels, mere slices of life but highly successful attempts at making art give meaning to life.

Like Green, Christopher Isherwood made his reputation before the war, though the books he is best known by – *Goodbye to Berlin* and *Mr. Norris Changes Trains* – have taken on a poignantly new significance since the war. They are studies of the Germany of the nineteen-thirties, though not hard-breathing and earnest concentrations on a significant period of modern history: what one primarily notes is their humour and lightness. Isherwood learned something from Forster here–the placing of melodrama on the margin. Look at Mr Norris with the stern eyes of the moralist, and he becomes a horrible example of depravity, what with his homosexuality, interest in flagellation, and addiction to crime. Isherwood makes him charming, a bubble-light figure of comedy. And comedy illuminates the other lost Berliners in both books, observed as they are–without any moral attitude–by 'Herr Issyvoo' himself, the mere camera-eye. The serious intention of Isherwood, the use of the novel-form to clarify tragic situations, was made manifest in his earlier, experimental, works, like *All the Conspirators* and *The Memorial*. By the time he came to the Berlin books, he had learnt that strong draughts required a bedside manner. It is astonishing how powerful a picture of the decay of bourgeois German society is drawn on the margin of entertainment. If we want to know what it was like to live in that autumn, the Nazi wind ready to puff its cheek, it is to Isherwood we must go and not the heavier, worthier chroniclers.

Unlike Upward, but like his collaborator in drama, W. H. Auden, Isherwood underwent a kind of conversion with the coming of the war. As Auden left behind his left-wing convictions and turned to Anglicanism, so Isherwood grew more interested in Quakerism and the philosophy of Indian Vedanta than in hopes of regenerating the world through political action. Like Auden, he became an American citizen, though his writing has not yet, as Auden's has, acquired an American accent. *Prater Violet*, a very slight story about making a film, still shows the camera-eye innocent, learning about life. *The World in the Evening* has an American setting, though with flashbacks to England, and it demonstrates a move forward to the moral preoccupations of the most recent Isherwood. This time the narrator is telling of himself, not merely clicking the shutter at others, and the arrested adolescent of thirty-six, wealthy Anglo-American Stephen Monk, seeks to discover the reasons for his failures in love. His first marriage, to a novelist, is disastrous; his affair with the Englishman Michael Drummond collapses; his second marriage is no more successful than his first. To say that these failures are due to Stephen's sexual ambivalence is not enough; answers have to be found in the need to equate love with a kind of moral strength, and, behind the mess of Stephen's love-life, the doctrines of the Pennsylvanian Quakers assert themselves.

A much bigger piece of later Isherwood is *Down There on a Visit*, in which the author once more appears as a character. Like *Goodbye to Berlin*, the book can be chopped into four easily separable pieces, though there is a unity which proclaims the work a true novel. Isherwood's approach to his persona is much more involved than in the earlier books: he is the Author looking back on various younger selves, towards which he feels both a son and a father, but the Author himself is a character created by the real Isherwood. The younger Isherwoods combine in the 'Visitor' who links four private hells made by personages who, though separated in time and space, have in common the rejection of the real world outside themselves: they have declared war on The Others. A more recent novel, *A Single Man*, has its setting wholly in California. It describes, in the classical manner of *Ulysses*, the events of a single day in the life of a university lecturer in English Literature–a British expatriate who is homosexual. It is a brief, taut novel, funny and pathetic, a manifesto of loneliness. In the homosexuality there is none of the guilt of *The World in the Evening*; the loved companion is dead, and there is none to replace him. The 'sane and normal' Californians are wittily caught, as are certain aspects of American academic life. The book entertains like everything of Isherwood's, and in the processes of enjoyment one may miss the art. But the art is powerful, a triumph of economy of means and grace of language.

This chapter is something of a mixed bag. I am emboldened to mention briefly an author, who just before *A Single Man*, published a novel called *A Singular Man*: the two are not to be confused. J. P. Donleavy is still best-known for his first novel, *The Ginger Man*, which was very popular, partly for the vigour of its language, certainly for its bawdy and anarchical Dublin student-hero. Plot is not important, but drink is and so is lechery.

OTHER MINERS

A Singular Man develops more boldly the element of fantasy in *The Ginger Man*. Its hero, George Smith, lives in a New York flat with a door of two-inch surgical steel; he is also building a mausoleum which he visits in a bullet-proof car. He has enemies; he is always receiving strange threatening letters from a man called J.J.J. He is rich, but he is also lonely. He is separated from a money-wanting wife and four children and is looked after by a Rabelaisian Negress and two secretaries. He achieves little in the book except a night of love with Miss Thomson, the blonde and beautiful secretary, but the essence of the whole structure lies less in what happens than in how things are described. Donleavy has developed an interesting prose-style which is, despite the echo of Joyce's rhythms, all his own:

'Smith in the cocktail bar. All blue and smoke where he sat in a club chair as they would seem to have it. Tinkle, the ice rocking in the glasses. People sparkling. Lamp-posts go by outside. Under which streams the snow. I wear my long red underwear. Calmly under the trouser leg. Waiter in light blue. Only white thing in sight is his towel.'

Add to this telegraphic prose a curious formality in the dialogue, so that the last thing to be shed, even in bed, is 'Miss' or 'Mrs', and you have a fine new medium for comedy. It is unique comedy, and it is in the service of the old Kafka obsession with loneliness, with difficulty of communication.

As this chapter is a kind of small monument to the difficulty of classifying certain novelists, their methods of mining into the human spirit all different, let us end with the most unclassifiable novelist of them all–the late Ivy Compton-Burnett. Her first novel, *Dolores*, appeared as long ago as 1911, but it was not until 1925 that she embarked on the highly original series of structures that begins with *Pastors and Masters* and ends with the remarkable *The Mighty and Their Fall*, published in 1961). Henry Green's titles follow a pattern of accidence, Miss Compton-Burnett's a pattern of syntax. *Brothers and Sisters*, *Men and Wives*, *A House and Its Head*, *Elders and Betters*–so the stream proceeds, all titles reducible to the paradigm '(Adj.) Noun AND (Adj.) Noun.' The

OTHER MINERS

novels themselves are similarly reducible to a paradigm–the breaking of the more violent of the Ten Commandments in respectable upper-class homes, the setting always in late Victorian or Edwardian times. There is a kind of trickery, the sense of a formula, but one cannot read just a couple of Miss Compton-Burnett's novels and think one knows them all: one needs the whole corpus, not just the underlying pattern. The technique is deliberately formal, even stilted:

'Something depended from Miss Starkie's skirts, of a nature to unravel when pulled, and her pupils were putting a foot on it in turn, and receding as its length increased.

' "Miss Starkie, you have suffered a mischance! Some part of your dress is disintegrating. The mischief should be arrested."

'Miss Starkie turned, paused and stooped, and set off in another direction.

' "Oh, a bush will serve me, Mr. Middleton. I can manage in a moment. Why did you not tell me, children?"

' "For a reason that is clear," said Hugo. "Some chances do not come again. Sometimes I regret my childhood. But only for light reasons." '

(That is from *The Mighty and Their Fall*) Usually the story is told almost entirely in dialogue, pithy, witty, strongly characteristic–in idiom and rhythm–of the speaker. Indeed, these novels cry out to be adapted for the stage, though nothing was done about this till 1965, when Julian Mitchell made a play–acclaimed by the critics–out of *A Heritage and its History*.

The piquancy comes from the tension between the upper-class formality and the nature of desires which, unspoken in real life, are grossly enacted here. There is no limit to the unnaturalness of the crimes committed within a family circle–murder, blackmail, adultery, incest. As with Greek tragedy, punishment is left to Nemesis, not to British justice. Indeed, the characters, swollen by formality of speech and great self-regard, have something statuesque about them, like personages in Racine or Corneille. Miss Compton-Burnett is totally self-effacing, offering no palliation, making no judgement. We never hear her voice, since her prose-style is

118

OTHER MINERS

carefully modelled on the bland cadences of an earlier age (very much earlier—Jane Austen is always coming to mind); it is itself one of the characters of the tragedy (if that term, with its loud heroic connotations, is really admissible here). She deliberately narrowed her range, working over the same ground again and again, bringing no new surprises. But within her limits she is beyond criticism.

See Bibliographical Note on p. 12

Ivy COMPTON-BURNETT (1892–1970)
Dolores. Edinburgh and London, 1911
Pastors and Masters. London, 1925
Brother and Sisters. 1929
Men and Wives. 1931
A House and its Head. London, 1935
Elders and Betters. London, 1944
A Heritage and its History. London, 1959
The Mighty and their Fall. London, 1961

J. P. DONLEAVY (1926–   )
The Ginger Man. Paris, 1955
A Singular Man. Boston, 1963
The Saddest Summer of Samuel S. New York, 1966
The Beastly Beatitudes of Balthazar B. New York, 1968

Maurice EDELMAN (1911–   )
Who Goes Home? London and Philadelphia, 1953
A Call on Kuprin. London and Philadelphia, 1959

Maurice EDELMAN (*continued*)
The Minister. London, 1961 (as The Minister of State, Philadelphia, 1961)
The Prime Minister's Daughter. London, 1964
All on a Summer's Night. London, 1969

Henry GREEN (1905–   )
Blindness. 1926
Living. 1929
Party Going. London, 1939
Caught. London, 1943
Loving. London, 1945
Back. London, 1946
Concluding. London, 1948
Nothing. 1950
Doting. 1952

Christopher ISHERWOOD (1904–   )
All the Conspirators. London, 1928
The Memorial. London, 1932
Mr Norris changes Trains. London, 1935 (as The Last of Mr Norris. New York, 1935)
Goodbye to Berlin. London, 1939
Prater Violet. New York, 1945

OTHER MINERS

Christopher ISHERWOOD (*contd.*)
  The World in the Evening.
    1954
  Down there on a Visit. 1962
  A Single Man. 1964
  A Meeting by the River. 1967
Arthur KOESTLER (1905–   )
  The Gladiators. 1939
  Darkness at Noon. London,
    1940
  Thieves in the Night. 1946
William SANSOM (1912–   )
  Fireman Flower. London, 1944
    (short stories)
  The Body. 1949
  The Face of Innocence. 1951
  A Bed of Roses. 1954

William SANSOM (*continued*)
  The Last Hours of Sandra Lee.
    London, 1961
  Goodbye. London, 1966
Rex WARNER (1905–   )
  The Wild Goose Chase. Lon-
    don, 1937
  The Professor. London. 1938
  The Aerodrome. London, 1941
  Why Was I Killed? London,
    1943 (as Return of the Travel-
    ler, Boston, 1944)
  Men of Stones. London, 1949
  The Young Caesar. London and
    Boston, 1958
  Imperial Caesar. London and
    Boston, 1960

X

Yin and Yang

Whatever title one contrives for a chapter dealing solely with women novelists, it is bound to sound arch or gallant or indulgent or contemptuous. This is perhaps because, as most women novelists are quick to tell us, the notion that art can be categorized according to the sex of the artist is not really tenable: thus, a novelist enters a sphere of the imagination where he or she becomes he-she, being granted equal knowledge of the lives of both (or all) sexes. The novelist is a hermaphrodite, prefigured in Greek myth in the seer Tiresias, who knew strange things and was man and woman at the same time. And yet we recognize two distinct, opposite and complementary, impulses in the novel, which we can designate by the Chinese terms *yin* and *yang*–the feminine and masculine poles in a pre-sexual, or if we like, metaphorical sense. The *yin* is the yielding, the *yang* the forceful; the *yin* is concerned with the colour and texture of life, the *yang* with its dynamic: the *yin* prose-style is careful, exquisite, full of qualified statements, while the *yang* is less scrupulous, coarser, more aggressive. Henry James was a *yin* novelist; Ernest Hemingway belonged to the brotherhood of the *yang*. In the greatest geniuses the two meet, are reconciled, fertilize each other.

But it is very rarely that any of our contemporary women novelists have much respect for the *yang*. Where they learn from men, it is usually *yin* writers: it is noteworthy that Henry James has been the greatest single influence on our senior women novelists. Take

YIN AND YANG

Elizabeth Bowen, for instance, passages from some of whose books could be inserted in novels by James without anybody's remarking on the intrusion of a feminine voice. All her books (there are not many of them) are exquisitely written, and this very exquisiteness is a limitation, since it is more easily placed in the service of the outer skin of life than used to probe into the fundamentals of human experience. Nevertheless, textures, colours, *nuances* of speech, surface subtleties–these are a legitimate concern of the novelist, the essential *yin* side which Sir Walter Scott recognized in Jane Austen, admiring and knowing himself incapable of it, chained as he was to the 'big bow-wow' stuff of the *yang*.

Critics are always seeing the influence of Jane Austen in the work of twentieth-century women novelists (not really so strange a bedfellow for Henry James), and Elizabeth Bowen may be said to exhibit the Austen touch–humour, delicacy, restraint, common sense, a limited social field. There is also an eschewal of concern with the great good-evil opposition, so that the antithesis of innocence is not guilt but experience. In *The Death of the Heart*, the diary of a girl of sixteen represents an as yet uncorrupted desire for love that is wholehearted and wholesome; the adult woman who reads it recognizes the corruption of time in herself–she has not become evil, she has merely yielded to the blunting of integrity which experience has brought about. She is the winter lake in Regent's Park that is the book's first, and very telling, symbol. One of Elizabeth Bowen's great gifts is the power to render the external world–time and space alike–so exquisitely that it seems to become itself a character, not a mere setting for human action. Her wartime novel, *The Heat of the Day*, gives us, for all time, the very feel and smell of London in the nineteen-forties, and perhaps this is a fault, for the characters are less convincing than their ambience. This is especially true of the traitor Robert Kelway, whose treason never once strikes us as more than a plot-device: people are less real than places.

Elizabeth Bowen's more recent novel, *The Little Girls*, shows her virtues and shortcomings as clearly as any of her works. Three women in well-preserved late middle-age return to a box that, as schoolgirls, they laid down for posterity's instruction: the box contains their 'treasures and fetters'. But is one ever justified in calling back the past? The nostalgia for innocence that informs *The Death of the Heart* can never redeem the world of experience, with all its capitulations to compromise and second-best. Besides, as the evocative and exact prose demonstrates, there is a kind of compensation for growing-up in the living current of the sensuous world. *The Little Girls* captures beautifully the texture and colour of life lived here and now—the aubergine-coloured jersey, the china in a tea-shop, the new houses growing up in a rural scene of childhood. The confrontation of innocence and experience in Elizabeth Bowen's best novels—*To the North*, *The House in Paris* may be added to those I have mentioned—is ultimately less memorable than the external world she delineates. This outer skin may symbolize the inner rind of human experience, but it always ends up as significant in itself.

British women novelists of Elizabeth Bowen's generation have for the most part resisted the urge to be 'contemporary': we note gaps of many years between the more recent books of writers like Rebecca West and Rosamond Lehmann, as though they were unsure of their audiences or found difficulty in making contact with the post-war world. Rebecca West is working on a novel-sequence of which only the first instalment has appeared—*The Fountain Overflows*, published in 1957, in which her theme is not the opposition between innocence and experience but the bigger one between chaos and order. Her portrait of a family in which the male principle (the father) stands for the destructive impulse, while the music-loving mother and three daughters represent a transcendent melodic world of peace and tranquillity, may be taken as a statement about *yin* and *yang* from the viewpoint of a *yin* writer. Rosamond Lehmann, who is closer to Elizabeth Bowen in acknowledging the influence of Henry James, has an impressive post-war novel to her credit—*The Echoing Grove*, published in 1953. This makes an exhaustive examination of the agony undergone by women in love and, very interestingly, seems to come to the conclusion that (though not in these words) much of the torture of the

YIN AND YANG

male-female relationship derives from lack of awareness of how much the *yin* and *yang* elements are shared by both sexes. We are all sexual mixtures (temperamentally if not biologically) and had better cease to regard ourselves as representing merely one or other of the two basic principles of the universe.

There has been a new wave, both in England and America, of women writers who strive to infuse the *yin* with some of the aggressiveness of the *yang*, with very disturbing results. We have seen how in Doris Lessing's *The Golden Notebook* there is a powerful expression of resentment of the male–not purely social (in the old suffragette manner) but sexual as well. Woman has a sexual need of man, but she objects to having this need; she wants to reject man, but she cannot, and so she seeks to dominate him, though a great deal of her sexual fulfilment must derive from being dominated. *Yin* and *Yang* are tangled up together, and the literary expression of the female dilemma is often harsh, sensational, explosive. A minor, near-popular, woman novelist who seems to blame male God for making woman what she is may be taken as exhibiting, in rather crude colours, this big contemporary theme on its simplest level. I refer to Edna O'Brien, who, in a trilogy beginning with *The Country Girls* and ending with *Girls in Their Married Bliss*, described the adventures of two young Irishwomen in London–adventures almost exclusively amorous, though told with a mixture of Irish whimsy and astringent humour. Man is represented as a weak self-regarding creature, sexually demanding and near-impotent at the same time. Male readers are intended to wince, but they soon grow mutinous.

In *August is a Wicked Month*, wronged, demanding, insatiable woman has visions of herself being made love to by all the men of the world at the same time. The quest for sexual fulfilment ends, after grotesque episodes of abandon in which nothing is left to the imagination, in the heroine's contracting venereal disease. We may take this as representing the only durable thing that man can give her. The book is a sour one, untouched by humour or tenderness. Here the *yin* has grown claws and learned to snarl, but at the same time it wonders why the *yang* has been scared away. It is

YIN AND YANG

good to find Miss O'Brien, in *A Pagan Place*, exhibiting other facets of her temperament. This is a moving and tender evocation of an Irish girlhood.

A cleverer writer is Brigid Brophy (daughter of the novelist John Brophy), whose agile mind has busied itself in many fields – sociology, morals, literary criticism, musicology (she is an expert on the operas of Mozart) – apart from the novel. She can be witty and cruel, especially when exploding male pretensions, though some of her victims (including the present writer) are occasionally puzzled by a virulence that seems out of all proportion to the object of the attack. Her fame (which approaches notoriety) seems to rest less on her fiction than on her pronouncements about marriage – both in the press and on television – but the big sex-theme occurs in at least one of her novels – *The Snow Ball*. Her earlier books – *The Crown Princess, Hackenfeller's Ape* and *The King of a Rainy Country* – are neatly written, witty, well shaped, sharply observant of contemporary manners, but *The Snow Ball* has been taken more as a female manifesto than as a novel of quality. Mozart's opera *Don Giovanni* obsesses her, but she seems anxious to invert its theme, creating a sort of Donna Giovanna who claims for herself the liberties of the Mozart hero. The victims of love are no longer women but men. Her logic is sound enough : man's sexual appetite is brief-lived, woman's rapidly renewable. Polygamy is absurd, since a man finds it hard enough to give sexual satisfaction to one woman : polyandry – in an age when man has no duty to beget, since we are already over-populated – is much more natural. Miss Brophy's sixth novel, *In Transit*, fights not just men but the whole of the twentieth century. She turns the modern world into an airport waiting lounge, in which a narrator who is a fusion of *yin* and *yang* – Evelyn Hilary O'Rooley – observes a fair selection of contemporary horrors, including a nun hunt and an air crash deliberately contrived to obtain human organs for transplant purposes. Language collapses along with traditional values, and Miss Brophy asserts her Irishness in Joycean puns and neologisms. It is rather an impressive novel, and it shows a distinct imaginative, moral and technical advance.

YIN AND YANG

The new willingness (though sometimes one may question whether it is really so new) of women novelists to discuss the physical and emotional needs of their sex finds many, strongly individual, manifestations. The torture of marriage, all neurosis and frustration, is powerfully presented in Penelope Mortimer's novels, particularly *The Pumpkin Eater*. The drive of a *yang* intellect emphasizes the essential femininity of Mary McCarthy's work, though it is a pity that *The Group* found so big an audience – by reason of its supposed sensationalism – among readers unqualified to appreciate the brilliance of *The Company She Keeps* and *The Groves of Academe*. *The Group* spoke with utter frankness about the sexual needs and aspirations of a clique of educated American women: one awed male critic has said that Miss McCarthy has done for the contraceptive what Melville did for the whale. We meet in her a new, very contemporary, phenomenon – the woman who sacrifices nothing of her female birthright when competing with, and often trouncing, men on their chosen ground of intellectual assertion.

It would be easy to categorize Iris Murdoch as one of the 'new women', but it would also be dangerous. In *A Severed Head* (a novel that seemed to mark a turning-point in her career) there is, among other things, the motif of man's yielding to superior woman – woman armed with a samurai capable of severing more than heads. But her work is very various and has attempted many themes and techniques. As Francis Hope has remarked, her first novel, *Under the Net*, looks like a refusal to write a novel at all: there is nothing like a plot, crises and resolutions are avoided; we are not encouraged to look for a moral or even an emergent generalization about life. Such a novel can be called picaresque, but it would be more accurate to term it existentialist: 'All theorizing is flight. We must be ruled by the situation itself and this is unutterably particular.' So the main character, Jake (Miss Murdoch's main characters, or at least narrators, are often male), moves from situation to situation in a curiously dreamlike postwar London, coping with events as they occur, engaging the problems of existence without philosophizing about essences.

YIN AND YANG

The Flight from the Enchanter is a link between this un-novel and her first conventional piece of fiction, *The Sandcastle*. In *The Flight from the Enchanter* there is a pattern imposed on the flux of separable events, so that the career of the character called Rainborough is systematically ruined and a death comes neatly near the end – all good plot material – but, at the same time, there is that residue of the inexplicable and uncontrollable which gives Iris Murdoch's work distinction – magical elements, symbols, ambiguities. These practically disappear when we come to *The Sandcastle*, though we cannot miss the symbolic intention of certain pieces of pure realism – the drowning of a car in a stream, the prophesying tramp at the door, the giddy climbing episode towards the end. But now Miss Murdoch is writing a fully contrived novel, with carefully drawn characters and neatly organized plot, and, instead of exhibiting the nature of life as a series of unconnected events, each of which requires a fresh technique of approach, she is making a general statement about it. The statement may be called existential, since it is about the nature of human choice, but we cannot help seeing the story as a mere illustration of a theory. Mor, the schoolmaster, married and middle-aged, falls in love with Rain Carter, a young painter, and is, as it were, appalled by his freedom to do so. This freedom is more than most of us can stand; we are so used to the habit of conformity. Moreover, one cannot flirt with freedom. Mor's in-between state, deceiving his wife if not his children, involves the learning of subterfuges which must break sanity. This is a tale of a recognizable aspect of the human condition, but it reads like a contrived parable rather than a genuine novel.

The Bell is probably the best of Miss Murdoch's novels, and, like all original works of art, it represents the end of a creative phase rather than a beginning. It is what the earlier novels were working towards – a synthesis of the traditional and the revolutionary. The story is thoroughly realistic yet at the same time loaded with symbols, the most potent of which is the bell of the title. This is named for the Archangel Gabriel and it is inscribed *Ego Vox Sum Amoris*; it lies drowned in a lake in the grounds of a

127

convent, the legend stating that it flew there miraculously. It is the still centre of a complex of human problems, the chief of which is summed up in the character of Michael Meade, the founder of a lay religious community on the family estate, where the convent also is situated. Meade has suffered a conflict between his homosexual tendencies and his desire to become a priest; the community he has founded is intended to be a way out of the conflict, a compromise and a compensation, but he learns the truth of the maxim: 'to leave the world is not to leave the temptations of the world'. There are other characters, all faced with the need to probe the limits of personal morality, to ponder the best means of ordering one's life – by abiding by essential rules or following the *Under the Net* way of existential living, so that one is 'ruled by the situation itself.' Dora and Toby, intruders into the community, are impelled to drag the bell out of the lake and then to ring it: it is the voice of love but also the cast metal of self-realization. It is more besides, since it is not in the nature of a poetic symbol to be capable of easy interpretation: there are levels of unconscious myth and magic to which it appeals. This is an intensely poetic novel and marvellously organized.

Miss Murdoch seemed to leave behind, when she came to the writing of *A Severed Head*, all that she had so far taught herself – except the ability to write taut English and to dredge that world of the strange and mysterious which had, so far, lain on the boundaries of the ordinary. In *A Severed Head* we never enter the house of the ordinary. The characters dress, talk, act like ourselves, but they are caught up in a purely intellectual pattern, a sort of contrived sexual dance in which partners are always changing. They seem to be incapable of free choice; they are totally in the puppeteering hands of their creatrix. The very title seems to indicate a deliberate and wanton cutting off of the heart and glands from a pattern-making intelligence. And yet we feel that it is not altogether a cerebral exercise. Martin, the wine-merchant, reaches the final figure of his dance when he yields to the mysterious Honor Klein with her Japanese sword (symbol of power, intelligence and cruelty). It is the mysterious *yin* spirit that stops the music and ends the pattern: man has little power to decide for himself.

In *An Unofficial Rose* and *The Unicorn* Iris Murdoch has given us two further studies in the patterning of love, more complicated than *A Severed Head* in that there are many more characters; at the same time she has, disturbingly, come closer to the orthodox concept of the novel–complete with plot-contrivances and even a kind of horror-sensationalism. *The Italian Girl* is a great disappointment. Its picture of a tortured family living in a house which, eventually and expectedly, is set on fire reminds one, in the banality of its situations and obviousness of its symbols of such a 'popular' novelist as Daphne du Maurier. *The Red and the Green* goes back to 1916 and the Irish Rebellion, and its mediocrity contrasts violently with the distinction of another woman's novel on the same subject–*The Last September*, by Elizabeth Bowen. For one thing, Miss Murdoch catches nothing of the flavour of Dublin talk; everybody converses with polite dullness. For another, she seems uninfected by the mad magic of the times, in which ordinary men became giants. The surface has nothing to do with reality, and the content has none of the glint of myth. Miss Murdoch's great period seems to be over, though one would be only too thankful to be confuted–as may well be possible–by the appearance of another book as good as *The Bell*. But she cannot go back to her early style, and to go forward seems to mean becoming just another popular woman novelist. All this is, perhaps, profoundly worrying.

Muriel Spark appeared, in her early books, to be a writer of the same stature of Iris Murdoch, though these books are hardly long enough to be called anything more than *novelle*. Yet the conciseness of the writing in works like *The Comforters, The Ballad of Peckham Rye, Memento Mori* and *The Prime of Miss Jean Brodie* gives a weight and toughness that make them seem bigger than they are. It is difficult to summarize her quality. Unlike Miss Murdoch, she writes from a Catholic point of view, and the elements of the uncanny or (as in *The Ballad of Peckham Rye*) the diabolic seem less fairy-tale whimsy than a return to a mode of thought which could accept God and the Devil as powers always ready to alter the texture of everyday life. In *Memento Mori*, old people receive supernatural telephone calls telling them that they must die; in *The Prime of Miss Jean Brodie*, a teacher exerts an uncanny influence over her pupils, and the device of what we may call the flash-forward shows how their lives work out. Miss Spark has a Godlike view of time, ranging easily into the future lives of her characters and showing her readers what is mercifully hidden from the characters themselves. Along with this goes a curious callousness in the disposing of them. There is a lot of cold violence – often mentioned obliquely, never dwelt upon – which tends to take grotesque forms, like smothering in hay or killing with a corkscrew.

The Girls of Slender Means has its full share of violence, but this seems symbolically related to the public outrage of war, in which violence is a norm, even a good. The setting is the May of Teck Club, founded for the girls of the title by the late Queen Mary when she was still the Princess of Teck. The year is 1945. An unexploded bomb is said to lie buried in the garden, but as this tale is constantly related by an old spinster with her share of eccentricities, no one takes much notice of this. Yet the girls themselves are eccentric: Pauline Fox has an imaginary weekly dinner with a great actor; Jane Wright sends letters to famous writers; Selina Redwood carries on a love affair on the next-door roof; Joanna Childe, disappointed in love, recites (with exquisite appropriateness, considering the year) Hopkins's poem 'The Wreck of the Deutschland'. Even the men in these girls' lives are haunted, one by fear of wire-tapping, another by his work in progress, *The Sabbath Notebooks*. And yet we can accept these strange people as making up a world like our own, since the world that has dropped an atom bomb in its own garden cannot really be accounted sane. Eventually the bomb goes off, dealing out wholesale death and destroying the club which is human society. But the management of the story is too subtle for simple allegory; we learn not merely of a phase of history but of the whole human condition. And yet Miss Spark refuses to be compassionate: as Joanna Childe starts to burn to death, the author chooses this time for a detailed description of the clothes she is wearing.

Muriel Spark must have felt that she was not doing justice to her talent by exercising it only in small fictional forms. Sooner or later she had to tackle a full-length novel, *The Mandelbaum Gate* (published contemporaneously with Miss Murdoch's *The Red and the Green*). The theme and setting are alike splendid. The heroine is half-Jewish, half-British county family, and she has been converted to Catholicism (this is Miss Spark's own position). She goes to Jerusalem to make a pilgrimage through the holy places, but Israel and Jordan share Jerusalem between them, snarling at each other through the Mandelbaum Gate which divides them. Barbara, the heroine, will be in danger in Jordan, since it must leak out that she has Jewish blood, and the plot concerns the attempt of a half-baked British consular official to get her safely back to the Israeli sector of Jerusalem. Much of the story is fantastic thriller-stuff, involving mad disguises, unexpected sexual exploits, discoveries of unsuspected espionage. The moral seems to be that in a mad world—which divided Jerusalem well enough symbolizes—we must become mad ourselves, throwing away our traditional allegiance to logic. Even the Catholic Church has its contradictions and divisions (as we see, for instance, from the attitude of the Italian Franciscans to the English priest saying Mass in the Church of the Holy Sepulchre), but there is eternal truth—the real Jerusalem—underlying all. The best analogue of a God who reveals Himself in strange ways is the wayward imagination of man. Unfortunately, *The Mandelbaum Gate* often summarizes better than it reads. Miss Spark never seems to do full justice to her fine theme; the prose is long-winded, as though anxious to fill up a given allotment of space; there is a lack of the old ruthlessness and magic.

Some of our women novelists are content to follow old paths in technique (paths older than those first trodden by Henry James), but this does not necessarily detract from the freshness of the fictional message. Elizabeth Jane Howard says: 'I write straightforward novels in the English tradition, am passionately against

YIN AND YANG

obscurity in any form'; she starts off with an idea instead of, after technical exploration, arriving at one. Thus *The Sea Change* is 'about how much people can change and how much they cannot'; *After Julius* is about 'the conflict and distinctions between public and private responsibility'. This may be regarded as the anti-poetic approach, but it is no less valid than Iris Murdoch's early use of half-understood complexities. Indeed, we have tended to regard clarity and common sense as essentially feminine properties in the novel—Alice in a land of male jabberwocks. Some of our traditionalists among women, like Storm Jameson, Lettice Cooper, V. Sackville West and—mistress of cool wit—Nancy Mitford, have made our sweating male experimentalists look gauche and uncomfortable. And the same may be said of their successors —the remarkable Margaret Drabble, Sylvia Clayton, Angela Carter and others who do not mince words. But, if the art of the novel is to progress, there will have to sweat and discomfort. The *yin* cannot have all its own way.

See Bibliographical Note on p. 12

Elizabeth BOWEN (1899–   )
The Last September. 1929
To the North. London, 1932
The House in Paris. London, 1935
The Death of the Heart. London, 1938
The Heat of the Day. 1949
The Little Girls. 1964
Eva Trout. New York, 1968
Brigid BROPHY (1939–   )
The Crown Princess. 1953
Hackenfeller's Ape. London, 1953
The King of a Rainy Country. London, 1956

Brigid BROPHY (*continued*)
The Snow Ball. London and Cleveland, 1964
In Transit. London, 1969
Angela CARTER
Shadow Dance. London, 1966
Heroes and Villains. London, 1969
Sylvia CLAYTON
The Crystal Gazers. London, 1961
Top C. London, 1968
Lettice COOPER (1897–   )
The Old Fox. London, 1927

YIN AND YANG

Lettice COOPER (*continued*)
We Shall have Snow. Leicester, 1966
Margaret DRABBLE (1939–   )
A Summer Bird-cage. London, 1963
The Waterfall. 1969
Elizabeth Jane HOWARD (1923–)
The Sea Change. London, 1959
After Julius. London, 1965
Storm JAMESON (1897–   )
The Pot Boils. London, 1919
The White Crow. London, 1968
Rosamond LEHMANN (1903–   )
The Echoing Grove. 1953
Mary McCARTHY (1912–   )
The Company She Keeps. New York, 1942
The Groves of Academe. New York, 1952
The Group. 1963
Nancy MITFORD (1904–   )
Highland Fling. London, 1931
Don't Tell Alfred. 1960
Penelope MORTIMER (1918–   )
A Villa in Summer. London, 1954
The Pumpkin Eater. London, 1962
My Friend Says it's Bullet-proof. London, 1967
Iris MURDOCH (1919–   )
Under the Net. 1954
The Flight from the Enchanter. 1956
The Sandcastle. 1957
The Bell. 1958

Iris MURDOCH (*continued*)
A Severed Head. 1961
An Unofficial Rose. 1962
The Unicorn. 1963
An Italian Girl. 1964
The Red and the Green. 1965
The Time of the Angels. 1966
The Nice and the Good. 1968
Bruno's Dream. 1969
Edna O'BRIEN (1932–   )
The Country Girls. 1960
Girls in their Married Bliss. 1962 (as The Girl with Green Eyes. Harmondsworth, 1964)
August is a Wicked Month. 1965
A Pagan Place. London, 1970
Victoria SACKVILLE-WEST (1892–1962)
Heritage. London, 1919
No Signposts in the Sea. 1961
Muriel SPARK (1918–   )
The Comforters. London and Philadelphia, 1957
Memento Mori. London and Philadelphia, 1959
The Ballad of Peckham Rye. London and Philadelphia, 1960
The Prime of Miss Jean Brodie. London, 1961
The Girls of Slender Means. 1963
The Mandelbaum Gate, 1965
The Public Image. 1968
Rebecca WEST (1892–   )
The Fountain Overflows. New York, 1956

133

XI

History and Myth

One of the fields in which women writers are said to excel is that of the historical novel. One doubts if they really do better at it than men, though it is certain that the most popular historical novels of the present age have been written by women–*Gone With The Wind*, by Margaret Mitchell, and *Forever Amber*, by Kathleen Winsor. Perhaps it is unfair to mention these two in the same breath, since the first is a serious evocation of the American Civil War, while the second is an over-sexed travesty of life in Restoration England. But, questions of merit apart (comparative or absolute), women historical novelists have shown a fearlessness, or temerity, in plunging into the past which men, much more cautious, can only view with a kind of regretful envy. This feminine boldness may spring from a conviction that life does not change much, and that to walk into history is merely to open an alternative door to the present. After all, the function and status of women have known few changes over the centuries: men dream new dreams, play with new toys, speak new dialects, but women go on being mistresses, wives, and mothers. We have only to re-meet Chaucer's Wife of Bath, Shakespeare's Juliet's Nurse and Samuel Butler's Mrs Jupp to be aware of how little the very rhythms, and even vocabulary, of women may alter over five hundred years. Woman is changeable, but it is man who changes.

The belief that history is no more than fancy dress has impelled some women novelists to write the most deplorable historical fantasies–like the endless sequence of Georgian novels by Georgette

134

HISTORY AND MYTH

Heyer or, earlier, Baroness Orczy's Scarlet Pimpernel stories. On the other hand, this inborn sense of familiarity with the past may, when added to a scholarly mind, produce remarkable work, like Helen Waddell's *Peter Abelard* or Bryher's conjurations of life in early Britain. Yet, so far as the serious historical novel is concerned, we may take it that a woman's problems are no different from a man's, that both face the same tangle of perplexities – balancing fact with imagination, scholarship with entertainment.

Why, when there is so much present clamouring to be written about, should a novelist concern himself with the past? One answer sounds rather like a quibble: the present is only a thin line between past and future; the future has not yet come into existence; therefore we have only the past to write about. In a sense, it is true that every novelist tries to enshrine a period in a book; thus every novelist is a historical novelist. But if we take that term 'historical' in its school sense – denoting a past long gone, a past that the writer, as well as the reader, must learn to understand – then we can get a more useful and particular answer. The historical novelist is, in fact, a historian to whom a talent for imaginative fiction has been fastened. He is not a novelist with an occasional taste for history.

Most novelists who concern themselves with their own time have attempted fiction about periods long past. Arthur Koestler wrote *The Gladiators* (the Slaves' Revolt in Ancient Rome), Evelyn Waugh wrote *Helena* (the discovery of the True Cross by the mother of the Emperor Constantine), William Golding has written *The Spire* (medieval England) and, with *The Inheritors*, has even dived into pre-history. In a sense, the motive of all three has been less to illuminate the past than to clarify some principle of politics, religion or morality by a technique of 'alienation' – giving us a new look, in fact, by means of an old (which means odd) setting. But past, future, or myth will do equally well: Koestler's Rome is matched by Orwell's fairy-tale farm run by animals or his vision of England in 1984. This is not the way of the true historical novelist.

Robert Graves springs to mind at once as a true example of a

135

HISTORY AND MYTH

writer who revivifies the past for its own sake, not for the end of preaching a contemporary lesson. Primarily a poet, he turned to the historical novel as a means of earning a living, but there is no pot-boiling flavour about *I, Claudius* and *Claudius the God*. His technique for telling a tale of the Roman past is austere, but it has been curiously fruitful–the plain flat narrative by an imagined witness of the historical events described, sometimes (as in the Claudius books) the chief protagonist himself. There is no attempt to work magic, to make the remote past highly scented or coloured as if it were here and now; the language and psychology are limited to the chosen past. Of Graves's many historical novels, perhaps the most astonishing are *King Jesus* and *Wife to Mr. Milton*. The first is a daring attempt to re-tell the story of the synoptic gospels (from the viewpoint of a contemporary of Christ), stressing Christ's secular claim to the crown of Jewry, playing down the miracles but by no means trying to explode the supernatural. *Wife to Mr. Milton* was written partly with a view to showing the great poet less as a champion of British liberty (it came out in wartime: 'Milton, thou shouldst be living at this hour . . .') than as a petty domestic tyrant who, seen through his first wife's eyes, could be rather ridiculous. That towering difficulty of the novelist who writes about England's past–whether to make a pastiche of archaic English or, like Hollywood films, to use the language of the present–is trumphantly solved here. Mary Powell (the wife) tells her tale in a kind of Timeless Feminine, as acceptable to our own day as to hers, though clearly modelled on the best letter-and-diary prose of the seventeenth century. David Caute, whose *Comrade Jacob* is the best novel about that same period to appear since the war, goes a different way, seeing the Civil War through the glass of twentieth-century English, but the result is totally convincing–we smell the Cromwellian time.

Another novelist who dealt consistently with the past was Alfred Duggan, drawn mainly to the Dark Ages and to Ancient Rome, though any period of transition, especially one not well documented, fascinated him. Perhaps the best of his many novels are *Conscience of the King, Leopards and Lilies, Three's Company,*

HISTORY AND MYTH

Founding Fathers, The Cunning of the Dove and *Lord Geoffrey's Fancy*. But, in his admittedly skilful hands, the historical novel tended to become a routine hack-job: one feels often that Duggan was not driven by a kind of scholarly necessity to bring the past to life; rather he accepted the novelist's treadmill and was happy that there was so much history to provide material for a book a year. But, since his untimely death, we have missed that busy pen; he was perhaps the only truly *professional* historical novelist that modern literature has seen—with the possible exception of the French 'writer and historicist' (so *Who's Who* describes her) Zoë Oldenbourg. Her work is well enough known in England and the United States, and she has been lucky in her translators (*The Awakened* was translated by Edward Hyams, *Destiny of Fire* by Peter Green). One of her interests has been the Albigensian movement in medieval France, and *Destiny of Fire* is a moving and sometimes shocking account of the persecution of the Albigensians, a sect which, seeing the universe as a continuing conflict between the God and the Devil, not as a beneficent creation merely pricked by evil, was accused of devil-worship by the powers of orthodoxy.

Peter Green, named above as a translator, has written two fine historical novels of his own. *The Sword of Pleasure* is a vivid re-telling of the life of Sulla, and *The Laughter of Aphrodite* is bold enough to take as its heroine the poetess of Lesbos, Sappho. It is to be noted that frequently novelists attracted to classical Rome or Greece will push back further than recorded history. Mary Renault began by writing novels of contemporary life but, in *The Last of the Wine*, she went to fifth-century Athens and the character of Socrates. More recently, she has made the mythical hero Theseus tell his story in *The King Must Die* and *The Bull from the Sea*. The aim of these two books seems to be to find a core of anthropological plausibility in the legend of the Minotaur and Theseus's slaying of it, just as Henry Treece's magnificent *Jason* attempts more than a fairy-tale re-telling of the adventures of the Argonauts.

As far as American historical novels are concerned, it is not fair

HISTORY AND MYTH

to think solely in terms of the thick best-sellers that dream of a bawdy old Europe or celebrate the miseries and glories of the Civil War. A young American academic, John Barth, has produced an eight-hundred-page novel called *The Sot-Weed Factor* (this is the old American name for a tobacco merchant) which has done something quite original in the historical field. As the American critic Leslie A. Fiedler has said, Barth, even in those novels of his which deal with the contemporary world, gives us fiction which has 'the odd effect of being worked up from documents, carefully consulted and irreverently interpreted'. In history he finds 'not merely the truth, not really the truth at all . . . but absurdity'. To be a scholar and yet mock scholarship requires courage. Barth's book recounts the adventures of an ugly young man called Ebenezer Coke who, in the last years of the seventeenth century, comes to America as official 'Poet and Laureate of Maryland', only to be engaged in the familiar distractions of early colonial history–politics, religion, sex, wars with the natives. Much of what Barth presents is a parody of the usual content of popular historical novels: a brother and sister recognize each other on the point of rape, an Indian and a white man find they have a common father. The resources of seventeenth-century English are scattered joyously over a great romp of pseudo- or anti-history; through the madness of the plot, if we can talk of one, we seem to see what the building of a new country is like. The wonder is that this should be done through a destructive technique and through the deliberate concentration on a very small portion of America–'the marches of Dorchester in Maryland'.

Perhaps the kind of historical novel that is needed in Britain is one rather like Barth's, except that our beginnings lie too far back to awaken wonder at them. There was a time when it seemed a great novel, or novel-sequence, might be written about the British Empire, but Kipling's talent was for verse and the short story; now the chance has gone. When one re-reads Tolstoy's great *War and Peace*, one is not happy about historical novelists who merely fiddle with classical remoteness, and when Boris Pasternak's *Doctor Zhivago* appeared (to the anger of the Soviet

Union), one wondered whether the failure of modern Britain to find some big fictional theme could be blamed on history itself rather than on the imaginative recorders of history. Britain has not been invaded by Napoleon, nor has it had a revolution as shattering as the Russian one of 1917. Perhaps such upheavals find historical justification in the art they produce. *Doctor Zhivago* is very great art. It describes the failure of the 1917 Revolution, but not in the crude black-and-white terms that the Soviet denouncers feign to see in the book. Zhivago, the hero, knows that such a failure is far more noble than an utter refusal to attempt to rebuild a human society: in this sense the book is hotly pro-Soviet and anti-West. The optimism of Pasternak is deeper and more humane than the official prescription, since it is based on an awareness of what the individual can do in the face of impossible odds: out of failure springs hope. But it is the glorification of the individual, the creation of a particular kind of twentieth-century hero that most offended, and still offends, orthodoxy. Striding into the future in *Doctor Zhivago* is no abstract factory worker but the figure of a poet—quintessence of articulate individualism—singing the epic struggle. Zhivago is a doctor, a useful though faceless member of society; he is also a poet, and it is as this—a container of society—that he claims the right to be noticed, heard, remembered. It is a very anti-collectivist notion and it was bound to offend. Russia has, by the crass strictness of her doctrines, denied herself the reflected glory of the greatest historical novel of the age.

Perhaps important historical novels must always be about outstanding individuals, not merely the feel, smell, texture, philosophy of a past age. Iris Murdoch's novel about Ireland on the eve of her own revolution—*The Red and the Green*—lacks a mammoth hero; the Graves novels do not, nor do the Russian masterpieces. In other words, the historical novel is at its best when it is fictionalized biography. But straight biography—with its documents, letters, willingness to let the subject speak his own words and those only—remains an easier and more popular way into the chambers of great men and women. One has to be a very bold novelist indeed to attempt to re-create Jesus Christ, Buddha, or William Shakespeare in full and convincing glory. Present Shakespeare in a novel (one or two of us did for his quatercentenary in 1964; John Brophy, in *Gentleman of Stratford*, tried it much earlier) and a great poet is diminished to a very ordinary man. I called my own Shakespeare novel *Nothing Like the Sun*, to emphasize the impossibility of conveying the authentic effulgence. There are many great novels but very few great historical (or historico-biographical) novels. It is safer to fictionalize the smaller reaches of history, with their comparatively small men, or to speculate on the reality behind myth, than to depict the men who give history its meaning. Even Tolstoy's Napoleon is a small man, swallowed and spewed by the true hero, Russia. And to make a hero of the great poet, one must be a great poet oneself: that is why *Doctor Zhivago* is the sort of book that comes so rarely. But one knows that there are many great historical novels that ought to be written; the difficulty is finding someone to write them.

See Bibliographical Note on p. 12

John BARTH (1930–)
  The Sot-Weed Factor. New York, 1960
  The End of the Road. New York, 1958
  Giles Goatboy. New York, 1966
  The Floating Opera. New York, 1956
  Lost in the Funhouse. New York, 1969
John BROPHY (1899–)
  Gentleman of Stratford. London, 1939
BRYHER (1894–)
  Roman Wall. New York, 1954
  The Coin of Carthage. New York, 1963

Anthony BURGESS
  See Chapter XVI, page 218
David CAUTE (1936–)
  Comrade Jacob. London, 1961
  The Decline of the West. 1966
Alfred DUGGAN (1903–64)
  The Conscience of the King. London, 1951
  Leopards and Lilies. 1954
  Three's Company. 1958
  Founding Fathers. London, 1959 (as Children of the Wolf, New York, 1959)
  The Cunning of the Dove. 1960
  Lord Geoffrey's Fancy. 1962
William GOLDING
  See Chapter V, page 71

HISTORY AND MYTH

Robert GRAVES (1895–   )
 I, Claudius. London, 1934
 Claudius the God. London,
   1934
 Wife to Mr Milton. London,
   1943
 King Jesus. 1946
Peter GREEN (1924–   )
 The Sword of Pleasure. London
   and Cleveland, 1957
 The Laughter of Aphrodite.
   1965
Arthur KOESTLER
 See Chapter IX, page 120
Margaret MITCHELL (1900–49)
 Gone with the Wind. 1936
Iris MURDOCH
 See Chapter X, page 133
Zoë OLDENBOURG (1916–   )
 The Awakened. Paris, 1956, tr.
   1957

Zoë OLDENBOURG (*continued*)
 Destiny of Fire. Paris, 1960, tr.
   1961
Boris PASTERNAK (1890–1960)
 Doctor Zhivago. Tr. 1958
   (Russian text published,
   Milan, 1959)
 The Last Summer. Tr. London,
   1959
Mary RENAULT (1905–   )
 The Last of the Wine. 1956
 The King Must Die. 1958
 The Bull from the Sea. 1962
Henry TREECE (1912–66)
 Jason, 1961
 The Windswept City. London,
   1967
Helen WADDELL (1889–1965)
 Peter Abelard. 1933
Evelyn WAUGH
 See Chapter IV, page 60

XII

A Sort of Rebels

Heroes like Zhivago are produced by societies in ferment; stable societies breed only anti-heroes. One of the most compelling literary phenomena of our time has been the emergence of the small good-hearted rebel, too feeble to make his protest against society seem more than a clown's gesture, not even articulate enough to clarify for himself what precisely is wrong with society, except that it is full of humbug. Lower-middle or working-class Voltaires crying '*Ecrasez l'Infâme!*' have grown out of societies quite unlike pre-revolutionary France; they are the children of communities with enough food and no poverty, fractious sons of the Welfare State.

In England, the first of the rebels seemed to make his appearance in William Cooper's *Scenes from Provincial Life*, published in 1950. Joe Lunn, science master in a grammar school, refuses to conform, either in taste or behaviour, with dull provincial society, though his rejection of the *bourgeois* way of life never goes so far as to be criminal. The trouble with him is that he believes in nothing strongly enough to wish to oppose it to the gods of the borough; he is an anarchist who would be less at home in an anarchistic society than he is in a *bourgeois* one. From the sequel (1961) called *Scenes from Married Life*, we learn what we all along expected to learn–that Joe has become a respectable civil servant and a reputable novelist, and that all that is now needed to brim his cosy content is the status of husband and father. Stendhal's Julien Sorel in *Le Rouge et le Noir*–the distant progenitor of all anti-heroes–goes the whole hog in his disruption of *bourgeois* solidity; the British rebels, starting with Joe Lunn, merely have a fling before settling down.

The most popular anti-hero of our time has been, without doubt, Jim Dixon in Kingsley Amis's *Lucky Jim*–an astonishing best-seller of the middle nineteen-fifties. Amis caught the public mood of post-war restiveness in a book which, though socially significant, was, and still is, extremely funny. Dixon is a lower-middle-class young man of no great pretensions to anything–charm, looks, learning, certainly not wealth. A stroke of luck has given him a job in a provincial university as junior lecturer in History, but a rebellious streak, which often comes out as maladroitness, qualifies his desire to conform and keep his job. Unfortunately his professor is a monumental fool much given to cultural week-ends, complete with madrigal-singing and recorder-blowing, and Dixon has other crosses to bear in high places. He asks little from life–enough money for beer and cigarettes, a nice undemanding girl-friend–but society has so organized things that he cannot have even this little. What he can have, what in fact is imposed upon him, is the great post-war sense of social purpose, hypocritical slogans about education, culture, progress. He asks for the bread of minimal comfort (along with the rest of a Britain that was sick of war and post-war austerity), but he is handed the stone of a spurious idealism.

Dixon is a radical, but radicalism is in his blood rather than his head. He detests privilege and phoney upper-class values, and he finds these wonderfully personified in Bertrand Welch, the son of his professor. To make things worse, Bertrand has a girl-friend whom Dixon hopelessly desires. One of the big themes of *Lucky Jim*–and it is a theme to be found in many English novels, as well as plays (John Osborne's *Look Back in Anger*, for instance) of the nineteen-fifties–is what anthropologists call hypergamy. This means, literally, 'marrying above oneself', and one of the great aims of the post-war rebels is to conquer a woman who belongs to a higher social class than themselves. This is an aspect of the perennial class motif which bedevils British fiction. Dixon achieves this

aim, and others as well. He perpetrates enormities terrible enough
to ensure his losing his university job (setting fire to Mrs Welch's
bedclothes, collapsing–after a rebellious manifesto–at a public
lecture), but he gets something better–the job that Bertrand was
after, as well as Bertrand's girl. He makes little dents in the
smug fabric of hypocritical, humbugging, class-bound British
society, but he is not big enough to portend its collapse. His is the
voice of decent protest, and it is a voice that a stable society ought
to listen to occasionally, though it never does.

Although we are intended to be on Dixon's side, we are also
intended to laugh at him, to pity his ignorance. There is a certain
ambivalence in *Lucky Jim* which is to be found also in Amis's
other novels. The author, like his anti-heroes, is against culture because culture has the wrong associations–with Professor Welch
and the rest of the phoneys. At the same time he cannot hide the
fact of his bookishness and musicality, and the Amis protagonist
always earns his living by purveying culture (as teacher, librarian,
journalist or publisher). In *I Like It Here*–Amis's least successful
novel–Bowen has to apologize to himself for mentioning Elgar
or Byron. The librarian hero of *That Uncertain Feeling* lives among
books but reads only science fiction and cheesecake magazines.
And yet the love-hate attitude to culture (it is not a matter of pure
indifference) permeates the very prose-rhythms. All of Amis's
novels, despite their gaiety, show up the sickness of a divided
society. Lewis in *That Uncertain Feeling* is, like Dixon, drawn to
an affair with a woman out of his class (a member of the Anglo-
Welsh ascendancy), but he does not end by conquering her, only
by scuttling back to where he belongs, with a working-class father
doing the Ximenes crossword.

If Amis proclaims any tradition at all, it is the venerable line
of English nonconformism to which Defoe and Fielding belong.
Take a Girl Like You presents a really 'good' middle-class
girl whose virtue is assailed but remains impregnable. *One Fat
Englishman* shows Roger Micheldene, a gluttonous, lecherous,
mean-minded British publisher visiting America. Roger is the
whole dance of the Seven Deadly Sins rolled into one detestable

bladder of lard; Amis the novelist of detached wit is also Amis the moralist, rarely judging but always giving plenty of scope to a comic nemesis. In Amis, people do not hop into bed lightly with each other; if they do–as John Lewis does in *That Uncertain Feeling*–they always suffer for it. Micheldene can do it, as he can snub, over-eat, pontificate, because he is the villain rather than the anti-hero. Dixon, Bowen and Lewis are, being so very much against humbug, really very much for middle-class virtue. And middle-class virtue defines itself not only in terms of opposition to highbrow pretentiousness, with its pose of amorality, but, as *I Want It Now* seems to show, in hatred of the rich. Man, implies Amis, is defiled by possessions–yachts and mansions equally with books and ideas.

It is not too much to ask for–that people should be good and that fags and booze should be not too expensive. Amis is even–though with a bit of a wrench–prepared to drop all claims to culture and be content with a nice read of science fiction. He has become a strong advocate of this form (which lies between highbrow literature and popular trash) and has written a critical book about it (*New Maps of Hell*) as well as, with Robert Conquest, edited several anthologies of it. One of Amis's most recent novels–a collaboration with Conquest–has shunted all pretensions to culture into little marginal jokes. The title, *The Egyptologists*, refers to a group of middle-aged men who go in for clandestine fornication under the guise of running a scholarly society (culture has found, at last, a way of making itself useful). But it is in the nature of things, as Amis sees them, that they should not get away with vice and deceit. You may play merry hell with culture, but you had better not blaspheme against orthodox morality. This is the message of the new rebels.

In 1966, Amis published a novel which, though very different from his comic-social ones, could be seen as a complement to them. Jim Dixon gave society a couple of bumbling knocks in the towser-face, but injustice and the rule of privilege would always be there. *I Like It Here*, as well as *That Uncertain Feeling*, seemed to warn about the dangers of grappling too hard with life: stay

A SORT OF REBELS

at home or you'll get hurt. Sooner or later, though, Amis had to write about getting hurt–nakedly, without playing for laughs, but under the guise of something popular, even fashionable. *The Anti-Death League* essays a masque of ultimate bitterness–not against human institutions but against God–in the form of a secret-weapon-and-spy story.

The setting is not the land of the Flemings (though, as his James Bond pastiche *Colonel Sun* shows us, he can be comfortable enough in that country) but England now, with a cold war and a yellow peril, the chief male interest distributed among the officers of No. 6 Headquarters Administration Battalion, which is engaged on something secret. Although the apparatus of security and intrigue, with something exciting imminent, is a mere fictional means to an end bordering on the eschatological, it would be unfair to give too much of the plot away. Take it that this army unit has (as it must have) collective death in view, and that some-one unknown–we find out at last, but we're expertly kept guessing –founds, among these potential killers, the organization of the title. Ayscue, the chaplain, is sent an anonymous poem for the unit magazine he is starting, and this is the first shot in a war against God. God speaks in this ode *To A Baby Born Without Limbs* and promises 'plenty of other stuff up My sleeve–Such as Luekemia and polio' (the misspelling is a deliberate blind).

God is death, the eternal butcher, full of the filthiest and most ingenious practical jokes. The young officer Churchill falls in love with Catharine Casement, who deserves this benison after a night-mare life with a sadistic husband; then God sneaks in sniggering with the gift of cancer of the breast. There are other divinely dealt nastinesses. Ayscue, who says he took orders the better to wage war on God, risks a prayer towards the end : 'Catharine. Don't do it to her. Let her get well and stay well. Please.' But, an earnest of His infinite badness, God at once has a stab, not at Catharine, but at a smaller and more defenceless life. So the book ends, and I can think of only one sourer ending–that of *Brighton Rock*. But, though Rose runs home to her final horror, Pinky, affirming the devil, has also affirmed a beneficent God. In this new Amis universe we're all in the hands of the Great Gangster. Can one really wage war against Him? One can make certain existential gestures, totally impotent, but that, apparently, is better than doing nothing.

John Wain's *Hurry On Down* has been regarded by some critics as being as good as, if not better than, *Lucky Jim*. The subject-matter suited popular taste, being as radical as Amis's: the anti-hero deliberately descends the ladder, rung by rung, from the roof of the middle classes (good family, good education) to the ground-floor of the workers, ending in the cellar of popular culture. There is no hypergamy here, only a dissatisfaction with the life of the *bourgeoisie* which finds logical expression in a shying away from it. What the early critics did not seem to notice about Wain's novel was its atrocious construction and indifferent style. More than ten years after Wain's début, the faults of his work seem more patent. *The Contenders*, with its fashionable provincial setting, depicts the rivalry of three Midland lads who, competing at school, smack at each other on their adult way to the top. A symbol of success is, as in *Lucky Jim*, the love of a high-class woman, but the true victory is attained by the fat comic unpretentious man who opts out of the race and settles for the kind of job (provincial journalism) and girl (working-class, though Italian) predestined for him by upbringing and temperament. 'Living in the present' (the title of Wain's second novel) is desirable, but it is even more desirable to stay in one's class. *The Contenders* is written in a pawky but undistinguished prose, and its editing, as well as construction, is remarkably careless.

If the new rebels look for a literature-substitute in science fiction, they find their music ready to hand in jazz. The significance of jazz to writers like Amis and Wain is perhaps extra-musical: though its harmonies and metres are fundamentally traditional and solid, the element of improvisation–both melodic and rhythmical–is anarchic, primitive, instinctual: it carries the right nonconformist overtones. Jeremy, the hero of Wain's *Strike the Father Dead*, leaves home during the war, dodges call-up, and becomes a jazz-cellar pianist. Revolting against his professor-father and all he stands for, he soon finds a father-substitute in a Negro

A SORT OF REBELS

trombonist (this is really hurrying on down to the atavistic, the dark gods who are our primal fathers). Later he discovers that his revolt is only part of a pattern that is relived from generation to generation: his own father left home and made a father-substitute out of his commanding officer in the First World War. And so at the end, when Jeremy and his jazz-colleagues are virtually hooted off the dance-hall platform by a new (rock-and-rolling) generation he recognizes that the process of parricide goes on, but that new and better values do not necessarily emerge from it. The rebel has become philosophical about rebellion.

Here, as in *The Contenders*, Wain evades the problem of narrative style by opting for a first-person colloquial which sounds weary rather than bright; he does not prune sufficiently, so that what should be sharp is often long-winded. What is worrying about his novels is his apparent reluctance to shed his faults, to learn by doing. Thus *The Young Visitors*–a not very exciting tale of East-West confrontation (some Moscow students come to London and learn all the expected things about capitalist *mores*)– marks no fresh departure, though the subject, like all his subjects, is excellent. Wain is a good poet and a really outstanding critic. The novel-form hides his fine taste and his clarity of thought. Perhaps, having done his work of singing the rebel of the fifties in, along with Amis and Iris Murdoch, he ought to consider giving up extended fiction (one can find few faults with his short stories).

Colin MacInnes is regarded as a sort of voice of the displaced, downtrodden, or misunderstood–the rebel (real or would-be) with a cause. 'Low life' may be regarded as the subject-matter of *City of Spades*, *Mr. Love and Justice* and *Absolute Beginners*, but there is no attempt to exploit the sensational in the manner of the popular novelist. *City of Spades* avoids showing Negroes as either brutish, innocent or quaint; it is moving and indignant in its presentation of racialism in the London of the fifties, but it is not merely propaganda. The aim of *Mr. Love and Justice* is to show what the world of the prostitute and the ponce is really like and to examine the conventional image of an incorrupt British police force. *Absolute Beginners* is sympathetic to the culture-patterns of teenagers. MacInnes knows the underside of London life, but, strangely, he does not seem to have a sharp ear for its language. Being unable to record faithfully the idioms of Negroes, small criminals and adolescents, he makes up dialects for them out of his head–at least, this is the impression one has when reading him. For all that, his work is psychologically accurate, very enlightening, and full of a real (and quite unsentimental) compassion.

The extent of the British public's continuing concern with class-divisions may be gauged by its response to John Braine's *Room at the Top*, a study in provincial hypergamy, but very different from Amis, and its sequel, *Life at the Top*. (There was not the same enthusiasm for the novel that came in between–*The Vodi*. This was less rich in class overtones, being mainly about the struggle of an individual soul to overcome repressive forces which were projected into a personal myth.) Braine's working-class hero, Joe Lampton, is not like Jim Dixon. Coming to work in a large provincial town from a slummy outpost of depression, he demands more than a sufficiency of material comforts and a chance to sneer at the pretensions of the *bourgeoisie*. He demands the best and (here comes hypergamy) gets it through the door of marriage with a magnate's daughter. His triumph over his upbringing and his natural instincts is, however, a sour one: the woman he really loves (a married woman who represents no exalted future for him) dies a horrible death when he abandons her. *Life at the Top* continues Joe's story. The top seems not so very high–a large suburban house, children, a car, a cocktail cabinet, an executive job with his father-in-law, business lunches in London, mutual adultery. The implied moral is clear: be true to your class. Braine has, perhaps temporarily, abandoned this theme, as has the British novel itself. *The Jealous God* brings out Braine's Catholicism, and his hero's ambitions are spiritual, not material. Inevitably, such a theme is less popular than that of the fleshly rat-race.

The class-struggle element in the novels of Alan Sillitoe is for the most part a retrospective one. The young hero of *Saturday Night and Sunday Morning* is a highly paid factory worker: he has more beer and fags than Jim Dixon will ever see. But he feels that his own comparative affluence emphasizes all the more the injustices done to his own class in the past. And the streets of working-class Nottingham are still not very pretty–inadequate sanitation and too many families to a house. Revolt continues to be a virtue: the deserting soldier, one of the hero's family, is supposed to have done something heroic. Sillitoe catches the grumbling and the touchiness, the traditional radicalism, the beer, fights, fornication and skittles in a novel whose form is imperfect but whose dialogue is very much alive. For perfection of form one has to turn to *The Loneliness of the Long-Distance Runner*, the title-story of a remarkable volume, in which we really learn what makes juvenile delinquents tick. It was a disappointment to see Sillitoe turning to Kafka-and-water in *The General*, and painful to watch him grappling unhandily with the problems of rather naïve polemical verse in *The Rats*. It was a relief to find him going back to the full-length working-class novel in *Key to the Door*.

Much of this novel is set in Malaya, where the hero is, at the beginning of the Malayan Emergency, surlily doing his National Service. There are flashbacks to working-class Nottingham and growls and whines about social wrongs; inevitably, it is the Communists in the jungle who have the monopoly of right, and it is assumed that the people of Malaya, who have allegedly smarted under British exploitation, would welcome a Communist régime. Yet we see practically nothing of these people; it is as though the whole land–with the exception of a Chinese prostitute and a rickshaw-driver or two–were bare except for the working-class lads in the services and their not very efficient officers. Anyone who knows Malaya must marvel at both the wilful ignorance and the incredible political innocence. *Key to the Door* is one of those rare books which are hard to judge artistically because they are so wrong-headed. The Malayan landscape is wonderfully rendered (there is plenty of rough poetry in Sillitoe), and there is a great deal of the radical vigour that distinguishes *Saturday Night and Sunday Morning*. But Sillitoe has no right to twist contemporary history for ends that are not purely artistic. His subsequent novel, *The Death of William Posters*, resembles the *Aaron's Rod* of his fellow-

A SORT OF REBELS

townsman (or near) D. H. Lawrence in that it shows a dissatisfied artist of working-class origins wandering in search of personal fulfilment. It is not the most satisfactory of Sillitoe's books. Reading it (so a critic has said) would be uphill work if the going were not so flat. This is not wholly fair. Sillitoe approaches Lawrence in what we may call the 'early morning' apprehension of life–the sense that the world is newly created, the dew fresh; the poetry of the body is very much there in his work, as is the poetry of the family, the snug human community. But he can be verbose, over-intense, sprawling and embarrassing. He has perhaps still to discover the disciplines of art.

The novels of Amis, Wain, Braine, Sillitoe have brought back to popularity the provincial setting which, in the view of metropolitan novelists, was unworthy precisely because it was provincial–meaning dull, uninformed, unfashionable. But, at this moment of writing, certain provinces of the British Isles (particularly Liverpool) are regarded as bright, progressive, trend-setting. The metropolitan way of speaking has yielded to the plebeian accent on stage and (small or large) screen; a television serial set in Salford heads the TAM ratings, London has at last realized that it has no monopoly of the full life, and the contemporary British novel has been driving home the lesson. Stan Barstow, like John Braine, is able to write powerfully of high passion in Yorkshire (*A Kind of Loving*), and Keith Waterhouse, another Yorkshire-man, has created a myth as valid for our age as Amis's Jim Dixon –the hero of *Billy Liar*, who muffles the impact of provincial reality by indulging in grandiose daydreams. Waterhouse is a fine novelist in whom humour serves an end of acute social and psychological observation–the New Town of *Jubb*, for example–though, with Willis Hall, he has given much of his talent to the drama. Stanley Middleton showed, in *Harris's Requiem*, the passionate musical life of the Midlands, though his later novels– *A Serious Woman*, for instance, and *The Just Exchange*–seem to play into the hands of the anti-provincials by showing the unmusical Midlands as perhaps duller than they really are. If we are to use the term 'provincial' in its most literal sense, the province

A SORT OF REBELS

of Wales (or principality, for the purists) has been well served fictionally by Emyr Humphreys, who has written his novels in English but also translated some of them into Welsh. In him the great world of film, drama, foreign travel marries the smaller one of the parish. What J. D. Scott has done for Scotland in his best novel, *The End of an Old Song*, is not to glorify that romantic nationalism which may be regarded as provincialism gone mad, but to disparage nationalism altogether as a kind of fascism. Ultimately, the task of the novelist is with the whole of man, not just man in his regional (or, for that matter, metropolitan) aspects.

America is too big, and too little troped to a single centre of life and culture, to produce anything that can be called a provincial novel. The Middle West of Sinclair Lewis's novels (*Main Street*, *Arrowsmith*, *Babbitt*, and so on) provided symbols for the whole of forward-looking, boosting, go-getting America; the South has produced a major literature which transcends region, and names like Ellen Glasgow, William Faulkner, Robert Penn Warren, Carson McCullers and Katherine Anne Porter appear among the fiction-writers. As for contemporary rebels in America, these are not concerned with shaking their fists at the limitations and pretensions of the little *bourgeoisie*; it is the whole structure and ethos of a materialistic society that they revolt against. The most spectacular of the rebels are the Beats, though their literary record is meagre and their works amateurish. The late Jack Kerouac was their chief novelist, and a title like *The Dharma Bums* seems to sum up the Beats' view of themselves—people with few possessions living quietly in fellowships, ostensibly lazy but actually highly interested in the techniques of Buddhist contemplation. Their rebellion is really a withdrawal.

A more significant rebel is to be found in J. D. Salinger's *The Catcher in the Rye*, though its hero, Holden Caulfield, is more a gentle voice of protest, unprevailing in the noise, than a militant world-changer. Holden tells his own story in a vernacular that has learned something from the Beats, very attractive, often funny, as often childishly pitiable. He is an adolescent who leaves his boarding-school to spend a week-end in New York, meeting taxi-drivers,

A SORT OF REBELS

a prostitute, his own young sister, finally a man whom he has always respected (one of the very few: nearly all adults are suspect) but who makes a homosexual pass at him. There is no real plot, only the acute observations of a boy alone in a world of hypocrisy and phoney values, a world which is a kind of comic hell because it needs love and does not know how to find it. This is what the inner voice of Holden is talking about, though indirectly and fumblingly–the need for honesty, which is a kind of love or at least the first attempt to find it, as well as the horror of the public American image which thinks it can get along without love. Love does not mean sex; Holden has a chill instinct towards celibacy: it is significant that the only people he meets who are really good are two nuns, women who do not have sexual connotations and who have put off the dirty world. Love, however, does seem to have something to do with death (he idolizes a dead brother) and with the innocence that dies with pubescence. Holden has misheard the words of Burns's song about coming through the rye; he sees himself as a body who catches in the rye–catches the innocent playing in a ryefield who are in danger of falling over the unseen edge of a cliff. But the dream-task of saving the innocents before the world corrupts them is a hopeless one; Holden escapes from its hopelessness into mental illness, and he is writing his story while under psychiatric treatment.

The Catcher in the Rye is one of the key-books of the post-war period. It was the culminating work of a series of stories, most of which carried the theme of a sick mind's redemption through the innocence of a child. Salinger's later works–*Franny*, *Zooey*, and *Raise High the Roof Beam, Carpenters*–have disappointed his admirers, though they are the books they should have expected. It required boldness to present an attempt at solving the world's problems through a positive creed of love, though Salinger's genuine crime is to close in, depicting a family of the elect (the Glass family) who are doing two things–ritually washing away the world's guilt, practising a synthetic religion that has elements of Christianity and Zen Buddhism in it. Holden at least confronts the dirty mass of sinning humanity, though it drives him to a

A SORT OF REBELS

mental home; the Glass family confronts itself. A latent sentimentality in *The Catcher in the Rye* comes out into the open in
the later stories, pawing with sticky fingers. But at least Salinger
has refused to repeat himself; a lesser author could have used
Holden Caulfield for ever.

Perhaps the impact that *The Catcher in the Rye* was able to
make, in the nineteen-fifties, on the young of both America and
Europe was too powerful to maintain its strength into the sixties–
a kind of *sforzato* piano chord, dying away. But the book was at
least a symptom of a need, after a ghastly war and during a ghastly
peace, for the young to raise a voice of protest against what the
adult world was doing, or rather failing to do. The young used
many voices–anger, contempt, self-pity–but the quietest, that of
a decent, perplexed American adolescent, proved the most telling.

See Bibliographical Note on p. 12

Kingsley AMIS (1922–   )
  Lucky Jim. 1954
  That Uncertain Feeling, Lon-
    don, 1955
  I Like it Here. 1958
  Take a Girl like You. London,
    1960
  One Fat Englishman. London,
    1963
  The Egyptologists. London,
    1965 (with Robert Conquest)
  The Anti-death League. 1966
  I Want it Now. London, 1968
  Colonel Sun. 1968 (under the
    pseudonym, Robert Mark-
    ham)
Stan BARSTOW (1928–   )
  A Kind of Loving. London,
    1960

Stan BARSTOW (*continued*)
  The Watchers on the Shore.
    London, 1966
  A Raging Calm. London, 1968
John BRAINE (1922–   )
  Room at the Top. 1957
  The Vodi, London, 1959 (as
    From the Hand of the Hun-
    ter, Boston, 1960)
  Life at the Top. 1962
  The Jealous God. London and
    Boston, 1965
  The Crying Game. London,
    1968
William COOPER (1910–   )
  Scenes from Provincial Life.
    London, 1950
  Scenes from Married Life. Lon-
    don, 1961 (with the above as

154

A SORT OF REBELS

William COOPER (*continued*)
  Scenes from Life, New York, 1961)

Emyr HUMPHREYS (1919–   )
  The Voice of a Stranger. London, 1949
  Outside the House of Baal. London, 1965

Jack KEROUAC (1922–69)
  On the Road. New York, 1957
  The Dharma Bums. New York, 1958
  Satori in Paris. New York, 1966

Colin MACINNES (1914–   )
  City of Spades. London, 1957
  Absolute Beginners. London, 1959
  Mr Love and Justice. London, 1960
  Westward to Laughter. London, 1969

Stanley MIDDLETON (1919–   )
  Harris's Requiem. London, 1960
  A Serious Woman. London, 1961
  The Just Exchange. London, 1962
  Wages of Virtue. London, 1969

J. D. SALINGER (1919–   )
  The Catcher in the Rye. 1951

J. D. SALINGER (*continued*)
  Franny and Zooey. Boston, 1962 (short stories)
  Raise High the Roof Beam, Carpenters; and Seymour: an Introduction. 1963

J. D. SCOTT (1917–   )
  The Way to Glory. 1952
  The End of an Old Song. 1954

Alan SILLITOE (1928–   )
  Saturday Night and Sunday Morning. London, 1958
  The Loneliness of the Long-distance Runner. London, 1959 (short stories)
  The General. London, 1960
  Key to the Door. London, 1961
  The Death of William Posters. 1965
  A Tree on Fire. London, 1967

John WAIN (1925–   )
  Hurry on Down. London, 1953 (as Born in Captivity, New York, 1954)
  The Contenders. 1958
  Strike the Father Dead. 1962
  The Young Visitors. 1965

Keith WATERHOUSE (1929–   )
  Billy Liar. London, 1959
  Jubb. London, 1963
  The Bucket Shop. London, 1968

XIII

Exports and Imports

Whatever faults of limitation are possessed by United Kingdom novelists, insularity cannot be said to be one of them. E. M. Forster's *A Passage to India*, D. H. Lawrence's *Kangaroo*, the African novels of Joyce Cary – these are accepted as modern classics. They may also be regarded as the creators of whole new national literatures in English. Few Anglo-Indian novelists would deny that *A Passage to India* has influenced them profoundly, and – here is one of the great mysteries of art – the few weeks that Lawrence spent in Australia were sufficient to inspire a novel that native-born Australians (often with generations of Australian experience behind them) regard as their literary starting-point. The novelists of the Commonwealth owe a great deal to British expatriates and travellers, and it is because of this that it is so difficult to separate out the qualities of the two kinds of 'exotic' novels in English – the novel by a native of the United Kingdom that probes into the essence of a British colony or dominion or protectorate; the novel by a native of one of these that, in the stream of fiction in English, looks at that essence as it expresses itself in a tradition he takes for granted. Could *Mister Johnson* have been written by an African? Could Balachandra Rajan's *The Dark Dancer* have been written by an Englishman? These are hard questions.

And yet they can be answered. We can take as a key-phrase 'a tradition he takes for granted'. A great deal depends on whether the writer is assuming the existence of an audience drawn from his own community, or a foreign one to which everything has to be

156

EXPORTS AND IMPORTS

explained. If I may give a personal example, when I wrote my *Malayan Trilogy* (called *The Long Day Wanes* in the United States), I addressed primarily an audience of English-speaking Malayans of all races—Malays, Chinese, Tamils, Eurasians, as well as expatriate settlers in the country; somewhere in the shadows I imagined a secondary audience of readers who had never been to Malaya. I assumed a knowledge of certain locutions, customs and habits of thought, and I did not attempt to explain them. I did not, for instance, say: 'Malays, being Muslims, are allowed four wives' or 'Friday is the Sabbath in Malaya'. I regarded such information as dangerous, since it would imply a cold outsider's attitude and turn my characters into interesting foreign specimens, not creatures of the same flesh and blood as the ignorant reader. Besides, this ignorant reader belonged to the secondary audience, and the secondary audience must puzzle out difficulties for itself. I saw myself as a Malayan writer entertaining Malayan readers and, indeed, intended to become a Malayan citizen. Later I was to change my mind, turn the primary audience into the secondary audience, and vice versa, and take to looking at the East from the outside.

There are other factors which make for differences between the expatriate's novel and the native's novel: the influence of the mother-tongue on writers who use English as a second spoken, though first written, language; custom and tradition (a Muslim writer will, for instance, have a radically different approach to marriage from a Catholic writer like Waugh or Greene); the view of what is comic and what is tragic. It is conceivable that many Indian novels—like those of R. K. Narayan—are less comic to a native than to an English audience. We ought never to assume that the use of English implies an acceptance of British values, or even British semantics. To take the simplest possible example, a sentence like 'I put on my suspenders and sat down to my breakfast biscuits' means one thing to an Englishman, quite another to an American. The statement 'He was very fond of pork' carries neutral associations for a Christian; for a Muslim there are bound to be connotations of disgust. Terms like 'love' and 'truth' and

157

EXPORTS AND IMPORTS

'loyalty' are too complex for quick analysis, but they will mean one thing to the West, quite a different thing to the East.

Let us consider very briefly, first, some of the English writers who are associated with the Eastern or African scene. Gerald Hanley has used African settings for such novels as *The Consul at Sunset*, *The Year of the Lion* and *Gilligan's Last Elephant*. His Africa is brilliantly realized and shows an acute insight into the native mind, but it is the white man who holds the centre of the stage. Sometimes, as in *Gilligan's Last Elephant*, it is a white man who loves an Africa already dead–safaris, no game laws, Negroes who hold no status higher than that of servant. Thomas Hinde, a younger writer, has sandwiched a couple of African novels between two groups of novels with home settings. The first of the groups contained *Mr. Nicholas*, *Happy as Larry* and *For the Good of the Company*, and these turned a critical eye on certain unattractive aspects of post-war British life. *Mr. Nicholas*, in particular, showed how the pattern of middle-class manners was changing in the early nineteen-fifties, with one set of convictions dying, another not yet come to replace it. The later group of novels–*Ninety Double Martinis*, *The Day the Call Came*, *Games of Chance* (two stories in one volume)–seemed to seek a release from the modern world in fantasy or mental disorder. The technique of all these works is notable for extreme economy, and the typical Hinde novel gains its effects from ellipsis rather than expansiveness. *A Place Like Home* and *The Cage* are about East Africa, but they studiously avoid 'atmosphere'. They both carry the theme (initiated in *Mr. Nicholas*) of the difficulty of adjusting to social change, though here the social change is more spectacular–the breakdown of colonial rule and the emergence of new (though not necessarily better) patterns of life in newly independent territories. The emphasis, though, is less on society itself than on the impact change makes on a mixed-up individual soul. The expatriate, through the need for adjustment, comes to a better understanding of his own nature. What is learnt is not comforting; reality never is.

Paul Scott, enchanted by India since his war days there, has

158

EXPORTS AND IMPORTS

evoked its essence in a number of novels from *Johnnie Sahib* on. Perhaps his finest achievement is *The Birds of Paradise*, in which a realistic attempt is made to analyse the mind of a man who, brought up on a dream of service to India, finds with the dissolution of that dream that there is little left in life to sustain him—only the way of the 'consumer' (this is becoming everybody's way in the West), not that older, nobler, way of the 'contributor'. The breakdown of an empire has, it is implied, been responsible in part for the enervation of British life. Scott's talent is at its best in this poignant study, but its variety is attested by *The Bender*—a superb comic novel based on contemporary England—and *The Corrida at San Feliu*, which is set in both Africa and Spain, with a brief glance at India, and creates, in the tortured novelist Thornhill, a genuine tragic figure. It seems that Scott can best realize the tragic divisions of human beings in a foreign setting, bringing these out through symbols taken from an exotic scene, sharpening them through the strangeness of the background.

Other writers who have looked East include Mary McMinnies, Katharine Sim, and Susan Yorke, all of whom have given us perceptive studies of Malaya in a state of transition. Susan Yorke has, in *Capitan China*, delved into Malayan history in order to illuminate the present; Mary McMinnies, in *The Flying Fox*, has woven a multi-racial tapestry of Malayans learning the 'new look' of independence around an old-type British expatriate figure—drunken, irresponsible, rootless; Katharine Sim's books—*Malacca Boy*, *Black Rice*, *The Jungle Ends Here*—tend more to the romantic and colourful for their own sake, though they show a remarkable understanding of the Malay mind. Farthest East of all, Francis King's *The Custom House* makes a valiant attempt at probing the mystery of the Japanese soul, but he neither excites our sympathy for it nor attempts to hide his own antipathy overmuch.

Only South Africa, among all the colonized territories of the Dark Continent, seems so far to have produced considerable novelists of European stock (as also, in Roy Campbell, a considerable poet). The father of these is undoubtedly William Plomer, born in the Transvaal, and writers like Alan Paton, Dan Jacobson, Daphne Rooke and Nadine Gordimer owe much to him. He was perhaps the first white writer to take the concept of negritude seriously, and, as early as 1926, he published a novel called *Turbott Wolfe*, whose theme was the need for black and white blood to mix, thus ensuring a liberal future for a South Africa not given over to purely white domination. This was an anti-apartheid book that appeared long before the doctrine of apartheid achieved world notoriety, and–needless to say–its plea for miscegenation is still well ahead of its time. Plomer did not, like his inheritors, settle to the vocation of a purely South African novelist. *Sado* is set in Japan; *The Case is Altered* and *The Invaders* are about England in the nineteen-thirties. Despite Plomer's variety of fictional settings and themes, a clear motif runs through most of his work–the sense of estrangement, of human beings looking for a home but not finding it. Races and classes meet and sometimes clash, but the antithesis is never resolved in a synthesis. *Museum Pieces*, published in 1952, presents a different irresoluble conflict–that between past and present. As the title suggests, generations grow old and appear as mere embalmable freaks to their successors. Toby d'Arfey, the hero, tries to adapt himself to change, bringing talents learned in the past to the various challenges of the present, but never succeeding in either accepting the present or being accepted by it. Plomer does not, however, see him as a pathetic or ridiculous figure. If *Turbott Wolfe* was red-hot in its plea for a new South Africa and *The Invaders* angry about unemployment in the thirties, the Plomer of *Museum Pieces* has learned a kind of humorous resignation, accepting much of the absurdity and tragedy which spring from man's divided nature as a cross that has to be borne.

Writers like Alan Paton, Dan Jacobson and–as we saw in a previous chapter–Doris Lessing have devoted most of their considerable skill to the annotation of the present racial position in South Africa. The danger of a strongly propagandist content in a novel lies in the fact that it may swamp the art, turning a piece of literature into a mere pamphlet. We all accept the injustice of the

EXPORTS AND IMPORTS

Negro's status in South Africa, and we have often first been made aware of it in novels like Paton's *Cry, The Beloved Country*. Knowing the position, our duty is to fight against it, and we do not need to be told the position again. What we look for now in the South African novel is something of more universal import–static, not angry, works of art which deal with individuals, of whatever colour, and not with the abstractions more proper to didactic writings.

Some strange and interesting things are coming from the Negro novelists of West Africa, and much of the strangeness and interest derive from the way in which the English language is used. Pidgin is being combined with standard literary English, and some of the rhythms and idioms of native African tongues are counterpointing, or fertilizing, English into what is virtually a new set of dialects. One of the most remarkable of the Nigerian novelists is Amos Tutuola, whose *The Palm-Wine Drinkard* has earned him an international reputation. He uses a naïve-seeming English which is really very subtle: it is a lucid and elastic medium for the presentation of themes drawn from native folk-lore, and it is irradiated with powerful humour. Cyprian Ekwensi has written *Jagua Nana*, which shows the impact of Western values on the tribal mind: the Nana of the title is a woman obsessed with luxurious importations of which the 'Jagua' stands as a symbol. Onuora Nzekwu has, in his *Blade Among the Boys*, a graver theme–the conflict between Ibo religion and Christianity in the upbringing of a sensitive and confused young man. The same seriousness is to be found in Chinua Achebe, an Eastern Nigerian whose first two novels–*Things Fall Apart* and *No Longer at Ease*–have made a large impact on Europe, as well as Britain and America. His third novel, *Arrow of God*, exhibits as well as any his predominant theme –the threat to native civilizations which the great world may call primitive but which are in fact vital, rich, and happy. It also shows a remarkable power in the rendering of Umuaro speech and thought. *A Man of the People* shows a fresh departure. It is a oitter yet funny satire on the corrupt government and personality cult which disfigure so many newly independent African states.

161

Achebe's wishful thinking epitaph on such régimes deserves to be quoted as a typical example of his rich idiom:

'. . . I do honestly believe that in the fat-dripping, gummy, eat-and-let-eat régime just ended–a régime which inspired the common saying that a man could only be sure of what he had put away safely in his gut or, in language ever more suited to the times: "you chop, me self I chop, palaver finish"; a régime in which you saw a fellow cursed in the morning for stealing a blind man's stick and later in the evening saw him again mounting the altar of the new shrine in the presence of all the people to whisper into the ear of the chief celebrant–in such a régime, I say, you died a good death if your life had inspired someone to come forward and shoot your murderer in the chest–without asking to be paid.'

English is not a universal literary language in India, and writers who work in English look outward rather than inward ('Indo-Anglians' whose primary audience is in the West). But what they export is India herself. Perhaps the finest of the Indian novelists is Raja Rao, whose *The Serpent and the Rope* tries to make out of English a medium appropriate to the Indian psyche by fusing into it the rhythms of Sanskrit. R. K. Narayan's work is very distinctive: it blends–in the early *The English Teacher* and the more recent *The Maneater of Malgudi*–qualities of humour and pathos which threaten to touch, but never do touch, sentimentality. And he is not afraid to mix fantasy with naturalism. A newer talent is that of Balachandra Rajan, whose *The Dark Dancer* and *Too Long in the West* are witty, profound and beautifully written. The latter book is a satirical study of modern Indian life as seen from the angle of Nalini, a girl who has returned to her remote muddy village from three years at Columbia University. She has, in fact, been too long in the West to take kindly to the throng of suitors who, in reply to her father's newspaper advertisement, have come to compete for her hand. Rajan uses the Indian attitude to marriage as a focus for some good-humoured but telling attacks on a too-conservative way of life that must learn to come to terms with the West. At the same time, the West has to take a few gentle slaps:

'In the evening she descended into the depths, filled with a sense

EXPORTS AND IMPORTS

of patriotism for her new home. She entered a restaurant that was aggressively American. Fine-looking types from Italy, Hong Kong and Trinidad were propped obligingly against the architecture, preventing it from collapsing into the street. She seated herself precisely on a swivelling stool that was designed for someone with fourteen-and-a-half-inch hips. She disdained to reach for the menu; she had already read articles about American cuisine and knew what she could order to qualify as a citizen.

' "I'll have Boston clam chowder," she said, "and roast, stuffed, young Vermont turkey. With golden-brown, melt-in-your-mouth Idaho potatoes. And king-sized, tree-ripened California peaches."

' "We got chop suey," the girl said, "and Swedish meat balls and Swiss steak. But we ain't got none of the fancy stuff you're wanting."

' "Then I'll have a hamburger," Nalini insisted, doggedly.

' "You want it with French fries?"

' "I want it," said Nalini, clenching her pretty teeth, "with potatoes that taste of American earth, fried in the only way they should be, in butter fresh as a New England welcome. And then I'll have pie like your grandmother used to bake it when America was real and itself."

' "You mean, home fried," the girl reproved her. "Why don't you say so instead of letting your hair down? And the pie's ten cents extra with French ice-cream."

'With a sigh of resignation, Nalini settled down to her international repast.'

If novels from southern India are, like Rajan's, notable for highly civilized compassion and humour, the north seems capable of something like violence and wild poetry. The most notable writer from the Punjab is undoubtedly the Sikh Khushwant Singh, whose *I Shall Not Hear the Nightingales* is a fine chronicle of life in a Sikh community in the period 1942-43. We have here a formidable novelist who writes too little.

The achievement of the Caribbean is very large—though, since the West Indies ought not be regarded as a homogeneous territory, it would be more proper to speak of achievements. Trinidad

EXPORTS AND IMPORTS

is not the same place as Jamaica. Trinidad has, however, produced the two best known of West Indian novelists, though the more considerable of these, V. S. Naipaul, set a recent book, *Mr. Stone and the Knights Companion*, in an English suburb and shows in it greater affinities with another V. S. (Pritchett, one of our best senior short-story writers) and even E. M. Forster than with any of his co-regionalists. Naipaul wrote such colourful and light-hearted novels as *Miguel Street* before achieving a Caribbean masterpiece in *A House for Mr. Biswas*, a work of great comic power qualified with firm and unsentimental compassion. *The Mimic Men*, combining the Caribbean and the London scenes, has an even greater depth and poignancy. Samuel Selvon, the other major Trinidadian, who, like Naipaul, is of East Indian descent, is a grimmer, less polished, writer, capable of vivid evocation of the Trinidad scene–*A Brighter Sun, An Island is a World*–and, as in *The Lonely Londoners*, much concerned with one of the big problems of our age, that of the integration of the coloured and the white races.

George Lamming–*In the Castle of My Skin, The Emigrants, Of Age and Innocence, Season of Adventure*–gives us an authentic San Cristobal. Edgar Mittelholzer, whose death–under tragic and violent circumstances–robbed Caribbean fiction of an ebullient talent, was perhaps guilty of over-production. The later rash of books, many of which had an English setting, could not compare with the flavoursome *A Morning at the Office* (his first novel), *Shadows Move Among Them, Children of Kaywana*. John Hearne–*Voices Under the Window, Stranger at the Gate, The Faces of Love*–is notable for very firm and economical prose, though *Land of the Living* (at the moment of writing his most recent work) shows a certain falling-off in construction and narrative style. Wilson Harris has written a remarkable Guianan tetralogy–*Palace of the Peacock, The Far Journey of Oudin, The Whole Armour, The Secret Ladder*–in which dense and poetic prose serves another great theme of our time – the invasion by the scientist, road-maker, bridge-builder of the resistant jungle, the confrontation of logic and magic. In *Heartland* Harris takes up the story again. Stevenson, who comes with his machinery to exploit the natural resources of up-river Guiana, is profoundly disturbed by this ancient world. The mysteries of the jungle are the mysteries of man's unconscious mind. Prose narrative gives out, incapable of further articulation, to match Stevenson's disappearance 'somewhere in the Guianan/Venezuelan/Brazilian jungles that lie between the headwaters of the Cuyani and Potaro rivers.' All we are left with is a handful of fragmentary poems 'so browned by fire that some of the lines were indistinguishable':

. . . world-creating jungle
travels eternity to season. Not an individual artifice –
this living moment
this tide
this paradoxical stream and stillness rousing reflection.

This living jungle is too filled with voices
not to be aware of collectivity
and too swift with unseen wings
to capture certainty.

Branches against the sky tender to heaven the utter beauty
. . . storehouse of heaven

Harris has the courage to realize the impossibility of conveying, through the ordinary devices of the prose-novel, states of mind corresponding to the horror and grandeur of primeval nature. His own work is on the border between logic and magic; he is one of the finest of Caribbean novelists.

English writers have, as we have briefly seen, travelled to Africa and the East to bring back their fictional reports; British colonialism has exported the English language, and a new kind of British novel has been the eventual flower of this transplanting. In the smaller, less strange, territory of Europe, the British novelist has found stimulating material and, occasionally opting for exile in Europe, has taken most of his subject-matter from his adopted land. John Lodwick, who died prematurely and is in danger of being neglected, lived in Spain and set some of his best work there. *Somewhere a Voice is Calling* and *The Starless Night* could not have been written by the casual literary tourist, taking his note-book to Valencia and Barcelona and conscientiously amassing local colour. They are a special kind of fiction, giving a violent English hero – one who could hardly survive for a day in suburban Britain – the only kind of background for the release of his passionate talents. Even *The Butterfly Net*, with its sharply caught post-war English setting, derives its zest from the fact that the narrative revolves about an exile, briefly come home on a visit, like Lodwick himself. Contemporary England is surveyed from a Continental aspect. It is the 'European' quality of Lodwick's writing that repels some readers. He is not afraid of rhetoric, grandiloquence; his knowledge of foreign literatures is wide; his irony is subtle; his mastery of the English language matches Evelyn Waugh's.

Some British novelists have been urged to distil the atmosphere of a foreign country through a period of academic residence in it, as Frank Tuohy has opened our eyes to certain aspects of modern Poland in *The Ice Saints* or (to leave Europe, though only just) P. H. Newby has notated the changes in post-war Egypt in *The Picnic at Sakkara* and D. J. Enright, in his *Academic Year*, has attempted a similar probing of the Islamic mind. It is curious that writers who have settled in Morocco – like Robin Maugham, Rupert Croft-Cooke, and William Burroughs – have had so little to say about the country, though Paul Bowles, who shares Tangier with them, has written a very authentic, violent, and flavoursome Tangerine novel in his *Let It Come Down*. But of all novels which pierce to the heart of a foreign country in a particular era, few can compare with Gabriel Fielding's *The Birthday King*, which is an imaginative penetration into the Germany of 1939–45. In its pre-occupation with 'the innocent malevolence of the Teutonic mind', it reads like some exceptionally brilliant translation of a great unknown liberal survivor of the Nazi régime. Fielding's earlier novels – *Brotherly Love*, *In the Time of Greenbloom*, *Eight Days*, *Through Streets Broad and Narrow* – have a strongly individual flavour, but it is the sinking of individuality, the turning of himself into an anonymous German, that makes *The Birthday King* not only his best work but one of the most remarkable novels of the post-war era. The publication of his latest novel–*Gentlemen in their Season*–does nothing to make one change this judgement.

It is proper to end with a mention of some foreign novelists who, reared in their own language, have adopted English as a literary tongue and done great things in it. Joseph Conrad is the great prototype here, but, in our own time, another Pole is doing things with English which would hardly be possible to a writer brought up solely in the English tradition. I mean Jerzy Peterkiewicz, whose *Isolation* opened a wider window on human sexuality than any English-born novelist had yet dared to do, and whose *The Quick and the Dead* made a strange comic fantasy out of Purgatory and Limbo. This latter was far too original an idea for some British sensibilities and, generally, it must be said that Peter-kiewicz is still waiting for the audience he deserves. Arthur Koest-ler showed, many years ago, how desperately the parochial spirit of the English novel needed a salutary contact with the European mind; writers like Peterkiewicz ought to be cherished.

One large European sensibility has engaged American paroch-ialism, with startling results. This belongs to Vladimir Nabokov, who, on the strength of *Lolita*, gained an international reputation in late middle age. Nabokov's first language is Russian, and his earliest novels were written in that language, though–as he is totally out of sympathy with the Soviet régime–they addressed an audience of cultivated *émigrés* like himself. A good number of these early novels have recently appeared translated–by, natur-ally, Nabokov himself–into the involved, dense, witty, learned, allusive English that disappointed the smut-bound readers of *Lolita*. One example is *The Defence*, published in 1964, which proved to be a worked-over version of *Zashchita Luzhina* ('Luz-hin's Defence')–first published in Russian in 1930. It is, as P. N. Furbank points out, a typical expression of the somewhat des-pairing philosophy of Nabokov: 'the only alternative to perversity, with its magical and terrible privileges, is banality'. The hero is a chess-player of the master class who can find only two approaches to life–the way of the jigsaw, fitting the shapeless scraps of the

EXPORTS AND IMPORTS

world together into a pre-ordained pattern, and the way of chess, or the perverse self-absorption in closed-in skills and strategies. His obsession with chess is as much an unclean thing (the way of the jigsaw is the sane way, everybody's way) as Humbert Humbert's obsession with the young girl in *Lolita*. If you reject banality – as, with the mind of most of Nabokov's heroes, you have to – you have to accept the punishment of perversity. When Luzhin, in *The Defence*, has suffered a nervous breakdown he finds no rehabilitation possible, since the obsession which caused the breakdown is his only possible way of life. He throws himself out of a window and, as he falls, sees the chess-board pattern of the window of the building; he sees also 'exactly what kind of eternity was obligingly and inexorably spread out before him'.

So Humbert Humbert in *Lolita* is, because of his choice and justification of a particular perversity (though the choice is preordained, woven into his personality), bound to meet disaster. He is obsessed not with young girls in general but with a particular kind of young girl he calls a 'nymphet', a rare order of being who is a sort of demon, a teenage siren of irresistible attraction. On Humbert's fatal fixation all the riches of the English language are poured; only a 'European' writer could so sack and pillage its resources without an ounce of puritanical compunction. Here is a specimen of Nabokov's style:

'. . . I did everything in my power to give my Lolita a really good time. How charming it was to see her, a child herself, showing another child some of her few accomplishments, such as for example a special way of jumping rope. With her right hand holding her left arm behind her untanned back, the lesser nymphet, a diaphanous darling, would be all eyes, as the pavonine sun was all eyes on the gravel under the flowering trees, while in the midst of that oculate paradise, my freckled and raffish lass skipped, repeating the movements of so many others I had gloated over on the sun-shot, watered, damp-smelling sidewalks and ramparts of ancient Europe. . . . Flashing a smile to the shy, dark-haired page girl of my princess and thrusting my fatherly fingers deep into Lo's hair from behind, and then gently but firmly clasping them around the nape of her neck, I would lead my reluctant pet to our small home for a quick connection before dinner.'

There is something in Nabokov's vocabulary that is contemptuous of the ordinary reader's difficulties (he will have to look up 'pavonine' and 'oculate'), just as there is something in his approach to the America of *Lolita* that is supercilious, world-weary, cynically 'European'. But his aim with this book was not merely to probe an obsession but to indulge in 'a love affair with the English language', and the style exalts the subject-matter. The style is the most allusive since James Joyce and, like Joyce, Nabokov is both pedantic and cosmopolitan at the same time. He has seen the world and despises it; only the most ingrown scholarship remains.

Pale Fire is both pedantry and a satire on pedantry. The core of the novel is a 999-line poem by an American author, John Shade—a sort of Robert Frost—which consists mainly of a rather moving meditation on the tragic end of the poet's daughter. After Shade's death, a foolish scholar called Kinbote (an exile from the mythical country of Zembla and a visiting professor of Zemblan at Wordsmith College, New Wye, Appalachia) edits this work, providing a preface and a detailed corpus of notes. But Kinbote has an *idée fixe*—the history of his own country—and he believes that Shade's poem, 'Pale Fire', is an allegory of this history, with Kinbote himself (fantasied into the deposed King Charles Xavier II) as the hero. The humour (and I ought to say now that Nabokov can be one of the funniest writers alive) consists in this disparity between the simple truth of the poem—all too intelligible—and the gross self-exalting hallucinations of the editor.

The interest of *Pale Fire* is perhaps mainly formal—here is a new way of writing a novel: in the form of a text with *apparatus criticus*—but one can see how it satisfies a need of Nabokov's which makes him both more and less than a novelist. It is the need to collect and exhibit curiosities, interesting fragments of life, for their own sake, not as elements in a narrative plot. As *Lolita* almost sinks under detail, so *Pale Fire* is deliberately detail and little else. It is the true pedantic instinct, though the pedantry is raised to high art. In Nabokov's masterly four-volume translation (with notes) of Pushkin's *Eugene Onegin*, the scholar can relax in a vast meadow of detail, knowing that the telling of a story has been handed over to someone else: his true joy is the amassing of bits of coloured glass, strangely shaped stones, old customs, weird words. It is perhaps significant that Nabokov is, as well as a scholar and a novelist, a butterfly-collector.

Perhaps his most attractive novel is one about a lonely, absorbed scholar in exile–sane, though, where Kinbote is mad. This is *Pnin*. The character of Timothy Pnin is one of the most amiable creations of modern fiction. A St Petersburg *bourgeois* who has come to teach in an American college, Pnin can never do anything right. He cannot master the intricacies of English pronunciation, the timetables of trains and buses, the gadgetry of modern America. And yet he represents a saner civilization than that represented by either Soviet Russia or capitalist America, and his devotion to scholarship (Russian literature) is genuine and profound. He deserves the characteristic lavishing of descriptive detail which bespeaks Nabokov's love of him:

'Ideally bald, sun-tanned, and clean-shaven, he began rather impressively with that great brown dome of his, tortoise-shell glasses (masking an infantile absence of eyebrows), apish upper lip, thick neck, and strong-man torso in a tightish tweed coat, but ended, somewhat disappointingly, in a pair of spindly legs (now flannelled and crossed) and frail-looking, almost feminine feet.'

Nabokov's biggest though not necessarily best novel to date is *Ada*, which has the expected verbal brilliance, pedantic learning wittily deployed, and a certain crotchetiness (he dislikes Borges and despises Freud and is happy to say so, though often with sly obliquity). But *Ada* goes further than his earlier works in not being content with the real world: he has to build an alternative one, in which Russia and North America fuse and time itself becomes very fluid. Indeed, the book resolves into an essay about time, in which the characters become so many footnotes. *Ada* is an uncompromising, coruscating, wholly original book, more likely to influence other novelists than to please ordinary readers. It will be

EXPORTS AND IMPORTS

a long time before lovers of the good yarn and the straightforward narrative are equal to its trickiness.

It is easy to disparage Nabokov's preciousness, his clogging of action with a luxuriance of self-indulgent detail, his curious despair that so often finds comic expression, the elements of perversity and pedantry which find outlet in heroes who are either ill-adjusted or frankly insane. But he is a major force in the contemporary novel, and an example of the manner in which an alien culture, the approach to English as to a strange but exciting tool, and what we may go on calling the European sensibility, are able to fertilize a tradition in danger of inanition through looking inwards and feeding on itself. He is an import for which America is rightly grateful. Exported back to Europe (which includes ourselves), he is beginning to influence the continent which he left behind. But there is no likelihood of his sweetening, with the breath of a rejected civilization, the thick air of the country which saw his birth and even the beginnings of his devotion to language.

See Bibliographical Note on p. 12

Chinua ACHEBE (1930–   )
Things Fall Apart. London, 1958
No Longer at Ease. London, 1960
Arrow of God. London, 1964
A Man of the People. 1966
Anthony BURGESS
See Chapter XVI, page 218
Paul BOWLES (1911–   )
Let It come Down. 1952
William BURROUGHS
See Chapter XIV, page 192

Rupert CROFT-COOKE (1903–   )
Give Him the Earth. London, 1930
Wolf from the Door. London, 1969
Cyprian EKWENSI (1921–   )
Jagua Nana. London, 1961
Iska. London, 1966
D. J. ENRIGHT (1920–   )
Academic Year. London, 1955
Gabriel FIELDING (1916–   )
Brotherly Love. London, 1954
In the Time of Greenbloom. London, 1958

Gabriel FIELDING (*continued*)
Eight Days. London, 1958
Through Streets Broad and
Narrow. 1960
The Birthday King. London,
1962
Gentlemen in their Season.
1966
Nadine GORDIMER (1923–)
The Lying Days. 1953
The Late Bourgeois World.
1966
Gerald HANLEY (1916–)
The Consul at Sunset. 1951
The Year of the Lion. 1953
Gilligan's Last Elephant.
1962
Wilson HARRIS (1921–)
Palace of the Peacock. London,
1960
The Far Journey of Oudin.
London, 1961
The Whole Armour. London,
1962
The Secret Ladder. London,
1963
Heartland, London, 1964
The Waiting Room. London,
1967
Tumatumari. London, 1968
John HEARNE (1926–)
Voices under the Window. Lon-
don, 1955
Stranger at the Gate. London,
1956
The Faces of Love. London,
1957 (as The Eye of the
Storm, Boston, 1958)
The Land of the Living. Lon-
don, 1961
Thomas HINDE (1926–)
Mr Nicholas. London, 1952
Happy as Larry. 1957

Thomas HINDE (*continued*)
For the Good of the Company.
London, 1961
The Cage. London, 1962
A Place like Home. London,
1962
Ninety Double Martinis. Lon-
don, 1963
The Day the Call Came, and
Games of Chance. London,
1964
Dan JACOBSON (1929–)
The Trap. 1955
The Beginners. 1966
Francis KING (1923–)
The Custom House. 1961
George LAMMING (1927–)
In the Castle of my Skin. Lon-
don, 1953
The Emigrants. London,
1954
Of Age and Innocence. London,
1958
Season of Adventure. London,
1960
John LODWICK (1916–59)
Somewhere a Voice is Calling.
1953
The Butterfly Net. London,
1954
The Starless Night. London,
1955
Mary MCMINNIES
The Flying Fox. London,
1956
Robin MAUGHAM (1916–)
The 1946 MS. London, 1943
The Link. New York, 1969
Edgar MITTELHOLZER (1909–)
A Morning at the Office. Lon-
don, 1950 (as Morning in
Trinidad, New York, 1950)
Shadows move among Them.

172

EXPORTS AND IMPORTS

Edgar MITTELHOLZER (*continued*)
London and Philadelphia, 1952
Children of the Kaywana. 1952

Vladimir NABOKOV (1899–   )
The Defence. Berlin, 1930, tr. London 1964
Lolita. Paris, 1955
Pnin. 1957
Pale Fire. 1962
Ada. 1969

V. S. NAIPAUL (1932–   )
Miguel Street. London, 1959
A House for Mr Biswas. London, 1961
Mr Stone and the Knights Companion. London, 1963
The Mimic Men. London, 1967

R. K. NARAYAN (1906–   )
The English Teacher. London, 1945
The Maneater of Malgudo. New York, 1961
The Sweet-vendor. London, 1967 (as The Vendor of Sweets, New York, 1967)

P. H. NEWBY
See Chapter V, page 72

Onuora NZEKWU (1928–   )
Blade among the Boys. London, 1962
Highlife for Lizards. London, 1965

Alan PATON (1903–   )
Cry, the Beloved Country. 1948

Jerzy PETERKIEWICZ (1916–   )
Fortune to Let. London, 1958
Isolation. London, 1959
The Quick and the Dead. London, 1961
Inner Circles. London, 1966
Green Flows the Bile. London, 1969

William PLOMER (1903–   )
Turbott Wolfe. 1926
Sado. London, 1931 (as They Never come Back, New York, 1932)
The Case is Altered. 1932
The Invaders. London, 1934
Museum Pieces. London, 1952

Balachandra RAJAN (1920–   )
The Dark Dancer. New York, 1958
Too Long in the West. London, 1961

RAJA RAO (1909–   )
The Serpent and the Rope. London, 1960

Daphne ROOKE (1914–   )
A Grove of Fever Trees. New York, 1950
Boy on the Mountain. London, 1969

Paul SCOTT (1920–   )
Johnnie Sahib. London, 1952
The Birds of Paradise. 1962
The Bender. 1963
The Corrida at San Feliù. 1964
The Day of the Scorpion. 1968

Salmuel SELVON (1924–   )
A Brighter Sun. London, 1952
An Island is a World. London, 1955
The Lonely Londoners. London, 1956
The Housing Lark. London, 1965

Katherine SIM (1913–   )
Malacca Boy. London, 1957
Black Rice. London, 1960
The Jungle Ends Here. London, 1961

Khushwant SINGH (1915–   )
I shall not Hear the Nightingale. New York, 1959

EXPORTS AND IMPORTS

Frank TOUHY (1925–)
  The Ice Saints. 1964
Amos TUTUOLA (1920–)
  The Palm-wine Drinkard. London, 1952

Amos TUTUOLA (*continued*)
  Ajaiyi and his Inherited Poverty
  London, 1967
Susan YORKE (1915–)
  Captain China. London, 1961

XIV

World Tour, etc.

So far our concern has been almost entirely with novelists who work in English, and, if we can rightly speak of matters of 'duty' in respect of an activity dedicated to pleasure, our primary 'duty' is to read Anglo-American or Commonwealth novelists. But, apart from that, most of us have to gain our knowledge of foreign writers from translations, and the greater the writer is, the more difficult he is to translate. This is because he is thoroughly *inside* his own language, exploiting its tones and rhythms and idioms and ambiguities. One of the important 'international' novels of our day is Boris Pasternak's *Doctor Zhivago*, which, so Edmund Wilson tells us, cannot properly be appreciated if we do not read it in Russian: this is because it is crammed with symbols resident in the language itself. Even the name of the hero has a special significance for the Russian reader. *Zhivago* means 'the living', and it carries overtones of a liturgical nature (in the twenty-fourth chapter of St. Luke in the Russian Bible, the angels ask the women who come to Christ's tomb: '*Chto vui ishchyetye zhivago myezhdu myer-tvuikh?*–Why do you seek the living among the dead?'). Similarly, Zhivago's first name, Yuri, is a form of 'George', and his aim in the novel is to destroy dragons. Wilson says, '*Doctor Zhivago* . . . is studded with symbols and significant puns . . . there is something in it of *Finnegans Wake* . . .'. And *Finnegans Wake* itself is a book that, though attempts to translate it into other languages have been made, cannot yield its true meaning in any language but Joyce's own.

WORLD TOUR, ETC.

I have myself seen, in translations of my own books, how the original can be misunderstood by the translator and thus be totally misrepresented in his version. To give one small example, I make a character in *The Wanting Seed* sneeze: 'Howrashyouare'. This was solemnly taken to be a statement–'How rash you are'–and not a noise, and 'How rash you are' was solemnly and literally translated. If we wish to read a novelist who is concerned with the manipulation of language, we ought to approach him–as we approach foreign poets–in the original. Otherwise we must take a translation only as an approximation.

The further away we travel from those languages of the Indo-Germanic group which (like the Romance and Teutonic and Slav tongues) we regard as sisters of English, the more difficult do we find it to translate literature into literary English, and this may explain our comparative ignorance about what is going on in the Japanese or Indonesian or Chinese novel. And, of course, there is a great paucity of translators from those languages. Probably the only Japanese novelist who is well known in the West is Junichiro Tanizaki, and his works–*The Key, The Makiota Sisters, Some Prefer Nettles, Diary of a Mad Old Man*–are acceptable because they deal with a Westernized Japan and have (*The Key* especially) a frank and lavish sexual content. That we read so few Chinese novels is undoubtedly due to the fact that Chinese writers are in a strong ideological grip and do not tell the real truth about life–only the truth as the Party sees it. The same is true about the fiction of most Communist countries, though–as we shall see–there are exceptions.

Of novels in Malay (either in its Malaysian or Indonesian form) there have been few: the tale, or long short story, has not yet grown into full-length fiction. But such novels as have appeared in Indonesia still wait for a Western audience. One exception is the remarkable *Twilight in Djarkata*, by Mochtar Lubis–a bitter indictment of the Soekarno régime, which sent its author to prison. The Tamil writers of Malaysia have written much verse and many short stories but, as far as one can tell, no longer fiction at all. And, with all these remoter languages, we have to face a hard but necessary question: have they produced enough work valuable enough to merit translation?

To come nearer home, Russia is big enough and productive enough to allow some works of universal import and artistic merit to squeeze through the ideological mesh, though one of the greatest novels of the century, Pasternak's, has been loudly and inevitably reviled by the Soviet gods. Nabokov has said: 'There is no Soviet literature', and Nabokov, like Dr Johnson, is a dangerous person to disagree with. Nevertheless, there is a powerful renaissance in the field of poetry taking place in Russia–a movement of young men who reject the correct ideological line–and where poetry flourishes the novel (in a country with so magnificent a fictional tradition) ought to flourish too. Yet many Russians believe, along with Aleksandr Solzhenitsyn, that the long novel is out of place in a technological age: the long evenings of reading aloud by the family fireside are dead and gone. It must be admitted that Soviet Russia has produced some very fine short-story writers, but it is perhaps significant that many of these belong to Tarusa, the writers' colony outside Moscow, where writers are almost a law unto themselves, resistant to the pressures of the 'official line'. It is perhaps significant also that *Pages from Tarusa*–a very interesting anthology compiled by Konstantin Paustovsky–was withdrawn from sale by the authorities, though not before a few thousand copies had been sold. There is nothing politically offensive in the compilation, but there is evidence of individuality, boldness, fearless speaking-up, and a willingness to be influenced by writers of the decadent West–particularly Ernest Hemingway.

Andrew Field has said that the short story 'predominates in Russia because Russian fiction is just awakening from a long period of dormancy, and it is only natural that the first steps in serious fiction should be taken in a form of a more limited scope'. Aleksandr Solzhenitsyn, champion of the short-story form, has nevertheless attempted the further step–towards the *novella*, or brief novel. His *One Day in the life of Ivan Denisovich*–a study of life in a Stalinist concentration camp–has been universally praised, but one wonders whether the praise was given to the subject-matter or to the style and form. It is a terse piece of writing that gains most of its effects from restraint, but there is a lack of individual life in the character of Ivan Denisovich himself: he is, like the factory-workers and collective farmers of the orthodox optimistic Soviet novel, too much of a type or abstraction. And his *Cancer Ward*, a bitter attack on Soviet repression, naturally unpublished in Russia, similarly seeks approbation for its political daring rather than its status as a work of art. A novel that breaks free from the themes of Soviet history is what is really needed to assure Western readers that the renaissance in literature is really proceeding.

One such novel—*A Starry Ticket*, by Vasily Aksyonov—is about real people, not about past wrongs and future glories. It is modelled on *The Catcher in the Rye* and hence is full of youthful revolt against phoney values; the traditional stiltedness of the Soviet novel dissolves into a jazz-pattern of slang. It is not a great novel, but it is an encouraging sign of new directions. And there is Vladimir Tendryakov, who—in works like *The Extraordinary*—is able to make a 'positive' character (atheist and good member of the Party) into a sympathetic and tolerant humanist. Perhaps the most hopeful sign of all is to be found in Abram Tertz's *novelle*, which take a thoroughly Western interest in probing the human mind, diagnosing sexual conflict and paranoia—admitting, in fact, to psychological subtleties that the mechanistic philosophy of the State would rather pretend did not exist. A new wave of novelists will certainly appear in Soviet Russia, so long as the anti-Stalinist liberal thaw persists. We must wait and, in the meantime, make do with little snacks of short stories.

The rest of the Iron Curtain countries seem to be exporting very little fiction. The most considerable post-war novel from Poland—*Ferdydurke*, by Witold Gombrowicz—proved to be a very late reissue. It has been published in Warsaw before the war and then, in 1939, was suppressed along with Polish liberty. Translated into Spanish and published in Buenos Aires in 1947, it found little favour when it re-entered an Eastern Europe suffering from a new tyranny. But, with the coming of the 'thaw', *Ferdydurke* was republished in Warsaw—in 1957, ten years after its first appearance. Most of its readers in the West have been baffled by it. Led to expect a trenchant satire on totalitarianism, they found instead a surrealistic fantasy which made game of all theories and offended the earnest Utopians through its Rabelaisian gaiety. In 1958 Gombrowicz's work was once more suppressed, and it had to wait for a French translation in 1959 before critics could start talking again of a work of 'capital importance' and 'a strange masterpiece'. It is difficult book to summarize, but, if it has a recurrent theme, it is the theme of depersonalization. The author's last words are 'There is no shelter from face except in face, and we can escape from men only by taking refuge in other men. And from the arch-bum there is no refuge. I fled, with my face in my hands.' With the turning of the world upside down, the human bottom is replacing the human face. Gombrowicz's argument seems to be that this depersonalization is a product of contemporary civilization in general, but the dictators (Nazi first, then Communist) thought that the author was getting only at them. Besides, this theme of 'anal tyranny' was unhealthy.

Perhaps Hungary's most important post-war novelist was Gusztáv Rab, now dead. He still awaits recognition in the West and deserves it on the strength of one novel alone—*Sabaria*. This develops very skilfully a theme which oppresses those Iron Curtain countries that have not succeeded in stamping out the opium-habit of the people—the conflict of Christianity and Communism. On the site of the old Roman city of Sabaria the Hungarian city of Szombathely stands. To it, on a 'cultural tour', go three men (a priest, an archaeologist and a lung specialist), but they find themselves involved in a strange happening—an old half-mad woman claims to have heard the voice of St Martin speaking to her from her sewing-machine. This is taken up by the State as a fabrication 'aimed at overthrowing the Socialist order in Hungary', and it is the Bishop of Szombathely who is blamed. The conflict between Church and State is not delineated in the usual black-and-white of a puppet-play. The tragedy of life lies in the fact that good and evil reside where they will, not where a uniform of an office leads us to expect; that a Church can contain selfish and corruptible priests and a Communist Party can show humanity. 'There's nothing wrong in lying to the Devil', says one of the priests, excusing his own crimes against the régime. Some of us might be tempted to answer that lying is always wrong. This is a very disturbing and beautifully written book.

Modern Greek fiction is best represented by the work of Nikos Kazantzakis, whose *Zorba the Greek* is well known through its film and stage adaptations. Perhaps his best book is *The Last Temptation*, which presents the life of Christ as a struggle to overcome the Devil which is in all men (incarnated in the flesh, the will, the desire for temporal gratification and power) and to achieve the Good which can be found only in the spirit. The author himself said: 'Within me are the dark immemorial forces of the Evil One, human and pre-human; within me too are the luminous forces, human and pre-human, of God–and my soul is the arena where these two armies have clashed and met. The anguish is intense.' The novel is alive with dialectical power; every page shouts with argument and mental struggle. In many ways *The Last Temptation* depicts the final stage of Kazantzakis's own fight to 'reconcile opposites and unite them in his own personality' (words of his translator, P. A Bien); it glows with the author's personality. Here is Christ's death from, as it were, the inside:

'His head quivered. Suddenly he remembered where he was and why he felt pain. A wild indomitable joy took possession of him. No, no, he was not a coward, a deserter, a traitor. No, he was nailed to the cross. He had stood his ground honourably to the very end; he had kept his word. The moment he cried ELI ELI and fainted, Temptation had captured him for a split-second and led him astray. The joys, marriages and children were lies; the decrepit degraded old men who shouted coward, deserter, traitor at him were lies. All–all were illusions sent by the Devil. His disciples were alive and thriving. They had gone over sea and land and were proclaiming the Good News. Everything had turned out as it should, glory be to God!'

'He uttered a triumphant cry: IT IS ACCOMPLISHED!

WORLD TOUR, ETC.

'And it was as though he had said: Everything has begun.'

Italy has, since the days of men like D'Annunzio and Pirandello, produced little literature that has made a world impact. Moravia, Vittorini, Pratolini, it has been said, are fine novelists but not true *maestri*, and the impression we gain from their work is of a lack of conviction (ironical, when we consider who lives at Rome), without which great literature is not possible. And yet post-war Italy had at least plenty to be bitter about—a war which it had not wished to fight, Nazi persecution, the mess of a broken society, the realization (a belated one) that there was great poverty in Southern Italy and Sicily, as well as age-old oppression. But, except for Carlo Levi's *Christ Stopped at Eboli*, very few of the bitter novels of disillusion have made much mark in the English-speaking countries. To many non-Italians, the Italian novel means mainly Alberto Moravia—the realism of works like *A Woman of Rome*, *The Time of Indifference*, and *Two Adolescents*, and the mature but hopeless philosophy of *La Noia* (*The Empty Canvas*). *La Noia* is, I think, a superb study of modern man's predicament—his sense of estrangement, his inability to find substitutes for the old values of life in a healthy society. *La noia* (emptiness, boredom) is imposed, in Moravia's philosophy, on all human acts: everything man does is less a product of the creative urge than an attempt to escape from *la noia*. Perhaps even God created man out of *la noia*.

As important as Moravia is Elio Vittorini, whose main aim is to present—in books like *Erica and Her Brother* and *La Garibaldina*—man's attempt to recapture dignity and happiness in a world torn by ideological strife. Vasco Pratolini is more explicit in his trilogy, *Una Storia Italiana* (*An Italian History*): he is not concerned with man in general but with man in Italy, specifically the Italian working man and his own contribution (Pratolini has been rapped for this by Marxist critics) to a Fascist decadence which has been most often blamed on the middle class alone. Political consciousness in Italy tends to infect artistic judgements, and Giuseppe di Lampedusa's *Il Gattopardo* (*The Leopard*)—that dignified and exact, though aristocratic, picture of Sicilian society—has been attacked as reactionary, even Fascist. But great art

WORLD TOUR, ETC.

transcends questions of partisanship. It also, alas, sometimes transcends translation, else Carlo Emilio Gadda's *Quel Pasticciaccio Brutto di Via Merulana* would be universally recognized as the Rabelaisian masterpiece it is.

Italy's partner in post-war disillusionment was Germany, and the disillusionment took extreme, desperate, essentially Teutonic forms in the first post-war novels. Works like Hermann Kasack's *The Town Beyond the River* and Elisabeth Langgässer's *The Indelible Seal* were full of visions of human depravity. These authors were right to see in the Nazi descent to the pit an image of the fall of man in general. Was there any hope for him? Elisabeth Langgässer (partly Jewish, but essentially a Catholic writer) thought that he could only be redeemed by God's grace, not through his own efforts at rehabilitation. Writers like Heinrich Böll have taken a less mystical and traditional, more common-sense, view of Germany's sickness. The first task that Böll (and Hans Werner Richter and other members of the organization of writers called 'Group 47') embarked upon was the virtual creation of a new literary language–one clean, spare, workmanlike, altogether purged of Nazi debasements. With this fresh, bare German they recorded the soldier's life and disillusionment (Richter's *The Vanquished*; Böll's *Where Art Thou, Adam?*), and they kept their eyes open for elements of corruption in the new Germany to which the soldiers returned. Böll's *Not Just at Christmas* satirizes the so-called German economic miracle; a German returning from exile asks, in *Billiards at Half-past Nine*, 'Am I wrong if I find the present Germans not less bad than those I left?' This latter book presents the whole history of the German middle class, from Kaiser to Hitler, in the compass of a few hours, using an easy, rather crude, symbolism. It finds little good in the solid, complacent burghers, and its reply to the homecoming German's question is: 'No.'

Apart from the guilt and bitterness derived from a consideration of Germany's immediate past, Germany has the further shame of her own division, its visible symbol that wall running across what was once a proud city. Uwe Johnson's *Speculations about Jacob* is about the relations between East and West Germany, its hero

WORLD TOUR, ETC.

Jacob–man suffering from that division which is man's 'wearisome condition'–caught between two forces and hence paralysed. *The Third Book About Achim* (Johnson's second novel) is about the attempt of a West German journalist to write the biography of an East German sports celebrity. But it cannot be written, for facts and opinions and rumours about Achim are, because of this same division, in such conflict that the truth cannot be found. Johnson's own style and construction are deliberately chaotic here. Generally speaking, his interest in technical experiment makes him difficult to translate; he is not so well known as another novelist of equal stature–Günter Grass.

Grass's first novel, *The Tin Drum*, is the imaginary autobiography of a mad dwarf who can recall the shameful past of the Nazi régime by beating his magic drum. Grass spares us nothing, but his approach lacks the grey guilt of so many German novels about the same period; he has handed over his narrative to a creature who is too innocent to be possessed of any ethical attitude to the events he chronicles. The book is a big, bawdy, sprawling triumph. The later *Dog Years* deals with Hitler's last days. In finding out what happened to the Führer's missing dog, we piece together–from all sorts of disjunct sources–the story of declining power and a desperate end. Again, we are impressed by a great satirical gift, mockery, bawdry, a powerful and idiosyncratic personality, but deplore the lack of real artistic unity. And one wonders what these gifted Germans will do when their recent history has been plucked bare of fictional feathers. (Grass's recent *Local Anaesthetic* is set in a dentist's surgery: the bad teeth of the world still seem to be those pulled out in 1945.) The Anglo-American novel has other things to do than atone for the past or blast national character. The works of Grass, Johnson, and the rest are remarkable commentaries on history, but a novel ought to be more than that.

The novelists of France have always had more influence on the Anglo-American tradition than those of any other country–with the exception of Imperialist Russia. In the nineteen-thirties the great name was André Malraux, whose *La Condition Humaine* was

WORLD TOUR, ETC.

regarded by some as representing the high-water mark in a new kind of fiction—the committed, or *engagé*. After the war, the work of the 'existentialist' writers—notably Jean-Paul Sartre and Albert Camus—represented an even newer kind of philosophical novel. And now the *nouvelle vague*—the new wave, associated with the so-called 'anti-novel'—is stimulating new attitudes to the art of fiction. The French take two things seriously in this field—ideas and technique—and when they talk or act we would do well to watch and listen.

The kind of novel that Jean-Paul Sartre has written exemplifies an attitude to life that was conditioned by the German occupation of France. That period was 'the age of assassins' foretold by the poet Rimbaud. As Sartre says, in his *What is Literature?*:

'We have been taught to take Evil seriously. It is neither our fault nor our merit if we lived in a time when torture was a daily fact. Chateaubriand, Oradour, the Rue des Saussaies, Dachau and Auschwitz have all demonstrated to us that Evil is not an appearance, that knowing its cause does not dispel it, that it is not opposed to Good as a confused idea is to a clear one. . . . In spite of ourselves, we come to this conclusion, which will seem shocking to lofty souls: Evil cannot be redeemed.'

By what may seem a paradox, men like Sartre recovered a sense of the dignity of human freedom (lost during the stale, tired period of the nineteen-thirties) at a time when they were least free. There was the Resistance; there was the ultimate and irreducible freedom to say 'No' to Evil. But if Evil is a reality, man has the power to say 'No' to other kinds of reality. In a Godless age (Sartre is an atheist) man can say 'No' to the whole structure of the universe, to history, to nature, to everything except his own capacity to deny. It is, in a sense, the freedom that Christians have ascribed to God, and, in possessing that freedom, man has replaced God.

Man is, exists, because he can say 'No' (Descartes taught this a long time ago), but what do words like 'is' and 'exist' mean, what is the nature of 'being'? Sartre, in a long book called *Being and Nothingness* which he wrote during the Occupation, said there were two kinds of being—being-in-itself (*en-soi*) and being-for-itself (*pour-soi*). Being-in-itself is the property (or essence) possessed by objects—a cigarette or glass of whisky is itself, no more. But being-for-itself is the essence of consciousness, which can look outside its own bounds, seeing into the future, looking back at the past —a free ranger, while an object is not free. Cease to be conscious, and you become a thing. Be conscious, and you need not necessarily be yourself in the sense that a cigarette is itself: you may transcend yourself or fall short of yourself. This *existence* is man's special attribute, his great glory, but at the same time it is tragic—existence shifts, is unsure, lacking the solidity of the self-contained thing that has being-in-itself. Man sees himself in a huge universe that ignores him—an insubstantial being-for-itself that can only achieve reality through the exercise of choice (like saying 'No' to Evil). Because man is free to choose, he will use this faculty to show that he exists, and he may well choose the hard way because (being free) the hard way is not *imposed* upon him by any power in the universe. Mary McCarthy, in her novel *The Groves of Academe*, gives us a light-hearted example of how this capacity for choice works out in everyday practice. We feel that the washing-up must be done—a duty, an obligation that faces us. But if we refuse to accept this duty (remembering our freedom of choice) we are able to approach the washing-up existentially: we will do it because—exercising our choice to do it —free action justifies our existence.

Sartre's plays, short stories and novels are passionate embodiments of a philosophy rather than genuine acts. In his first novel, *Nausée*, which portrays that age of *salauds* (or 'stinkers') which preceded the Second World War and the call to heroism and action, the hero Roquentin discovers existence through disgust (hence the title). But the disgust is more philosophical than we are used to in a novel. Roquentin sees a chestnut-tree in a park and is overwhelmed by a sense of its absurdity—an excessive mass of being-in-itself with no ultimate reason for existing. It is an expression of the *yin* (big, blooming, fruitful but passive), while Roquentin, like his creator, is on the side of the *yang*—the hard, spare, creative masculine force. The seeking out and realization of this force–the will to accept freedom–is the theme of the *roman fleuve* called *Les Chemins de la Liberté* (*The Roads to Liberty*), a work of which three volumes have already appeared. Sartre has great gifts, but there is something of the sprawl and excess of that chestnut-tree in his writing. Characters and events crowd upon each other, and we never become aware of the disciplined, essentially artistic, aim of the true novelist. It is Sartre the philosopher who really counts. His influence on the novel is more important than his actual achievement as a novelist.

Albert Camus is a thinker, like Sartre, but he has joined the classic writers (he died prematurely) as a great novelist, not as a great philosopher. Books like *The Plague, State of Siege, The Just Assassins* are primarily studies of real people and places–they impress as fiction–and only secondarily imaginative expressions of ideas. Camus's ideas are intelligible enough, though to appreciate them we must have some knowledge of the writer's own background. Born of working-class French Algerians, he knew early privation, and tuberculosis cut short what might have been a distinguished academic career. He rejected the optimism of Christianity and preferred to see man as a victim of the natural order, an absurd figure to whom the only sure reality is death. But something can be salvaged out of the hopelessness, the early book *Nuptials* seems to say: a pagan acceptance of nature, the joyous exercise of the senses. The collapse of France reinforced his pessimism, though, like Sartre, he found a kind of salvation in action, in working for the Resistance. In *The Myth of Sisyphus*, man is presented as a creature condemned (like Sisyphus of the Greek legend) to pushing a heavy weight up a steep hill, only to see it fall down again. Sisyphus is in hell, damned to this hopeless task for all eternity; man finds release from it in death. An empty universe, man as an absurdity, the necessity for action–these form the central themes of Camus's fiction.

The absurdity has something heroic in it, as *The Plague* shows. This may be taken as an allegory: the plague that descends on an Algerian city is an occupying tyranny, and men come alive through stoicism, courage, and the exercise of charity–redeemed from

WORLD TOUR, ETC.

absurdity by action. *The Stranger* (Camus's earliest, and some say best, novel) is about a man who breaks out of a constitutional apathy and nihilism by, for no apparent reason, shooting an Arab to death. Condemned to the guillotine, he is urged by a priest to believe in an after-life, and now for the first time he shows passion. Rejecting survival after death with great vehemence, he realizes that his apathy was due to his passive acceptance of the fact of death as the end of everything. Now he accepts this fact actively: it is a positive basis for engaging life. If death seems to make life meaningless, it is up to the human will to impose meaning. But, ironically, it is too late for him to start to live life again.

What we admire in Camus, apart from the skill of the novelist, is the courage and honesty with which he tries to attack the nothingness which seems to be the human lot. The human condition is absurd, the universe is indifferent to man; why not then commit suicide? But this is to play into the hands of the enemy; moreover, a suicide is an individual act which may or may not be performed –it cannot be posited as a general philosophical principle. We are left–as in Sarte–with the necessity of being human, which means performing the acts of a human being.

Sartre and Camus take a bold hard look at reality; Jean Genet seems to lock himself up away from it, spinning fanciful cocoons about himself. But reality for Genet really means society–the society which rejected him as an orphaned child, condemned to live in public institutions. Genet took to an anti-social life of crime and homosexuality and learned to admire criminals, the rejected men of the world, those who oppose what the world calls normality. The best introduction to his perverse but highly idiosyncratic work is the novel *Our Lady of the Flowers*, whose aim seems to be to purify, scent and embellish the lives of the imprisoned and rejected, to transform (to use his own words) 'by means of the language, reputedly base matter into what is regarded as noble matter'. A character wishing to go to the lavatory talks of his 'two bouquets of violets'; a character who picks his nose plucks from his nostrils 'acacia and violet petals'. This enflowering of the sordid indicates a desire to remain cut off from action, from the dirty human realities: if one acts, one must act only through the imagination. Genet's work, admired by Sartre, seems to have little to do with the more fashionable literary movements of France: he is very much on his own.

The practitioners of the *Nouveau Roman*–or the anti-novel, as it is sometimes called–claim to derive their approach to life from Sartre's *Nausea* and Camus's *The Stranger*. What they take is the element of absurdity, but it goes much further than Sartre's existentialism or Camus's stoicism. The universe ignores man, true, but let us not think of the universe as a remote abstraction: the very objects that surround man are part of the universe, and man's existence is a matter of complete indifference to them. The novels of Alain Robbe-Grillet–especially his best known, *Jealousy*–are interested in solid objects, not in vague flights of metaphysical or religious or psychological or political speculation. They represent the end of the old pathetic fallacy, in which objects threw back a radar echo of man's own emotions: the world of man and the world of things have lost the fanciful, even sentimental, link that was forged by human egoism. In *Jealousy* (which is a thrilling enough 'human' story if we are bold enough to skip) Robbe-Grillet is almost geometrical in his approach to the exterior world. Things are themselves, not symbols or metaphors, and Robbe-Grillet is devoted enough to things to be called a *chosiste*.

With this concentration on objects, the pace of the novel slows down. It reaches its slowest in the works of Nathalie Sarraute, who goes beyond the mere representation of objects and concerns herself with what she calls *tropismes*–the responses of the human mind to external stimuli. A novel called *Tropismes* was published by her as early as 1939–an account of the responses of a group of middle-class women to the daily routine of their lives. As response has little to do with the apparatus of 'character', Mme Sarraute is able to present the minds of all these women as one mind–a collective psychological machine. Her much more recent *Le Planétarium* shows a number of consciousnesses–each with a name, each speaking for itself–circling like lonely planets until a chance event causes them all to collide. Mme Sarraute is still concerned with that psychological area which Henri Peyre sees as containing 'formless, nascent moves, slow repetitions of our mental organs, elementary reactions of our flesh or of our nerves which never reach the stage of half-conscious elaboration in our brains'. We are moving away, with both Mme Sarraute and Robbe-Grillet, from the concept of a novel with solid recognizable characters who are involved in conventional plots on a thoroughly conscious level, the world of things but dimly seen, or when seen, only acceptable as symbols.

The anti-novel can, as it melts character into sheer perception, also melt that time through which character moves, remoulding it. In the novels of Michel Butor (like *Passing Time*) the dimension can be reversed: we can live our memories backwards. Soon it no longer becomes necessary to see the novel itself (the printed book) as a model of the old dreary temporal treadmill (start at page one and work through to the end). A novel can be like a dictionary or encyclopaedia, to be opened at any page. We must welcome any attempt to broaden the outlook of the novel, to make something truly contemporary (too many of the modern novelists we call important do little that Dickens and Thackeray did not do), to absorb the new views of the world that the sciences are giving us. But it is dangerous to move the novel too far out of the sphere of enjoyment: any work of art must be a compromise between what the writer can give and what the reader can take. Unless, that is, novel-writing is to become a mere rarefied hobby conducted in a little family circle or a salon of sympathetic friends.

This kind of French experimentation in the novel is not new. Laurence Sterne (whom many Continental writers acknowledge as their master) turned the fabric of conventional fiction inside out in *Tristram Shandy* in the eighteenth century. Virginia Woolf was playing with time and character in the nineteen-twenties. Philip Toynbee, in the late nineteen-thirties, attempted a multiple-view novel called *Tea With Mrs. Goodman*, in which a single event is looked at over and over again, but from different angles. In *The Garden to the Sea* we have the 'fracturing' of personality in which

WORLD TOUR, ETC.

Robbe-Grillet is so much interested. Toynbee has gone further than the French novelists in jettisoning–in the novel-sequence beginning with *Pantaloon*–the use of prose, finding verse a subtler medium for the rendering of *nuances* of thought (in effect, returning to an older tradition–that of Robert Browning's *The Ring and the Book* and Elizabeth Barrett Browning's *Aurora Leigh*). Even Eric Linklater, who, on the strength of such books as *Juan in America* and *Magnus Merriman*, is regarded as a 'popular' novelist, a highly literate entertainer, attempted in *Roll of Honour*, a 'static' novel of reminiscence: a retired schoolmaster muses about some of his old pupils, dead in the war, and muses not in prose but in free verse.

Still, some recent British novels show the influence not of native but of French example. Christine Brooke-Rose, after fine 'orthodox' books like *The Languages of Love* and *The Middle Men*, produced a complex anti-novel in *Out*, which is set in an imaginary future England ruled by coloured people but, instead of indulging in the abstractions of fantasy, meticulously records the surface of life:

'A fly straddles another fly on the faded denim stretched over the knee. Sooner or later, the knee will have to make a move, but now it is immobilized by the two flies, the lower of which is so still that it seems dead. The fly on top is on the contrary quite agitated, jerking tremulously, then convulsively, putting out its left foreleg to whip, or maybe to stroke some sort of reaction out of the fly beneath, which, however, remains so still that it seems dead. A microscope might perhaps reveal animal ecstasy in its innumerable eyes, but only to the human mind behind the microscope, and besides, the fetching and rigging up of a microscope, if one were available, would interrupt the flies.'

And so on. Christine Brooke-Rose, like the anti-novelists in France and, for that matter, like James Joyce, does not see why observation of the texture of life should be speeded up, and hence falsified, by the needs of the ordinary 'plotted' novel, with its swift action and contrived relationships and neat resolutions. The same is true of Rayner Heppenstall's *The Connecting Door*, which has a special authenticity as a British example of the anti-novel, since Heppenstall has written a fine book (*The Fourfold Tradition*) on the French new wave. Again the rule is texture, close notation of surface, refusal to be hurried. The narrator-hero does not even have a name.

It is perhaps too soon to deliver judgement on the work of William Burroughs, the American expatriate, since some of his books–suppressed for various reasons, though the chief one is alleged obscenity–require long brooding on, and availability must precede brooding. *The Naked Lunch* has at last appeared in England–a straightforward but amorphous satire, bitter as Swift, on the world inhabited by the drug-addict, a rapacious world that eats the weak (the drug-addict) and preys on the needy (the drug-addict). Burroughs's strength lies in his uninhibited prose, his ability to attack the nerves, but this prose is, in *The Naked Lunch*, in the service of a didactic aim (as in Swift's satires, which are not really novels), not an artistic one. It is in books like *The Ticket that Exploded* that Burroughs seems to revel in a new medium for its own sake–a medium totally fantastic, spaceless, timeless, in which the normal sentence is fractured, the cosmic tries to push its way through bawdry, and the author shakes the reader as a dog shakes a rat:

'Wooden pegs in another room forgotten memory controlling the structure of his Scandinavian outhouse skin–The man flicked Ali's clothes–Prisoner pants with wriggling movement stood naked now in green mummy flesh, hanging vines and deflated skin –Death kissed him–His breath talked to the switch blade–He dropped Ali on the last parasite from the shelf before news-reels shut off–Looked like frog eggs–He was shoving the eggs–Poo Poo snickered, coming alive in his rectum like green neon . . .'

What is the book about? It is about Mr and Mrs D., Green Tony, Iron Claws, Sammy the Butcher, Willy the Fink, the Subliminal Kid, Izzy the Push, Limestone Jones and Hamburger Mary–members of the Nova Mob, 'a gang of cosmic thugs tracked from planet to planet by Inspector Lee of the Nova Police'. In other words, a kind of mad science-fiction, literature as

WORLD TOUR, ETC.

a total release from the bondages of gravity and inhibition alike, sometimes baffling, often exhilarating.

We must welcome experiment in the novel, and we must allow it to go as far as it wishes–in the direction of Burroughs's present work in progress, which has three streams of consciousness written in three parallel columns, or the counterpointing of a story in the main text and a commentary in footnotes, or the dissolution of the traditional reading procedure (as in Butor or in *Pale Fire*– which, says Nabokov, ought to be read in two copies at the same time: one for the poem, one for the commentary), or the cracking of character and plot and dialogue and all the glories of the conventional novel. But it would be a pity to throw overboard all that the novel has learned throughout the slow centuries of its development. This is something that John Barth, in writing his massive experimental epic *Giles Goatboy*, seems to realize. The really great revolutionary novel–like *Ulysses*–encloses the past before moving on into the future.

See Bibliographical Note on p. 12

Vasily AKSYONOV (or Vasilii AKSENOV) (1932–   )
A Starry Ticket. Moscow, 1961, tr. London, 1962.
It's Time, my Friend, it's Time. tr. London, 1969
Heinrich BOLL (1917–   )
Where art Thou, Adam?, Frankfurt-am-Main, 1955, tr. 1955
Not just at Christmas. Frank-am-Main, 1952
Billiards at Half-past Nine. Cologne, 1959, tr. London, 1961

Christine BROOKE-ROSE (1923–   )
The Languages of Love. London, 1957
The Middlemen. London, 1961
Out. London, 1964
Such. London, 1966
Between. London, 1968
William BURROUGHS (1914–   )
The Naked Lunch. Paris, 1959
The Soft Machine. Paris, 1961
The Ticket that Exploded. Paris, 1962
Nova Express. New York, 1962

WORLD TOUR, ETC.

Michel BUTOR (1926–   )
Passing Time. Paris, 1957,
   tr. New York, 1960
Niagara.
Albert CAMUS (1913–60)
The Stranger (or The Outsider).
   Paris, 1942, tr. 1946
The Plague. Paris, 1947. tr. 1948
The Fall. Paris, 1956, tr. Lon-
   don, 1957
Carlo Emilio GADDA (1893–   )
Quel pasticciacio brutto di via
   Merulana. Milan, 1957
Jean GENET (1909–   )
Our Lady of the Flowers.
   Lyons, 1948, tr. Paris, 1949
Funeral Rites. 1947, tr. London
   1969
Witold GOMBROWICZ (1904–   )
Ferdydurke. Warsaw, 1937,
   tr. London, 1961
Pornografia. Paris, 1960,
   tr. London, 1966
Cosmos. Paris, 1965,
   tr. London, 1967
Gunter GRASS (1927–   )
The Tin Drum. Darmstadt,
   1959 tr. London, 1962
Cat and Mouse. Berlin, 1961,
   tr. 1963
Dog Years. Neuwied, 1963,
   tr. 1965
Local Anaesthetic. Neuweid,
   1969, tr. 1970
Rayner HEPPENSTALL (1911–   )
The Connecting Door.
   London, 1962
The Shearers. London, 1969
Uwe JOHNSON (1934–   )
Speculations about Jacob.
   Frankfurt-am-Main, 1959,
   tr. 1963
The Third Book about Achim.

Uwe JOHNSON (*continued*)
   Frankfurt-am-Main, 1961,
   tr. New York, 1967
An Absence. Frankfurt-am-
   Main, 1964, tr. London, 1969
Hermann KASACK (1896–   )
The City beyond the River.
   Frankfurt-am-Main, 1949,
   tr. London, 1953
Nikos KAZANTZAKIS (1885–1957)
Zorba the Greek. 1946,
   tr, London, 1952
Christ Recrucified. tr. Oxford,
   1954
The Last Temptation. 1959,
   tr. New York, 1960
Giuseppe di LAMPEDUSA
   (1896–1957)
The Leopard. 1958, tr. 1960
Elisabeth LANGGASSER (1899–
   1950)
The Indelible Seal. Hamburg,
   1946
Carlo LEVI (1902–   )
Christ stopped at Eboli. 1946,
   tr. 1947.
Eric LINKLATER (1899–   )
Juan in America. 1931
Magnus Merriman. 1934
Roll of Honour. London, 1961
A Terrible Freedom. London,
   1966
Mochtar LUBIS (1922–   )
Twilight in Djarkarta.
   tr. London, 1963
André MALRAUX (1901–   )
La Condition Humaine. Paris,
   1933, tr. as Man's Fate, New
   York, 1934, and as Storm in
   Shanghai, London, 1934
Alberto MORAVIA (1907–   )
The Time of Indifference.
   Milan, 1929, tr. 1953

WORLD TOUR, ETC.

Alberto MORAVIA (*continued*)
Woman of Rome. Milan, 1947, tr. 1949
Two Adolescents, tr. New York 1950:
Agostino. Milan, 1945, tr. London, 1947
Disobedience. Milan, 1948, tr. London, 1950
The Empty Canvas. Milan, 1960, tr. 1961
Boris PASTERNAK
See Chapter XI, page 141
Vasco PRATOLINI (1913–)
An Italian History:
Metello. Florence, 1955, tr. London and Boston, 1968
La Scialo. Milan, 1960
Konstantin PAUSTOVSKY (1893–68)
Pages from Tarusa.
Gusztáv RAB (1901–63)
Journey into the Blue. Paris, 1959, tr. 1960
A Room in Budapest. Paris, 1960, tr. London, 1962
Sabaria. tr. London, 1963
Hans Werner RICHTER (1908–)
Die Geschlagenen (The Vanquished). 1949, tr. as The Odds Against Us, London, 1950, and as Beyond Defeat, New York, 1950
Alain ROBBE-GRILLET (1922–)
Jealousy. 1957, tr. New York, 1959
In the Labyrinth, tr. New York, 1960
Nathalie SARRAUTE (1900–)
Tropismes. Paris, 1939, tr. London, 1964
The Planetarium. Paris, 1959, tr. New York, 1960

Jean-Paul SARTRE (1905–)
La Nausée. 1938, tr. 1949 as Nausea (New York) and The Diary of Antoine Roquentin (London)
The Roads to Liberty:
The Age of Reason. 1945, tr. 1947
The Reprieve. 1945, tr. New York, 1947
Iron in the Soul. 1949, tr. 1950 (as Troubled Sleep, New York)
Alexandr SOLZHENITSYN (1918–)
One Day in the Life of Ivan Denisovich. Russia, 1962, tr. London, 1963
Cancer Ward, tr. 1968
The First Circle, tr. 1968
Junichiro TANIZAKI (1886–)
Some Prefer Nettles. 1928, tr. New York, 1955
The Makiota Sisters. 1943–7, tr. New York, 1957
The Key. 1956, tr. 1961
Diary of a Mad Old Man. 1962, tr. New York, 1965
Vladimir TENDRIAKOV (1923–)
The Extraordinary. Moscow 1962
Abram TERTZ (1925–)
The Trial Begins. tr. London, 1960
The Makepeace Experiment. Paris 1963, tr. London 1965
Philip TOYNBEE (1916–)
Tea with Mrs Goodman. London, 1947 (as Prothalamium: a Cycle of the Holy Grail, New York, 1947)
The Garden to the Sea. London, 1953
Pantaloon. London, 1961

194

Elio VITTORINI (1908–66)
    Women on the Road, tr. London, 1961:
        Erica and her Brother. 1956

Elio VITTORINI (*continued*)
    La Garibaldina. 1956
        (tr. New York with The Dark and the Light, 1961)

XV

American Themes

That last chapter was, of course, ineptly named. I have neglected to say anything about the novel in Spain, Scandinavia, Finland, Lithuania and, for that matter, Upper Slobovia. I make no apology: this book is not an encyclopaedia, and I have a number of gaps in my reading, though I know Halldor Kiljan Laxness in Iceland (his *Paradise Reclaimed* is an interesting novel) and Rado-mir Konstantinovič in Jugoslavia (*Exitus* is a moving study of the death of Christ) and Tarjei Vesaas in Norway (try his *Is-Slottet*, translated as *The Ice Palace*). One important omission was deliberate: I mean the Jewish novel. But the Jewish novel can be two things: the novel written in one of the Jewish vernaculars, like Yiddish or Hebrew; the novel written by a Jew, on Jewish themes, in the language and country of the Gentile. The great modern Yiddish novelist is Isaac Bashevis Singer, and the best introduction to his work (all of which has been translated into English) is *The Magician of Lublin*, a story of a late-nineteenth-century Polish Jewish Don Juan who, after a life of self-indulgence, ends as a devout and penitent ascetic. Other novels of his are remarkable—*The Spinoza of Market Street*, for instance, and *The Slave*—and they represent an exploitation of thought and language which is thoroughly modern and very unusual in Yiddish fiction, which is one of the most conservative media in all literature.

Singer is an American, but his work is not American. He chooses neither to use the American language nor to describe the American scene. His concern is with Jewish tradition, religion, custom,

AMERICAN THEMES

character; the Gentile or *goy* has no place in his writing. He does not belong to the stream of the American novel, then; not even to the stream of the Jewish-American novel. But what is the Jewish-American novel? It is an American book like other American books, but it is more interested in Jews than in Gentiles. It is a more distinct *genre* than the Anglo-Jewish novel, if we can say that the Anglo-Jewish novel really exists. The work of Brian Glanville –like his long novel *Diamond*–is evidently motivated by the desire to say what the experience of British Jews is like, tight family groups in a Gentile community, though his admirable *A Second Home*, which is about the London stage (and it is perhaps the best novel there is about the London stage), has an actress heroine who seems, to this Gentile reader, to be only accidentally Jewish; the fact of her Jewishness is of far less importance than the fact of her being an actress. The novels of Gerda Charles, especially her excellent *A Slanting Light*, are not, again, of primary interest because they are by a Jewish author: they are books about people, and if they show non-English characteristics (which may or may not be Jewish), these may be said to belong to a tradition of passion and warmth which has, for the most part, become alien to Anglo-Saxon novelists.

Jewish-American novelists, on the other hand, seem to form a group whose need is to clarify the relationship of the Jew to the Gentile community in which he lives; in their work there is often a plea to belong, or a protest against not being allowed to belong. Their heroes are lonely men, but not tongue-tied ones: they inherit a great social tradition of talk and argument and humour. On a higher level than that of mere race, the Jewish novel is about the man who is seeking integration into a society which he can never trust, and whose values he rejects. Perhaps a prototype of the contemporary Jewish-American author is that important novelist of the nineteen-thirties, Nathaniel West, whose *Miss Lonelyhearts* and *The Day of the Locust* are full of the anguish of rejected humanity and the debasing of true values (love and beauty) by the gods of money which America worships. Another Jewish-American pioneer of the same period was Henry Roth, whose *Call It Sleep* is one of the most astonishing chronicles of childhood ever written–the initiation of the sensitive Jewish child into New York's slum-world, the degradation of the immigrants– with their proud traditions and fine language–into gutter-crawling mouthers of a deformed quasi-English. But the song of protest of the contemporary Jewish-American author comes at a time when the battle is nearly won; it is no longer purely a racial or partisan cry: it is a cry on behalf of all misfits in a heedless monstrous society.

The Jew has had, and still has, enough enemies without the gate. There is also an enemy within–the loving but devouring Jewish mother. The Jewish-mother novel to end all is the work of another Roth–Philip. This is *Portnoy's Complaint*, a fine tragi-comic work which wonderfully fulfils the promise of *Goodbye Columbus*, *When She Was Good*, and *Letting Go*. *Portnoy's Complaint* has caused something of a scandal since it deals frankly, but in a spirit of outrageous comedy, with the hitherto taboo theme of adolescent masturbation. But the basic subject is the debilitating influence of the cannibal mother, ambitious for her son but unwilling to let him order his own life, productive of the disease of Roth's title. For Alex Portnoy is, incurably but comically, sick, with a complex syndrome of which twisted sexuality is only one aspect. His mother sits in his belly like a cancer.

The most considerable of the American-Jewish novelists is Saul Bellow, but there is only one book by him that seems to deal with a specifically Jewish question, and that is *The Victim*, which is about anti-Semitism. The anti-Semitic theme was a popular one in the immediately post-war American novel, but it was often treated in a superficial manner–as, for instance, in Arthur Miller's *Focus*, where a man is mildly persecuted because he *looks* like a Jew (whatever a Jew looks like), and the basic reasons for anti-Semitism are not really considered. In *The Victim*, Bellow shows that the Jew and the Jew-baiter are, in a sense, necessary to each other. Albee, the anti-Semitic deadbeat, accuses the Jew Leventhal of getting on in the world at his, Albee's, expense. Leventhal sees that, although the particular accusation is groundless, there is truth in the general thesis that everyone gets on at the expense of others; Albee thus becomes a desirable focus of Leventhal's ordinary human guilt. And Albee's and Leventhal's sharpened awareness of the boundaries between themselves is a means of asserting identity. Albee becomes a parasite on Leventhal, but the mutual enmity emerges as a kind of symbiosis: parasites clings to host, and clinging is an aspect of need, which is another form of love.

Bellow's trademark is the popular-novel theme which is, through great richness of language and subtlety of insight, transformed into something anti-popular, if not unpopular (Bellow is no côterie novelist). The popular anti-Semitic theme is thus radically altered in *The Victim* and *Dangling Man* is an American war-novel with no war in it. Surely, says Bellow, the pain and hardship and danger can be taken for granted; much more interesting and psychologically fruitful is the position of the man waiting to enter on the war experience, dangling in the void between civilian security and 'supervision of the spirit'. *Augie March* could be taken as a picaresque novel in the native Mark Twain tradition, but the hero is a Jew—and illegitimate—not an Anglo-Saxon inheritor of Huckleberry Finn innocence and irresponsibility. Augie's integration into American society is achieved through a rejection of it. He *uses* America, taking odd eccentric jobs, indulging in crime even, recording many sexual successes but fleeing from orthodox success —the place in the community, the security, family warmth. Somehow, despite the boisterous ending, we are not wholly convinced that Augie is going to be happy. Irresponsibility has, in the Anglo-Saxon picaresque tradition, to be earned out of responsibility. Bellow is protesting too much about the Jew's capacity for being a joyfully lonely Columbus.

The hero of *Henderson the Rain King* is not a Jew. A Gentile millionaire in his middle fifties, Henderson leaves America for an Africa which is not on any map: it is perhaps the dark continent of his own unconscious mind. The successful American has everything an American can need, but there is a deep inchoate 'I want' which can only be understood after the ritual rebirth of the descent into the dark. Henderson, the consumer, returns to America as a contributor, humbly learning to be a doctor in middle age. On the surface, *Henderson the Rain King* looks like a romantic adventure story, but that is the Bellow way – the use of the popular form to make surprising statements about the human soul. The successful man (which every Jewish immigrant has traditionally wished to be) cannot be a Bellow hero. *Seize the Day* (the failed salesman theme, so easy to sentimentalize) celebrates the unworthy. Tommy Wilhelm, brought up to believe that money is the only measure of value, finds himself with no money; in this sense he is a failure. But this kind of failure is another descent into the dark, where human terms apply, not statistical ones. *Herzog*, perhaps Bellow's best novel to date, creates a fine Jewish victim who is bigger than the victors who 'run things'. A flood of words, rich and dialectical, celebrates the dignity of man: man the victim complains perpetually, but ironically, comically, with great self-awareness but no self-pity. Herzog is not what America would call a success, but he is very much alive. The same may be said of the eponym of *Mr. Sammler's Planet*, though he is old and bewildered by the contemporary world. At least he brings the weapon of intellect to tackle the unthinking chaos of complex but brutal American society.

Herbert Gold is another Jewish-American novelist of Bellow's stamp, though technically more uneven. *Birth of a Hero*, *The Optimist* and *Therefore Be Bold* proclaim, in the very positive titles, Gold's main aim – to let human beings define themselves, become aware of identity through deliberately engaging the world. The Jew, especially, is conscious of the need to be tested, in an America where anti-Semitism is of a different order from the atrocious pogroms of Europe: Gold's Jews step forward, to understand and be understood; they do not creep into dark immigrant holes, hoping to escape notice. The books of Bernard Malamud are harder to summarize. In many ways they are more traditional than either Bellow's or Gold's (*The Fixer* reads like some nineteenth-century Russian novel superbly translated), showing a kinship with the older Yiddish literature, in which the world of spirit impinges on that of the flesh and, without surprise, we see the supernatural (disguised as surrealism) closing in, the world of objects dissolving, the very identities of people becoming unsure. In *The Assistant*, with its setting in a New York slum full of very poor Jews, a *goy* hoodlum who beats up the grocer Morris Bober returns to the shop to run it while Bober is still recovering. He is actuated by remorse, but this does not lead directly to a positive wish to be good (the moral struggle is really what all Malamud's books are about); he backslides, he remains himself, but somehow the workings of what we can only call grace lead to the new life (signalized by his becoming an orthodox Jew, complete with circumcision). The new life, the road to a kind of sainthood, is approached always in terms of irony and bitter naturalism; Malamud is devoid of either conventional piety or sentimentality. His hero Levin, in the novel called, appropriately, *A New Life*, becomes a saint not through the denial of the flesh (eventually the way of the *goy* penitent in *The Assistant*) but through the assertion of its rights. A comic, foolish, accident-prone college lecturer, Levin commits adultery. It is a sin, of course, but it leads to love; eventually it leads beyond love to disinterested responsibility— the true spiritual love one human being ought to feel for another. Malamud has great gifts of language, though not of construction (his novels tend to the episodic); there is Jewish warmth, humour, irony, compassion in all his writing, expressed in supple prose-rhythms and exactly caught American speech.

The other great wronged race of the world is the Negro, and, in American fiction, its wrongs have been shouted very loudly. The most spectacular of the Negro novelists is undoubtedly James Baldwin, whose *Go Tell It on the Mountain* presents the two opposed Negro attitudes to the white community which persecutes him—the older one, which (literally) preaches acceptance of injustice as an unalterable part of the Negro condition (and, by implication, of the human condition generally); the newer one, which holds that injustice must be fought against and that the Negro must never rest until he has overcome it. In this very finely wrought novel, the struggle is not primarily between white and black but between two generations of black—the sons against the father. The father is a sin-obsessed preacher; the boys want to cleanse themselves of human guilt in order to pursue the struggle for justice. What is remarkable about the book is the way in which the whole conscience of a people is presented, along with the sense of its history of bondage, as a living force. That Baldwin is not wholly preoccupied with the Negro condition, but with the condition of all whom a monolithic white society exploits or rejects, is clear from *Giovanni's Room*, which has a Paris setting and deals with a tragic homosexual relationship, and more particularly from *Another Country*, which presents a kind of underworld of afflicted–men and women, whites and blacks, heterosexuals and homosexuals.

Baldwin's theme here is that these dividing terms, which society imposes on itself and regards as fundamental categories, are of no importance in face of the only things that really count–the establishment of satisfactory human relationships, the pursuit of love. What does it matter if white sleeps with black, or man with man? If our deepest individual needs are satisfied, we are incapable of seeing life in terms of arbitrary divisions. If a society grants primacy to these divisions, thus blocking the individual's right to fulfilment, then society must be fought tooth and nail, for society is evil. The intensity with which Baldwin, through the mostly tragic lives of his characters, makes these points is of a kind likely to, and intended to, shock. His verbal technique is one of extreme violence, a kind of literary rape.

Perhaps the most important post-war American novel on the Negro condition in an intolerant white society is Ralph Ellison's *Invisible Man*. The Negro-narrator calls himself invisible because 'people refuse to see me. . . . When they approach me they see only my surroundings, themselves, or figments of their imagination–indeed, everything and anything except me'. The reality of the narrator, who stands not only for all Negroes but for all the oppressed, is ignored; he appears to the outside world as a mere *thing*–to be tolerated, patronized, jeered at or kicked. The technique, which has elements of dream in it, like Kafka, and makes large use of symbolism, is a fluid, picaresque one. Parts of the book can be taken as allegorical, such as the episode in the paint factory whose slogan is 'Keep America pure with Liberty Paints'. The job of the hero (who is nameless) is to make white paint by dropping some magical substance into black liquid. The black liquid, stirred by a black finger, is essential for the pure white: the Negro keeps America pure by becoming a scapegoat for its sins. There are apocalyptic visions of wholesale destruction, sacrifice, the End of the World; there is a dream of running that ends in castration, the escape to a symbolic black hole where the Negro is truly invisible, though that cellar is, like a coal cellar, the eventual source of heat and light. The moral of the book is subtle, not at all the orthodox plea for integration: 'Why, if they follow this conformity business they'll end up by forcing me, an invisible man, to become white, which is not a colour but a lack of one.' What we all need is the glory of diversity. When we can all see the glory, there will be no need for talk of toleration.

Categorization is always dangerous, especially when one sees that most post-war American fiction–and not just that of the Negroes and Jews–is about the cry of the minority. The typical hero is a child or adolescent, bearing a half-realized innocence through the dirty world, or else a freak who is really a saint, as in Carson McCullers's *The Heart is a Lonely Hunter*, or else one to whom love is forbidden by the ordinances of the world, as in *Giovanni's Room* or Vidal's *The City and the Pillar*. The novels of Truman Capote seem to want to escape altogether from the world, weaving beautiful but precious prose (*Other Voices, Other Rooms* and *The Grass Harp*) around childhood or the quasi-childhood of the introverted, although *Breakfast at Tiffany's* comes up for air into a real New York, letting Holly Golightly (a child, despite her forcing into the adult world through a marriage at fourteen) loose in it.

The power of the work of James Agee, who died prematurely in 1955, comes from an ability to present, with the exactness of total recall, the experiences of childhood–the impact of the death of a father in *A Death in the Family*, the reformatory boy's entering into the agony of Christ's death in *The Morning Watch*. The fantastic inner country of the self is the theme of much of James Purdy's

AMERICAN THEMES

writing–*Malcolm*, *The Nephew* and *63: Dream Palace*. *Malcolm* may be read as an allegory of growing up into an era, our own, which offers nothing; but the child's image of its corruption is derived from within, from fantasies begotten by his own mind.

Do these gestures of drowning, not waving, sum up fairly the main themes of the contemporary American novel? Certainly, the novelists we admire most have little of the optimism of Walt Whitman in them; the America they observe is not an expansive land of opportunity, liberalism, liberty. But the typical American novel has always been possessed of a love-hate attitude (to use an expression now condemned by Mr Edmund Wilson) towards America itself, which is always ultimately the American writer's subject-matter, even when, as in Thomas Pynchon's remarkable epic fantasy *V*, escape is made to an alternative (and near-mythical) civilization. Thomas Wolfe, in his *Look Homeward, Angel* and *Of Time and the River*, hymned America with the muscular lyricism of a larger-than-life Whitman (but Whitman himself is a larger-than-life Whitman), singing of the 'gigantic American earth . . . this broad terrific earth that had no ghosts to haunt it' but changing into a minor key for 'the world of flimsy rickets' the earth bears 'upon its awful breast'. America is two things–a potential and an actuality–and the actuality can never live up to the potential. The vast resources of the country, its scenic beauty, the racial wealth of its population promise so much and, indeed, fulfil something of the promise, but never enough. A small country like England can be forgiven smallness of soul, but not a big country like America. That is why the persistent American theme is one of protest.

Yet subject-matter is not everything. The exhilaration we feel when we approach much American fiction comes very often from the sheer artistry. The popular British image of an American novel is of something big, clumsy, sexy, and best-selling. This would be corrected if only writers like Peter de Vries–whose *The Blood of the Lamb* is a joyful masterpiece made out of great personal pain– and John Hawkes (*The Lime Twig*; *Second Skin*) and the brilliant John Updike (*The Centaur*; *Rabbit, Run*) were read more than the late Grace Metalious (though, with *Couples*, Updike has achieved

AMERICAN THEMES

the best-seller list—perhaps for the wrong reasons: the general public has lapped up the sex and ignored the style). *Peyton Place* is no more typical of contemporary American fiction than the *Angélique* books are of French or the James Bond books of British. Literature is primarily the exploitation of language. On the soil of contemporary American fiction the English language may yet achieve its strongest and most beautiful growth.

See Bibliographical Note on p. 12

James AGEE (1909–55)
  The Morning Watch. 1951
  A Death in the Family. New
    York, 1957
James BALDWIN (1924–   )
  Go Tell it on the Mountain.
    New York, 1953
  Giovanni's Room. New York,
    1956
  Another Country. New York,
    1962
  The Fire Next Time. 1963
  Tell Me How Long the Train's
    been Gone. 1968
Saul BELLOW (1915–   )
  Dangling Man. New York, 1944
  The Victim. New York, 1947
  Seize the Day. New York, 1956
  The Adventures of Augie
    March. New York, 1953
  Henderson the Rain King. 1959
  Herzog. New York, 1964
  Mr Sammler's Planet. 1970
Truman CAPOTE (1924–   )
  Other Voices, Other Rooms.
    1948

Truman CAPOTE (*continued*)
  The Grass Harp. New York,
    1951
  Breakfast at Tiffany's. 1958
  In Cold Blood. 1966
Gerda CHARLES
  A Slanting Light. 1963
Ralph ELLISON (1914–   )
  Invisible Man. New York, 1952
Brian GLANVILLE (1931–   )
  Diamond. 1962
  A Second Home. London, 1965
  The Olympian. 1969
Herbert GOLD (1924–   )
  Birth of a Hero. New York,
    1951
  The Optimist. New York, 1959
  Therefore be Bold. New York,
    1960
  Fathers. 1967
John HAWKES (1925–   )
  The Lime Twig. New York,
    1961
  Second Skin. Norfolk, Conn.,
    1964
Radomir KONSTANTINOVIC
  Exitus, tr. London, 1966

205

AMERICAN THEMES

Halldor Kiljan LAXNESS (1902–)
Paradise Reclaimed. Reykjavík,
1960, tr. London, 1962
Bernard MALAMUD (1914–)
The Assistant. New York,
1957
A New Life. New York,
1961
The Fixer. New York, 1966
Pictures of Fidleman. 1969
James PURDY (1923–)
63: Dream Palace. London,
1957 (privately distributed,
U.S., 1956)
Malcolm. New York, 1959
The Nephew. New York,
1960
Eustace Chisholm and the
Works. New York, 1967
Thomas PYNCHON
V. 1963
Henry ROTH (1906–)
Call it Sleep. 1963
Philip ROTH (1933–)
Goodbye Columbus, New
York, 1959
Letting Go. New York, 1962
When She Was Good. New
York, 1967
Portnoy's Complaint. 1969

Isaac Bashevis SINGER (1904–)
The Magician of Lublin,
tr. New York, 1960
The Spinoza of Market Street,
tr. New York, 1961
The Slave, tr. New York, 1962
John UPDIKE (1932–)
The Poorhouse Fair. 1959
Rabbit, Run. New York, 1960
The Centaur. 1963
Of the Farm. New York, 1965
Couples. New York, 1968
Tarjei VESAAS (1897–)
The Ice Palace, tr. London, 1966
Peter DE VRIES (1910–)
The Blood of the Lamb. 1962
Let me Count the Ways. 1965
Nathaniel WEST (1902–40)
Miss Lonelyhearts. New York,
1933
The Day of the Locust. New
York, 1935
Thomas WOLFE (1900–38)
Look Homeward Angel. New
York, 1929
Of Time and the River. New
York, 1935
Carson MCCULLERS (1917–)
The Heart is a Lonely Hunter.
Boston, 1940

XVI

On the Margin

Though, at the beginning of this book, I attempted a definition of the term 'contemporary', I still find great difficulty in deciding which authors are merely modern and not contemporary at all, even where some of them are in vigorous production. John Steinbeck is a good example of an American novelist whose characteristic work came before the war in novels of protest like *The Grapes of Wrath*—a bitter study of the dispossessed sharecroppers of Oklahoma, hopefully migrating to the promised land of California—and the wholly unrepeatable achievement of *Of Mice and Men*, with its tragedy of the giant of a man who is, in his weakness and gentleness, as helpless as a mouse and doomed to be crushed by the world. Steinbeck's post-war books, like *The Wayward Bus* and *Travels with Charley*, represent a falling-off from his earlier standards, and the Nobel Prize he was awarded in the nineteen-sixties commemorated an old achievement. Katherine Anne Porter's only large-scale work, *Ship of Fools*, is a very recent production, but it cannot compare with her *Flowering Judas*, an early volume of stories, nor with the trilogy of short novels that includes *Pale Horse, Pale Rider*. And William Saroyan, though he has written novels and continues to write stories, is still, for most of us, the author of that brilliant volume of the late nineteen-thirties—*The Daring Young Man on the Flying Trapeze*.

Katherine Anne Porter and William Saroyan present an additional problem to the one of gauging their contemporaneity, though it is still, like that, merely a problem of classification. How

ON THE MARGIN

do we categorize the work of writers who produce the occasional novel but are best known for their short stories? One of the finest British writers of fiction is undoubtedly V. S. Pritchett, but his main achievement is in the story, and his novel *Mr. Beluncle*—excellent though it is—is not the work we should best wish to remember him by. On a smaller scale, H. E. Bates, despite fine novels like *The Jacaranda Tree*, has so rare a talent for the short story that one rather resents his working in the larger form. And what can one say of W. Somerset Maugham? Thinking over his large *œuvre* at the time of his death, I was not inclined to change my opinion of *Cakes and Ale*, which I had always regarded as one of the best novels of the twentieth century. But is it really, despite its length, a novel at all? With its episodic digressions and its surprise ending—reserved for the very last line—it seems rather an attempt at a novel by a writer who was essentially a short-story specialist. It is as this latter that Maugham must claim his place among the classic British writers. We may admire *Of Human Bondage*, despite its careless prose—a rare fault in Maugham; we may show surprise at the modernity of *The Razor's Edge* (its author was seventy when he wrote it); but we go back again to the collections of stories as examples of total triumph in a very difficult art.

Though we regard a novelist as a writer whose trade is the production of novels—in the plural—we must still take seriously those authors who have been limited, either by circumstances beyond their control, of which death is the least compromising, or by deliberate self-denial, to the production of a single novel. Samuel Butler's *The Way of All Flesh* was his one exercise in the novel-form (*Erewhon* and *Erewhon Revisited* are fables), and it is a great and seminal work. Nevertheless, we do not call Butler a novelist—rather a philosopher and fabulist who left, a posthumous gift, one fine novel to the world. Similarly, we regard Boris Pasternak as a poet whose *Doctor Zhivago* is, besides other things, a final commentary on his poetry. Sometimes, as with Lampedusa, a single novel, coming late in life, seems less the practice of an art than a distillation of years of human experience. A man has to write a very good book to be known by that and that only.

It often happens that we, the readers, make up our minds that a quite prolific novelist is to be known by a single work. This is true of Norman Douglas, whose *South Wind* blows, for many, his other writings off the scene. And it is true of Stella Gibbons, who produced in her youth a book which satirized the brooding country novel, all loam and heavy inarticulate passion, with such light-hearted brilliance that we wish to ignore her many other writings and think of her only as the author of *Cold Comfort Farm*. This was her first novel, and it may be taken as an instance of talent asserting itself early with such force that there was never quite enough force again. There are plenty of other examples. We take Elias Canetti as the author of *Auto-da-Fé*–that strange dream-book about a scholar's descent to the underworld–and of nothing else. We tend to ignore L. H. Myers's many novels and concentrate on *The Root and the Flower* alone. It is not always a matter of finding only one book by a particular author worth reading. It is rather that we think (often mistakenly) that the essence of an author is concentrated in one book, and that the other books cover the same ground. There are many people who profess to be admirers of William Golding, but they read only *Lord of the Flies*. They know that Golding's chief theme is the primacy of evil, and they are quite satisfied with this particular form of its expression; they think they will find nothing new if they read *Pincher Martin* or *The Inheritors*. The character in Waugh's *The Loved One* who says that you do not have to read much Henry James, since all his books are about the same thing, is half right. Read *The Ambassadors*, and you can confidently say that you have read Henry James. But surely a profound theme needs tackling again and again? A painter may paint nothing except apples, but there are innumerable facets of apples to be treated artistically, even though the apple remains only an apple.

The writer, then, who is known for one novel, or for whom the writing of a novel is a secondary trade to some other branch of imaginative literature, tends to be shunted to a margin of critical consideration. But there are other categories of fiction-writers who are either ignored or pushed down into a footnote, and one of these categories contains those writers who are most widely read – I mean the men and women whose primary purpose is to entertain. Ian Fleming is a good example here, and so is Nevil Shute. We recognize the main difference between the fictional entertainment and the serious novel from the work of a man who writes both – Graham Greene. The serious novels probe into the world as it really is; the entertainments falsify the world, manipulate it. And yet, in Greene, the two forms interpenetrate; and in the work of the writer who has no serious pretensions we often gain a new image of the world, an insight into human character. Fleming's entertainments may be examined by future generations as accurate notations of the dreams of the flabby affluent society. Nevil Shute's *No Highway* touched the real world of aeronautic technology and, presenting the theory of metal fatigue as a cause of structural failure in aircraft, proved genuinely prophetic. The same author's *A Town Like Alice* commemorated, in an imaginative form, acts of wartime heroism that posterity might otherwise have ignored. The rather badly written romances of Denis Wheatley contain accurate information about black magic. But the factor in fiction-for-entertainment which sets it outside the limits of literary inquiry is the concentration on content, not form; matter, not manner. There is rarely any attempt to use language imaginatively (clichés go down better with a mass-audience), and the true texture of life is always subordinated to the contrivance of plot. The popular novel is not an examination of the nature of reality; it is an escape-shaft out of reality, a device for engendering easy thrills or pleasant dreams.

There is nothing wrong in this use of the techniques of fiction, so long as we all know what is happening, and so long as the author is honest about his purpose (he usually is). But the reader himself may confuse the very different purposes of the entertainment and the serious novel, and suburban literary societies may hold discussions on the Art of Daphne du Maurier or demand lectures on Nicholas Monsarrat, Master of the Yarn of the Sea.

ON THE MARGIN

Fortunately, in that purest of all entertainment-forms – the book intended to make us laugh – there is rarely anything to provoke a misplaced earnestness. The stories and novels of P. G. Wodehouse do perfectly what they set out to do, and their humour does not ask for close analysis. We prize many humorous books, reading them often but never pretending they are great art as Tolstoy or Proust is great art – books like Jerome K. Jerome's *Three Men in a Boat* or Gerald Kersh's *Fowler's End* (one of the funniest of post-war novels, and strangely neglected). We recognize the time for the Strauss waltz and the time for the Strauss symphonic poem, but, while we write a long essay on *Till Eulenspiegel* or *Also Sprach Zarathustra*, we bring to *The Blue Danube* the tribute of unanalytical enjoyment.

Another field of entertainment which makes no larger literary claims (though it may take pleasure in literary embellishments) is the detective novel, popular again after its brief supersession by the spy-novel. The intellectual reader can take great pleasure still in the pre-war detective stories of Dorothy L. Sayers, or the post-war donnish offerings (with a don or certainly a scholar as the investigator) of writers like Michael Innes (J. I. M. Stewart the professor) or Nicholas Blake (C. Day Lewis the poet) or Edmund Crispin (Bruce Montgomery the composer). In America the crime novels of writers like Dashiel Hammett and Raymond Chandler represent a severe and serious craft (or did: only an older generation seems now to read them). At this moment of writing, Patricia Highsmith purveys highly wrought thrills, and she has distinguished intellectuals like Arthur Koestler in her palpitating audience. And then there is Simenon, inimitable and fecund practitioner of a tough, economical, altogether naturalistic kind of *roman policier* which many 'serious' novelists would give their eye-teeth to be able to write.

Can the gap between the entertainment and the serious art-form be bridged? Some say that science fiction will do it, though not the science fiction of the pulp magazines. H. G. Wells set a standard here, proclaiming an ancestry in one of the fathers of the novel – Daniel Defoe, whose *Journal of the Plague Year* is a prototype of the stricken-city theme of *The War of the Worlds* or *The Food of the Gods*. Post-Wellsian specialists in science fiction are serious intellectuals whose concern is with prophecy as well as with entertainment; the works of Isaac Asimov in America and Brian Aldiss in England are no easy fripperies for a loose-end evening; they demand concentration as Henry James demands it. And Ray Bradbury thinks the themes of science fiction worthy to have showered on them all the riches of most poetical and sophisticated language.

Still, the works of the science fiction specialists remain on the margin of aesthetic examination, and we have to leave criticism in depth to pioneers like Kingsley Amis. We are left with one other margin—that to which are relegated works of promise, though the boundary between promise and achievement is not always easy to define. A year or so ago I would have said that Simon Raven was a promising novelist, on the strength of books like *The Feathers of Death* and *Brother Cain*. But now he is a writer of some achievement. He is working on a long novel-sequence called (it is a pity that this title has already been used—by the popular novelist hero of Herman Wouk's *Youngblood Hawke*) *Alms for Oblivion*. This, which traces the fortunes of England's upper middle class after the war, has already a fine solidity about it, as well as highly individual prose and most civilized wit. Julian Mitchell was also a writer of promise when he had produced only *Imaginary Toys* and *A Disturbing Influence*. But now he has written *As Far as You Can Go* —a splendid picture of contemporary America from the viewpoint of a young Englishman—and *The White Father*, which takes a very honest look at an England that has jettisoned its values along with its Empire. The book brings about a surprising but convincing *rapprochement* between sceptical modern youth (which at least does not subscribe to humbug) and the bewildered colonial civil servant whose purpose in life—to protect the weak—is being taken away from him.

Some critics have been suspicious of Frederic Raphael's prolific Muse. In rapid succession he produced *The Earlsdon Way*, *The Limits of Love*, *A Wild Surmise*, *The Graduate Wife*, and *The*

ON THE MARGIN

Trouble With England and confounded the fault-seekers by maintaining one of the highest levels of craftsmanship that the contemporary British novel has seen. He is brilliant at conveying atmosphere (especially that of foreign places) and he has the rare gift of being able to characterize through dialogue alone. We still await some big, important, work from him–at present it is sometimes hard to see the substance for the cleverness–but there is no doubt that this will come. It may be said of David Storey that, after his violent and moving novel about a rugby football player, *This Sporting Life*, he became firmly established with *Radcliffe*, a very original study (despite the evident indebtedness to D. H. Lawrence) of sexual obsession. Robert Shaw, the actor, is on his way to distinction. His first two novels–*The Hiding Place* and *The Sun Doctor*–were very impressive; *The Flag*, the first novel of a sequence, promises one of the big English panoramas of modern social history. As for Andrew Sinclair, who was much praised for his first novel, *The Breaking of Bumbo*, one can only say that he has not lived up to its promise in *My Friend Judas* and *The Hallelujah Bum* (a beatnik-type novel of America, indebted to Kerouac, less effective than Mitchell's *As Far as You Can Go*). He remains–even after the very ambitious *Gog*–a novelist of promise. Jeremy Brooks, promising in *The Water Carnival*, has come to considerable stature in *Jampot Smith* and *Smith, as Hero*: he has created one of the few really large picaresque characters of the post-war novel.

And so some writers move from the margin to the page, where they take their place with the long-established, having assured us that their talents are expanding and that the books will come. Some remain on the margin, their future unsure; some–the majority– are still crawling towards the margin. Novels pour from the presses, piling up on the reviewer's table, tumbling on to the study floor and scaring the cat. All show competence, some talent, some few very exciting talent. Any literate person with flair and cunning can produce a first novel of some sort; the test comes not with the second (which is expected to be disappointing) but with the third or fourth or fifth. As for acceptance among the established–no one knows how this comes about. Critics concur in praising, reviews get longer and climb to the top of the reviewer's article, sometimes –with the very best novelists–the honour of a *solus* review is accorded. But critics and reviewers cannot ensure that a book is widely read and kept in print. This is up to the public, and the public's taste is imperfect and fickle. Fine novelists like James Hanley (brother of Gerald), whose serious art is dedicated to the spartan task of expressing states where communication is fragmentary or blocked; like (to go to the dead) Ford Madox Ford, whose greatness the public will not recognize; like Elizabeth Taylor (not the film-star); like Alfred Grossman (an American whom America will not publish, though England will)–such writers need the advocacy of a few devoted critics even to be moved from the margin to the main stream. Excellence, in an age much given to the ephemeral and flashy, is no guarantee of acceptance. An act of faith in the capacity of the excellent to flash forth widely at last, even after a century, has to be backed by innumerable acts of propaganda. It is not always easy to become a great novelist. . . .

The writing of this little book proceeded *pari passu* with the writing of my novel *Tremor of Intent*, and it has been revised during the painful composition of *M.F.*; I have been re-reading other men's work as a relaxation from my own. I do not now think that this was altogether a good thing to do, since–being reminded of the excellence of so many of my contemporaries–I have tended to lose heart at not being able to emulate them. And I have also been newly depressed at the amount of fiction there is in the world, the greater part of which I have not read. Why, I kept asking myself, should I wish to add to an already excessive heap of words and plots and characters? There are various answers, one of which is that I have to do it: there are half-invented people and half-conceived actions in my brain, and these have to be completed and released into novels for the sake of my own comfort. And I have to do it for another reason: it is the trade I have taken up, and I must practise it in order to pay the rates and the electricity and food bills, as well as the Inland

ON THE MARGIN

Revenue. Every year I must offer my wares, along with thousands of other professional writers, so that I may live.

Like most novelists, I like to regard my books as works of craftsmanship for sale, objects as well made as I can make them. The deeper issues–aesthetic or social or metaphysical–are not my concern; they are strictly for the commentators. A carpenter makes a chair for both use and ornament; the professional novelist hopes that his offering will provide refreshment for the mind and at the same time raise the mind closer to the eternal values of truth and beauty (which, as Keats reminds us, can be regarded as the same thing–different views of reality). The problem of every professional craftsman is the reconciliation of these humble aims with the pressures of time. Only the amateur–carpenter or novelist –has all the time in the world; the professional sometimes has to hurry. If he is commissioned to write a book, that book must be delivered (just as a set of chairs must be delivered) by an agreed date. He must say: 'Tomorrow I go out of circulation for a while; I must start a new novel.' This, and his habit of gathering material in the hope that it may be useful for a novel, makes him seem cold-blooded to those who have a more romantic view of art– the Muse descending only when she decides to, the long wait–in an exophthalmic trance–for inspiration. Novels are created by men and women who put bottom to chair and pen to paper.

When I first began to write fiction it was, as with most novelists, a refined hobby that, as I got deeper into it, began to demand more time and application than was right for a hobby: it began to wish to be a full-time job. But there is probably no greater happiness in this world than that derived from writing, in a void, for pure pleasure–to see whether places and people, speech and action, can be fixed on paper and then, like a lesser divine creation, rise from that paper and live. When I wrote my first novel, *A Vision of Battlements*, I had no artistic aim other than to recall my wartime life in Gibraltar and stamp that life, in a suitably depersonalized form, on to paper. I was not even concerned about an audience. But when I wrote my first published books–the three which make up my *Malayan Trilogy* (called *The Long Day Wanes* in the United

States)–I had a strong urge to communicate an image of a Far Eastern British protectorate in a phase of transition, and so I wrote for an audience (a primary one of Malayans, a secondary one of everybody else). I was encouraged by good reviews to wish to consider the writing of fiction as a secondary profession (my primary one was that of a Colonial Civil Servant), and so every book I wrote from then on was aimed at a cultivated readership and designed to further–through at least good craftsmanship–my reputation as a novelist. The subject-matter I chose was cognate with that of the three first published novels–the state of transition in British colonial territories; the impact of a self-indulgent England (which no longer cared about its dying Empire) on a sensibility much modified by living in the Far East. *Devil of a State* was about an imaginary caliphate in East Africa (a kind of fantasticated Zanzibar); *The Right to an Answer* (much influenced in its language by Nabokov, whom I had been reading for the first time) was a study of provincial England, as seen by a man on leave from the East, with special emphasis on the decay of traditional values in an affluent society.

Then I was invalided out of the Colonial Service and, back in England, found that literature had been forced upon me as a career: the days of the hobby and the semi-professional approach were over; I had to write in order to live. In a single year I wrote *The Doctor is Sick*, *The Worm and the Ring*, and *The Wanting Seed*, which were eventually published under the name of Anthony Burgess. I also wrote two other novels–*One Hand Clapping* and *Inside Mr. Enderby*–under the pseudonym Joseph Kell. The pseudonym was, I was told, necessary in order to hide evidence of over-production. Critics and publishers alike look sourly on the prolific writer, forgetting how large was the annual output of men like H. G. Wells, Henry James, Hugh Walpole and–to go farther back–Anthony Trollope, Sir Walter Scott, and Charles Dickens. For my part, I see only good in fecundity. I can never forgive E. M Forster (who has set a puritanical standard of spare output) for writing only five novels and subsisting on the reputation they earned into old age. There are two good reasons for writing much, if one can. The first is the need to earn; the second is the fear of an untimely death, which will prevent the half-formed books in one's mind from being realized. We know not the day nor the hour. I may be killed in a train accident when taking this revised book to my publisher in London. You can see whether or not this has happened by reading the blurb on the dust-jacket. If it is not mentioned, I am probably still alive. Anyway, we must all write what we can and, alas, as quickly as is consistent with good craftsmanship.

Critics say that there are certain persistent themes in my novels –the need to laugh in the face of a desperate future; questions of loyalty; the relationships between countries and between races. I am not qualified myself to discuss my work in terms of subject-matter; I have enough to do in trying to write well, which is not easy: the writer concentrates on his craft, the critic looks over his shoulder at his art, such as it is. All I can say is that the novel is a form to which I am committed, that I am interested in the progress of the novel, that it is the only important literary form we have left and that I am proud to be involved in its continuing life and development. I know that all my contemporaries would express a similar pride, while admitting to a certain desperation. Here is the daily treadmill; here is the job to be done. Are we doing it as well as we can? Should that sentence, which has already been re-written ten times, be re-written yet again? Is that character necessary? Is that scene really funny? Will people like the book when it is finished? More important, will they buy it?

As, I hope, this little handbook has shown, there are enough people in the world prepared to brave the novelist's depression and anxiety and self-doubt for the sake of the occasional elation and, more, for the sake of assisting in the evolutionary development of one of the noblest of the arts. The contemporary novel is not doing badly. Soon, when we least expect it, it will do not merely better but magnificently. Any one of us may, astonishingly, prove the vehicle of some great unexpected masterpiece which will burn up the world (meaning the people who read). That dim hope sustains us.

ON THE MARGIN

See Bibliographical Note on p. 12

Brian ALDISS (1925–   )
Non-stop. London, 1958
Report on Probability A.
London, 1968
Barefoot in the Head.
London, 1969
Isaac ASIMOV (1920–   )
I, Robot. New York, 1950
A Whiff of Death. London,
1968
H. E. BATES (1905–   )
The Jacaranda Tree. 1949
Down the River. London, 1968
Ray BRADBURY (1920–   )
The Silver Locusts. London,
1951
Something Wicked this Way
Comes. New York, 1962
Jeremy BROOKS (1926–   )
The Water Carnival. London,
1957
Jampot Smith. London, 1960
Smith, as Hero. London, 1965
Anthony BURGESS (1917–   )
Malayan Trilogy (as The Long
Day Wanes, in U.S.A.):
Time for a Tiger. London,
1956
The Enemy in the Blanket.
London, 1958
Beds in the East. London,
1959
The Right to an Answer.
London, 1960
The Doctor is Sick. London,
1960
Devil of a State. London, 1961
One Hand Clapping. London,
1961 (under pseudo. Joseph
Kell)

Anthony BURGESS (*continued*)
The Worm and the Ring.
London, 1961
The Wanting Seed. London,
1962
Inside Mr Enderby. London,
1963 (as Joseph Kell)
Nothing like the Sun. 1964
A Vision of Battlements.
London, 1965
Tremor of Intent. 1966
M.F. 1971
Elias CANETTI (1905–   )
Auto-da-Ffé, tr. London, 1946
(as Tower of Babel, New
York, 1947)
Norman DOUGLAS (1868–1952)
South Wind. London, 1917
Stella GIBBONS (1902–   )
Cold Comfort Farm. London,
1932
Alfred GROSSMAN (1927–   )
Acrobat Admits. New York,
1959
The Do-gooders. London,
1968
James HANLEY (1901–   )
The Last Voyage. London,
1931
Say Nothing. 1962
Jerome K. JEROME (1859–1927)
Three Men in a Boat. Bristol,
1889
Gerald KERSH (1909–   )
Fowler's End. 1957
W. Somerset MAUGHAM
(1874–1965)
Of Human Bondage. 1915
Cakes and Ale. 1930
The Razor's Edge. 1944

218

Julian MITCHELL (1935–   )
  Imaginary Toys. London, 1961
  A Disturbing Influence. London, 1962
  As Far as You Can Go. London, 1963
  The White Father. London, 1964
  A Circle of Friends. London, 1966
  The Undiscovered Country. London, 1968
L. H. MYERS (1881–1944)
  The Root and the Flower. 1935
Katharine Ann PORTER (1894–   )
  Pale Horse, Pale Rider. 1939 (with Old Mortality, and Noon Wine)
  Flowering Judas, and other stories. 1936
  Ship of Fools. 1962
V. S. PRITCHETT (1900–   )
  Mr Beluncle. 1951
Frederic RAPHAEL (1931–   )
  The Earlsdon Way. London, 1958
  The Limits of Love. London, 1960
  A Wild Surmise. London, 1961
  The Graduate Wife. London, 1962
  The Trouble with England. London, 1962
Simon RAVEN (1927–   )
  The Feathers of Death. London, 1959
  Brother Cain. London, 1959
  Alms for Oblivion:
    The Rich pay Late. London, 1964

Simon RAVEN (*continued*)
  Friends in Low Places. London, 1965
  The Sabre Squadron, London, 1966
  Fielding Gray. London, 1967
  The Judas Boy. London, 1968
William SAROYAN (1908–   )
  The Daring Young Man on the Flying Trapeze, and other stories. New York, 1934
Robert SHAW (1927–   )
  The Hiding Place. London and Cleveland, 1959
  The Sun Doctor. 1961
  The Flag. 1965
  A Card from Morocco. 1969
Andrew SINCLAIR (1935–   )
  The Breaking of Bumbo. 1959
  My Friend Judas. London, 1959
  The Hallelujah Bum, London, 1963 (as The Paradise Bum, New York, 1963)
  Gog. London, 1967
John STEINBECK (1902–   )
  Of Mice and Men. New York, 1937
  The Grapes of Wrath. New York, 1939
  The Wayward Bus. New York, 1947
  Travels with Charlie, 1962 (a travel book)
David STOREY (1933–   )
  This Sporting Life. 1960
  Radcliffe. London, 1963
Elizabeth TAYLOR (1912–   )
  At Mrs Lippincote's. 1945
  The Wedding Group. 1968

Index of Authors

Figures in bold type indicate bibliographical entries.

INDEX OF AUTHORS

INDEX OF AUTHORS

Index of Titles

INDEX OF TITLES

INDEX OF TITLES

INDEX OF TITLES

INDEX OF TITLES

INDEX OF TITLES

INDEX OF TITLES